Writing and Revising the Disciplines

Writing and Revising the Disciplines

Edited by

JONATHAN MONROE

CORNELL UNIVERSITY PRESS

Ithaca and London

First published 2002 by Cornell University Press
First printing, Cornell Paperbacks, 2002

Printed in the United States of America

LIBRARY OF CONGRESS CATALOGING-IN-PUBLICATION DATA

Writing and revising the disciplines / edited by Jonathan Monroe.
        p. cm.
    Includes bibliographical references.
    ISBN 0-8014-8751-X (acid-free paper)
    1. English language—Rhetoric—Study and teaching—New York (State)—Ithaca.
  2. Academic writing—Study and teaching—New York (State)—Ithaca. 3. Interdisciplinary approach in eduction—New York (State)—Ithaca. 4. Cornell University. I. Monroe, Jonathan, 1954-
    PE1405.U6 W73 2002
    808'.042'0710747—dc21

                                                                    2001003247

Contents

PART THREE   THE HUMANITIES

Preface

IN the 2001 edition of *The Best College for You*, Cornell's John S. Knight Institute for Writing in the Disciplines led the volume's co-publishers, *Time* magazine and *The Princeton Review*, to name Cornell their "College of the Year" among private research universities. In my dual role as Director of the Knight Institute (formerly the Knight Writing Program) and professor of comparative literature (my home department since arriving at Cornell in 1984) I have sought to assess and reevaluate, with the help of a broad cross-section of willing colleagues, the relationship between writing and disciplinarity across a broad range of academic disciplines. Imagining the final decade of the twentieth century to be an especially promising vantage point from which to survey the disciplinary fields and writing cultures in Cornell's "centrally isolated" corner of the Ivy woods, I wanted to learn what I could *in situ* about how far and to what ends writing in and across the disciplines had evolved. *Writing and Revising the Disciplines* seeks to document the state of the art of writing at Cornell at the turn of the millennium through contributions by nine distinguished Cornell scholars from as many different disciplines.

Conceived as a kind of family portrait or snapshot of the disciplines represented, the volume focuses on changes over time in the discursive contexts and writing practices of the three traditional areas of academic inquiry broadly defined: the physical sciences, where writing is often thought to be an ancillary activity of incidental importance; the social sciences, where writing's role is commonly understood as perhaps integral but primarily instrumental; and the humanities, where writing is more readily perceived as defining if not constitutive of each discipline's particularity. Six of the nine essays were originally presented at Cornell as "Knight Distinguished Lectures," a series of talks I organized under the auspices of the Knight Institute during the 1998–99 academic year. Talks by Jonathan Culler, Larry Palmer, and Roald Hoffmann launched the series in fall 1998, with those by Dominick LaCapra, Isaac Kramnick, and David Mermin following in spring 1999. Ron Breiger, who has since moved to the University of Arizona, and Margaret Rossiter have also contributed essays. Hunter Rawlings originally presented his contribution on the occasion of the December 6, 1999, symposium in honor of Cornell President Emeritus, Dale Corson. The occasion of the Corson symposium has special resonance for the concerns of the present volume in light of the fact that Corson was Cornell's president during a pivotal transitional time in the history of writing in the disciplines and the teaching of writing at Cornell. It was during Corson's tenure as president, in 1966, with the social pressures of the day inflecting academic work and academic writing in new directions, that Cornell moved away from a form-based, "composition" approach housed exclusively in the English Department, to the content- and discipline-based model that has continued to evolve at Cornell over the past three decades, and that now involves participation from some thirty departments each semester across all levels of the curriculum.

Readers familiar with Strunk and White's slim classic, *The Elements of Style*, may still associate Cornell and the teaching of writing with that book's enduring legacy. Yet since that influential volume first appeared (1918), Cornell has been the site of a remarkably sustained and successful experiment that has taken the teaching of writing down paths Strunk and White could scarcely have anticipated. Open to a wide range of disciplinary interests and discourses, the Knight Institute has proven an especially intriguing place for a comparatist such as myself to pursue field-related labor. Following a farsighted University-wide decision in 1966 to move toward a discipline-specific approach to writing instruction, participation has grown to include some thirty departments each semester. *Writing and Revising the Disciplines* has its beginnings in the fundamental conviction—shared by the teaching of writing at Cornell for the past three decades and what have come to be called since the mid-1970s "writing-across-the-curriculum" (WAC) and "writing-in-the-disciplines" (WID) approaches—that careful attention to the relationship between writing and learning is not the responsibility of any one discipline, but of all disciplines. As the property of all the disciplines, writing is a concern, in short, that does not and will not go away. For as soon as we think we've got it, the struggles for assertion in writing that shape all fields have a way of reminding us that we always have more to learn about writing, which is to say about learning, which is to say about writing and learning together—not apart from each other, but together.

Thanks in large measure to a three-year pilot grant from the John S.

and James L. Knight Foundation in December 1996, and a subsequent grant for endowment from the Foundation in December 1999, the Knight Program has been able to launch a series of initiatives that have transformed the Program itself into the John S. Knight Institute for Writing in the Disciplines. In the years since its creation in spring 1997, Cornell's annual Consortium for Writing in the Disciplines has allowed the Knight Institute to play an increasingly influential role in encouraging curricular reform and discipline-based approaches to the teaching of writing at a broad range of institutions, from such highly selective schools as Davidson, Duke, Pennsylvania, Princeton, Harvard, Johns Hopkins, Rice, and the University of Michigan, to public institutions such as Arizona State University West, California State University at Monterey Bay, Dull Knife Memorial College (a Native American community college in Lame Deer, Montana), Florida A&M, SUNY-Oswego, and the University of New Hampshire, to urban schools such as Temple, Queen Mary College of the University of London, and the American University of Paris. Through the Consortium, and through its hosting in June 1999 of the fourth national Writing across the Curriculum conference, which brought to the Cornell campus some four hundred participants from forty-seven states and seven foreign countries, the Institute has helped encourage the development of writing in the disciplines throughout the nation and abroad.

As an integral part of the Ivy League university where, in the words of founder Ezra Cornell, "any person can find instruction in any study," a university that is both private and public (as the land-grant university for the State of New York), the Knight Institute occupies a unique position from which to engage the developmental needs of a broad range of institutions. Yet while the Consortium has enjoyed a remarkable influence both nationally and internationally, the success of the Cornell model, and its sustainable influence on higher education generally, continue to depend on the Cornell faculty's commitment to the importance of writing as a richly complex, heterogeneous activity that is integral to learning and thinking across all disciplines, from cornerstone to capstone. In consulting with universities across the United States through my work with the Knight Institute, in particular in my visits to relatively new institutions that have participated in the Institute's rotating two-year collaborations since 1997, I have been struck by the proliferation of new names and acronyms for emerging fields of study. As one moves west and to younger institutions especially, such as Arizona State University West and California State University at Monterey Bay, familiar names and departmental designations often seem to be dissolving and recombining into new fields and subfields that threaten—or promise—to replace older, more traditional ones.

In the context of such rapidly accelerating change within the academy, one of my principal goals in bringing together *Writing and Revising the Disciplines*, and in organizing the "Knight Distinguished Lecture Series," has been to encourage interdisciplinary dialogue about writing at the highest levels of discipline-based practice that shape the fields in which college and university faculty of all ranks, as well as undergraduates and graduate students, must continue to find their way. In seeking to avoid the (to some extent unavoidable) trap of imposing questions framed by my own disciplinary formation as a comparatist and writing program administrator, I asked each author informally to conceive of the task of writing for this collection along a broad continuum. Part career autobiography, part exploration of the history and current state of the particular discipline or disciplines in question, each essay includes analyses of pieces of writing the authors consider exemplary and to some extent defining within their respective fields. From the vantage point of Cornell's particular local culture, the nine essays taken together serve to map out both continuities and shifts in their respective fields over time, as well as the parameters of disciplinary self-understanding and the diversity of writing practices within and across fields at a time of revolutionary change within higher education and society at large.

Writing and Revising the Disciplines

Introduction: The Shapes of Fields

Jonathan Monroe

BECAUSE poetry, more than any other genre, has shaped my own disciplinary formation concerning questions of writing, revision, and disciplinarity, and because it has been my primary location in my years as a member
of the Cornell faculty in comparative literature, I begin with a poem:

As It Is

The first discipline
of a discipline is, or
should be, not to forget
that it has not always been
a discipline.
       It is this
forgetting that makes up
the discipline, makes it
what it is, a thing
unmade and not
made up in the eyes
of those who
really make it,
hear it as it is,
necessarily fictional,
but a thing they need
to forget in order to
get on with remembering
what it is they don't need
to forget to go on with.

It is a thing
not itself not a thing that claims
things are the way they are,
have been and will be
always as they never were,
never can be again
once the forgetting starts
getting remembered, once
the dismembering
of its members achieves
a critical
mass, a celebration
perhaps of the need
to congregate, to gather
together under future stars
whose covert revelations
have yet to be revealed,
which is to say, re-
membered as if
forgotten.[1]

Paraphrasing—revising, rewriting—Heraclitus, that philosopher before philosophy, we might say we never write in the same discipline twice. For nothing is more certain in the lives of the disciplines, whatever the field, whatever the institutional setting, than that they are forever changing. In my own field of literary studies, what might be called the dominant mode of writing has changed at least a handful of times in the past several decades, in no small measure through the influences of other fields, from linguistics and political theory to psychoanalysis, from history and philosophy to cultural studies. The cross-disciplinary currency of the word "culture" itself owes its success to a recognizable disciplinary pedigree—that of the field of anthropology—at a time when that discipline has undergone its own crisis of convictions, a crisis that is unavoidably and inextricably, as George Marcus has observed, a crisis of writing.[2]

1. Jonathan Monroe, in "Poetry, the University, and the Culture of Distraction," the introductory essay to "Poetry, Community, Movement," ed. Jonathan Monroe, *Diacritics* 26, nos. 3–4 (fall-winter 1996): 3–30. For a recent assessment of contemporary poetry within larger fields of cultural production, see also my "Avant-Garde Poetries after the Wall," *Poetics Today* 20, no. 4 and 21, no. 1 (winter 1999–spring 2000): 95–128; the introductory essay to "After Shock: Poetry and Cultural Politics since 1989," part of a double issue of *Poetics Today* titled "Poetics of Avant-Garde Poetries" for which I served as guest editor along with Brian McHale and Meir Sternberg.

2. George Marcus, "Ethnography through Thick and Thin: The Possibilities and Limits of Anthropological Writing after 'Writing Culture,' " in *Ethnography through Thick and Thin* (Princeton: Princeton University Press, 1998), 231–53.

In 1995—a year before the publication of Bill Readings's *The University in Ruins* and a year after the publication of *Academic Discourse: Linguistic Misunderstanding and Professorial Power* (first published a full three decades earlier by Pierre Bourdieu, Jean-Claude Passeron, and Monique de Saint Martin as *Rapport Pédagogique et Communication* [1965])—I set out on an anthropological mission of sorts.[3] In documenting the states of writing in and across the disciplines at this particular historical juncture, *Writing and Revising the Disciplines* shares with *The University in Ruins* a certain elegiac perspective. The styles of self-representation characteristic of a given discipline depend to a great degree on that discipline's particular histories, cultures, appropriations, and transgressions. In the *Philosophical Investigations,* articulating in part a sense of entrapment within the discipline of philosophy, Ludwig Wittgenstein wrote: "'A 'picture' held us captive. (*Ein* 'Bild' *hielt uns gefangen*). And we could not get outside it, for it lay in our language and seemed to repeat it to us inexorably."[4] With this statement in mind, I asked each of the contributors to *Writing and Revising the Disciplines* from the outset at least to consider, if not necessarily directly address, the following questions: What first drew you to your discipline and what has retained your interest in writing within that discipline over time? How would you describe your entry and development within the field of writing you represent? How have you envisioned and revisioned your own writing practices over the course of your career, and how has writing figured more generally within your field? What are or were your field's captivating powers? Have there been periods when you found yourself an unwilling, perhaps unwitting, captive to these powers? If so, how did you escape captivity, or didn't you? What in your field have you found most liberating? Are captivity and liberation appropriate metaphors for figuring your relation to the discipline as you understand it? Which other metaphors or categories might you prefer as most defining?

In tandem with these questions, intended as suggestions to prompt a narrative of each author's inscription within his or her particular discipline, I invited each contributor to consider as well the following: How much or how little do writing practices within your field vary as to focus, range, style, and mode of presentation? What is the first thing you would want an undergraduate, graduate student, or colleague to understand about the current state of your discipline? Which approaches, concerns,

3. Bill Readings, *The University in Ruins* (Cambridge: Harvard University Press, 1996); *Academic Discourse: Linguistic Misunderstanding and Professorial Power,* trans. Richard Teese (Stanford/Blackwell, 1994); originally published as *Rapport pédagogique et communication* (Paris: La-Haye, Mouton et Cie, 1965).

4. Ludwig Wittgenstein, *Philosophical Investigations: The English Text of the Third Edition,* trans. G. E. M. Anscombe (New York: Macmillan, 1968), 115.

and strategies might be characterized, in Raymond Williams's helpful terms, as residual, dominant, and emergent? How does the discipline currently position itself in relation to other disciplines, and how are these other disciplines perceived? How have the writing practices of your discipline changed (and not) over the course of your career? What continuities and discontinuities do you see? Does a narrative of progress define your sense of writing (and perhaps righting) the discipline? How open is the field of your discipline's writing practices? What constraints—institutional, cultural, economic—currently govern and shape them? What examples of writing in your field would you single out as representative at crucial moments in the field's history and your own relationship to the field? Which texts have played the most critical role in your discipline's self-understanding and in your understanding of your own writing practices, as well as in the past, present, and future of the discipline itself and its cross-disciplinary engagements? Where does writing in your discipline seem headed at present, and where would you like it to go?

In taking up these and related questions, *Writing and Revising the Disciplines* tells a collective story of the captivating power of writing in the disciplines, but also of the capacity to be set free by, from, and through disciplinary constraints to new modes of writing—writing not yet written, writing that arises from what Readings has called a necessary and desirable *dissensus* to reshape fields of inquiry both within and outside the university. Since all of the essays are by senior scholars who have attained uncommon distinction within their fields, they share an inherently retrospective dimension. At the same time, all clearly seek in the past a common ground or frame of reference for renewal and rejuvenation of their respective discipline's languages and forms of inquiry within the shared context of what is called, with ancient resonances, the "academy," or "higher" education.

If nationality is one kind of glove through which we reach out to the universe, disciplines and departments are the academic equivalent within the pluriverse of the university, territorial entities shaped by internal divisions and border disputes, intra- and interdepartmental diplomacy. The world of the academy Readings has read as "in ruins" gets parceled out, divided up, shaped, and reshaped daily through acts of writing, acts in which faculty, graduate students, and undergraduates all participate. In Stephen Jay Gould's *Time's Arrow, Time's Cycle: Myth and Metaphor in the Discovery of Geological Time* (1987), time itself—the importance of which might be said to extend beyond the parameters of any particular discipline—figures as a quintessential disciplinary metaphor, a metaphor for geology itself *as* discipline, which presents itself as the Discipline of Disciplines, the discipline that goes to the core of the great questions of all the disciplines as to the core of the planet we live on. In exploring the question of time, Gould is self-consciously, elaborately, exuberantly bound up with questions of writing and disciplinarity. The arrows and cycles of which he writes are not just themes but meta-themes, not just themes to be addressed within the discipline but themes that address the nature of the discipline of geology and the inseparability of geology as a discipline from the way geology gets written. Geology and writing geology are, or become, one. [5] As Gould recognizes, the place he is himself carving out for his ideas within his chosen field is inseparable from the ways geology as a field has been written, the stories it has told itself, the myths and metaphors that have shaped it from both inside and outside. He is aware at one and the same time of the difficulty of revising the dominant stories, and of the necessity of doing so to keep the field and its writing (which he understands as virtually one and the same) alive. We might say that the danger of "parochiality" which Gould winningly acknowledges as a part of his own particular discipline—the culture of geology through which he reaches out to the world beyond the academy—has become, in an era recently described as "postdisciplinary," an urgent concern of all disciplines which no discipline can any longer afford to ignore.[6]

At Cornell, writing and the teaching of writing have been understood now for many years as a university-wide concern, a responsibility shared by faculty and graduate students alike with the strong support of both the College of Arts and Sciences and the University's central administration. Yet even with Cornell's long standing tradition, it is only in recent years that what could accurately be called an acute self-awareness of the implications of this tradition has been actively cultivated and explicitly discussed in a programmatic way. *Writing and Revising the Disciplines* marks an attempt to make explicit and further increase this level of self-awareness, at Cornell and elsewhere, about the diverse writing practices in which scholars engage across the disciplines, often, if not typically, without manifest awareness of the discursive frames, conventions, and constraints that shape the writing fields, or fields of writing, each discipline necessarily cultivates. If writing and the teaching of writing are to be given the priority they deserve, writing must be understood in the most capacious sense, not merely as a matter of mechanical skill, grammar, or style narrowly conceived, but as a matter of profound intellectual importance and resonance, a concern that reaches to the heart of, and indeed informs at all stages, the shapes fields take. At a time when the missions of universities

5. Steven J. Gould, *Time's Arrow, Time's Cycle: Myth and Metaphor in the Discovery of Geological Time* (Cambridge: Harvard University Press, 1987).

6. See William Eggington and Peter Gilgen, "Disciplining Literature in the Age of Postdisciplinarity: An Introduction," *Stanford Humanities Review* 6, no. 1 (1998), vii–xiii.

themselves are increasingly in question and many of the academy's most established disciplines are undergoing ever-accelerating change, increased dialogue of the kind Cornell's approach to the teaching of writing encourages across the disciplines is essential to avoid the sometimes debilitating compartmentalization and atomization that often characterize intellectual efforts shaped by acts of writing and revision at their very core.

The decision at Cornell in 1966 to distribute responsibility for the teaching of writing across the disciplines has contributed over time toward a rich appreciation of the diversity of writing practices and the integral role these play in the ongoing process David Bartholomae has called "inventing the university."[7] As commentary of the kind produced by such scholars as Marcus and Gould on and in their respective fields of anthropology and geology reminds us, what is called "writing" is not a subject that can be taught once, fixed, and forgotten in a single required (first-year or other) course, but the concern of everyone involved in the teaching that goes on within a college or university at all levels of the curriculum, an ongoing concern of faculty, as well as of graduate students, of sophomores, juniors, and seniors, as well as of entering students. The field of "Writing across the Curriculum" or "Writing in the Disciplines" continually runs the risk, as does every field, of devolving into something more parochial than it aspires to be.[8] Its strength continues to reside, in

7. Originally published in 1985 (in *When a Writer Can't Write*, ed. Mike Rose, [New York and London: Guilford], 134–65), a year after the publication of *Teaching Prose*, "Inventing the University" remains a touchstone in this regard for what I understand to be the Knight Institute's central mission: not to encourage students simply to emulate or reproduce disciplinary discourses, but to learn to understand and differentiate among them so as to turn them to their own uses. For two additional excellent discussions of how intellectually constraining the drive can be for what I've elsewhere called "expository correctness," see Bartholomae's "What Is Composition and (If You Know What That Is) Why Do We Teach It?" 11–28 in *Composition in the Twenty-first Century: Crisis and Change*, ed. Lynn Z. Bloom et al. (Carbondale, Southern Illinois University Press, 1996); and "'Stop Being So Coherent': An Interview with David Bartholomae," *Writing on the Edge* 10, no. 1 (fall/winter 1998): 9–28.

8. The desirability—and the stakes—of conflating the two terms remains an open question, and contested ground, a matter of at times intense internal fracturing and positioning within the field (or is it *fields*). See, for example, the two lead articles in *College English* (May 2000): "Clearing the Air: WAC Myths and Realities," by Susan McLeod and Elaine Maimon, and "Writing beyond the Curriculum: Fostering New Collaborations in Literacy," by Steve Parks and Eli Goldblatt. For a representative sample of other work relating directly to WAC/WID concerns, see especially Carol Berkenkotter and Thomas N. Huckin, eds. *Genre Knowledge in Disciplinary Communication: Cognition/Culture/Power* (Hillsdale, N.J.: L. Erlbaum Associates, 1995); Sharon Crowley, *Composition in the University: Historical and Polemical Essays* (Pittsburgh: University of Pittsburgh Press, 1998); Toby Fulwiler and Art Young, *Writing across the Disciplines: Research into Practice* (Upper Montclair, N.J., Boynton/Cook, 1986) and *Programs that Work: Models and Methods for Writing across the Curriculum* (Upper Montclair, N.J., Boynton/Cook, 1990); Anne Harrington and Charles Moran, eds. *Writing, Teaching, and Learning in the Disciplines* (New York: Modern Language Association of America 1992); Julie Thompson Klein, *Crossing Boundaries: Knowledge, Disciplinarities, and Interdisciplinarities* (Charlottesville: University Press of Virginia,

this regard, in its (or is it "their") closeness to the variety and depth of writing practices that go on within, among, and across particular fields, each parochial to its others, if not to itself, each in danger of becoming captive to the enchantment of its own self-representations. Given the current pace of change in the academy, even the broad traditional terms designating the tripartite organization of the present volume—the "physical sciences," the "social sciences," and the "humanities"—cannot help but register, as each essay in *Writing and Revising the Disciplines* does individually, as at once picture and frame of scholarly activities and forms of writing that have emerged from, exemplify, and exceed individual disciplinary, cross-, and even anti-disciplinary formations. How much longer, the essays compel us to ask, will the more established fields survive? What will become of them? How recognizable and representable will be not only specific fields—"literature," "government," physics"—but also " "writing," "revising," and "disciplinarity" as such by the end of the century? Will the disciplinary "pictures" the end of the twenty-first century inherits from the close of the twentieth be as beholden to, or as different from, themselves as those the twentieth century inherited from the nineteenth? And what of the pictures we have of what is called "higher education" generally? At the hinge of the present, where historical amnesia registers as perhaps less urgent an issue than the question of the past's continuing relevance, the essays that follow function not so much as a "stay against confusion," but as a barometer or point of reference in a climate and horizon of accelerating change.

As a comparatist, I was first drawn to directing the Knight Institute because of its distinctive interdisciplinary character. It is this character that has allowed me to understand my work as director not as a detour from field-related concerns, but rather as a continuation by other means—in this case the ubiquity of writing in and across the disciplines—of field-specific interests in questions of disciplinarity and cross-disciplinary interaction. Though teacher-scholars in the humanities, as compared to the sciences, can overestimate the centrality to learning of what we call writing, writing is clearly an area of profound concern to virtually all fields, which are themselves constantly rewriting and revising what it is we under-

1996); Richard Miller, *As If Learning Mattered: Reforming Higher Education* (Ithaca, N.Y.: Cornell University Press, 1998); Paul A. Prior, *Writing/Disciplinarity: A Sociohistoric Account of Literate Activity in the Academy* (Mahwah, N.J.: L. Erlbaum Associates, 1998); Donna Reiss, Dickie Selfe, and Art Young, *Electronic Communication across the Curriculum* (Urbana, Ill.: National Council of Teachers of English, 1998); David Russell, *Writing in the Academic Disciplines, 1970–1990: A Curricular History* (Carbondale: Southern Illinois University Press, 1991); and Barbara Walvoord, "The Future of WAC," *College English* 58, no. 1 (January 1996), 58–79, and *In the Long Run : A Study of Faculty in Three Writing-across-the-Curriculum Programs* (Urbana, Ill.: National Council of Teachers of English, 1997).

stand by writing in, with, against, outside of, across, and beyond the disciplines as they currently understand themselves. The writing issues our students confront, from entering students to advanced undergraduates, to graduate students, to the most distinguished scholars, remain in fundamental respects the same issues, including especially the process of socialization or acculturation into a particular field that may have recognizable beginnings—though beginnings can be notoriously difficult to pin down and tend toward the mythical—but has no end in sight for as long as one continues to be committed to the production of knowledge in that field. For as cultural studies and other disciplinary and interdisciplinary approaches have helped us to understand, the production of knowledge and the production of culture, the writing and revising of knowledges and cultures, go hand in hand. I was struck by a case in point in this regard on first speaking with Cornell's Nobel chemist, Roald Hoffmann, about writing the talk that has since become "Writing (and Drawing) Chemistry." Early on in the conversation, Professor Hoffmann pointed out that scholars in the humanities haven't quite figured out how to make collaboration an integral part of their professional (and writing) lives as scientists have. While writing across the Curriculum has played an important role in encouraging collaborative approaches to writing and learning in courses throughout the disciplines, authentically interdisciplinary collaboration among faculty remains in the humanities the exception rather than the rule, whether within or across fields. Through Cornell's hosting of the fourth national Writing across the Curriculum Conference in June 1999 and the annual summer consortium for writing in the disciplines, the Knight Institute has come to play an increasingly influential role in national and international discussions concerning the state of the art of writing instruction and the diversity of disciplinary and cross-disciplinary writing practices.[9] In seeking to further encourage this dialogue in *Writing and Revising the Disciplines*, I have been preoccupied by one question above all: What do we talk about when we talk about writing? The essays

9. Significant lag time may exist between the development of a practice and the deliberate cultivation of a self-reflexive relationship to that practice. Just as Cornell's decision to distribute responsibility for the teaching of writing across nine humanities departments in 1966 preceded the *naming* of the practice now known as "writing across the curriculum" in the early 1970s, it took another two decades after this explicit naming for the movement to become institutionalized on a national scale, as it did in the first national WAC conference in 1993. The first three biennial national WAC conferences were each hosted jointly by Clemson, the College of Charleston, and the Citadel. In 1997, Cornell was selected as the first university to host the conference in a venue other than Charleston. On the strength of the conference's continued success at Cornell, in June 1999 the decision was made to make the conference an annual event starting in the year after the fifth national conference which was hosted jointly in 2001 in Bloomington, Indiana, by the University of Indiana, the University of Notre Dame, and Purdue University.

that follow provide nine distinctive answers, each complex in its own right, each expanding in various directions the sense of what such a response might necessarily involve, whether from the perspective of the distinguished professor of physics, David Mermin, who has for a number of years taught a course on relativity and chaos theory in the Knight Institute's "Writing in the Majors" program, or from the more panoramic perspective offered by Cornell's president, Hunter R. Rawlings III.

In beginning with Mermin's "Writing Physics" and concluding with Rawlings's "Writing the Humanities in the Twenty-First Century," *Writing and Revising the Disciplines* deliberately traces a counterintuitive trajectory, from the single discipline associated perhaps least readily with writing to the broad field of inquiry most commonly associated with it, from a particular field of inquiry one might think made up exclusively of numbers and equations to one defined at its core by diverse practices of "writing" more commonly understood.[10] As Mermin points out in his tone-setting contribution, whether in its most apparently elementary or its most esoteric formulations—or articulations—solutions to the problems of physics never have been merely a matter of "writing up," as distinct from "writing" in the strongest sense. And while the pointed qualification "(and Drawing)" in Roald Hoffmann's title and the examples in his piece suggest the constraints of "purely" verbal articulations, they direct the reader to a much needed re-visioning of the field of chemistry as Hoffmann perceives it, a restyling or rewriting at once verbal and visual, in which recourse to the use of personal pronouns has implications, for "science" as well as "humanity," extending far beyond our knowledge of the bonding properties of any particular molecular structure.

As is clear from the first section's final essay, by Margaret Rossiter, writing the history of science and technology studies over the past three decades has indeed been a very personal matter, one in which personal pronouns, as inflected through gender, have figured not just incidentally but as a matter of survival. As the only essay in the collection by a woman, Rossiter's essay is vital in chronicling the difficulties through which women have written themselves into the academy—the necessity and serendipity of grant writing, for example, as a means of sustaining intellectual work in the face of an otherwise unwelcoming, intensely gendered workplace that has consistently undervalued and ignored the work of female scientists and scholars, at times actively discouraging them, all too often leaving their work wholly undocumented, without a trace, "unwrit-

10. For an exemplary analysis of discursive conventions and writing practices in the sciences in particular, see Charles Bazerman's *Shaping Written Knowledge: The Genre and Activity of the Experimental Article in Science* (Madison: The University of Wisconsin Press, 1988).

ten." Regrettably, although two additional women had committed to the project of writing the histories of their own inscriptions into their particular disciplines, neither was able to complete her contribution, one unfortunately for health reasons, the other for the happier reason that Cornell has welcomed her into increasingly prominent administrative positions that put her proposed contribution indefinitely on hold. As disappointing as I have felt the absence of these two additional essays—one in linguistics and one in women's studies—the proportion of eight male scholars to one female in the nine essays included here attests to the relative scarcity even now, not only at Cornell but throughout higher education, of senior women scholars. In documenting the re-gendering of the academy and of writing in the academy over the past three decades, Rossiter's lone female voice reflects both how far the academy has come and how far it has to go in establishing conditions for women to rise to the highest echelons of achievement and recognition I had in mind in launching the "Knight Distinguished Lecture Series" that gave rise to this collection.

As Isaac Kramnick's opening chapter, "Writing Politics," in the volume's central section on the social sciences makes clear, gender is one of a number of intensely "personal" factors that inform the shapes writing takes in a disciplinary context. In light of the section's second chapter, Ron Breiger's "Writing Sociology," the word "factor" itself might be said to carry a sociological, scientific charge with implications that are closely related to Hoffmann's concern with normative writing practices in the physical sciences and the way writing of all kinds gets written. In this sense, the scientific, or sociological (one would not probably say humanistic) factoring in of criteria of value, of what merits writing up or down and what can be written off, is not an incidental matter. For any discipline's explicitly articulated terms of value, its sense of what counts and what doesn't, deeply shapes that discipline's self-understandings and writing practices and the forms of knowledge such practices inscribe and disclose. As the section's final chapter, Larry Palmer's "Writing Law," makes clear in its exploration of the very different, mutually illuminating languages and writing strategies of critical race theory and the literary fiction of a writer such as Dostoevsky, the complex relationship between writing and social practice within and beyond the academy, in the classroom and in the courtroom, demands vigilant attention, challenging at times our capacity to distinguish the very boundaries between professional exegesis and personal engagement.

In moving from the self-distancing, New Critical forms of exegesis of the literary critic Cleanth Brooks, through the linguistically attentive, rhetorical criticism of Paul de Man, to the self-consciously gendered, social, and cultural criticism of Barbara Johnson, Jonathan Culler's "Writing

Criticism" documents how far writing in the humanities evolved over the course of the twentieth century and the legacy of questions it has left behind. As the penultimate piece in the volume's final section, Dominick LaCapra's "Writing History, Writing Trauma," suggests, what we talk about when we talk about writing, revising and revisioning the disciplines, can scarcely be thought, at this historical juncture, without factoring in the Holocaust and the inhumane, genocidal habits of humanity in the past century. In closing with classics professor and Cornell president Hunter Rawlings's reflections on the future of the humanities in the research university of the next century, the volume takes up the challenge of this inhumane legacy within the present context of what Rawlings calls the "culture of money," a culture that currently frames any and all writing practices, including not only those in the physical and social sciences most manifestly concerned with technology and the global economy, but also those that are situated within the university's emphasis on liberal arts values and writing generally.

In directing the Knight Program and now the Knight Institute, I have felt it perhaps my most important task to help cultivate an ongoing conversation among faculty and administrators at Cornell and elsewhere that would contribute to a sense of shared responsibility for the teaching of writing, and above all for the enhancement of learning through writing, across all disciplines and at all levels of the curriculum. With these purposes in mind, I have sought especially to encourage faculty across the disciplines to articulate for themselves and their students a richly nuanced, pedagogically responsive and responsible understanding of the diverse writing practices that shape the fields in which they alone are the true professionals. The professionalization of the teaching of writing in this sense thus involves above all the ongoing development of a continually evolving self-awareness among faculty from all disciplines of the diverse intellectual investments and rhetorical strategies that shape their various fields, fields students routinely encounter within an *interdisciplinary* context in the course of taking four or five courses each semester, often, especially in their first two years, across as many departments. Accordingly, one of my primary motivations in bringing together *Writing and Revising the Disciplines* has been to encourage faculty from the various disciplines to speak for themselves, from the disciplinary perspectives they alone can represent most effectively. In asking each of the distinguished authors here included to contribute, I wanted above all to elicit essays that would give a sense of the diversity of writing practices across the disciplines, essays that would not homogenize the sense one might have of what we talk about when we talk about writing, but rather convey the struggles for self-understanding that are invariably a collective as well as an individual matter within every field and subfield, every discipline and department the university finds room to accommodate. Access to overlapping and competing arenas of culture, whether at its centers or its margins, hinges a great deal on the shaping power of early access to education and the reading and writing communities such access encourages. Whatever the various disciplines may or may not have in common in their reading and writing practices—and this is itself one of the open questions the volume seeks to explore—all disciplines are subject over time to a continual process of re-visioning. The essays that follow seek to engage this process across levels and for a broad audience situated both within and outside each discipline, and to do so in a way that might shed light on the nature and culture of disciplinary practices and self-definitions for the three major intellectual constituencies within the university: from undergraduates striving to grasp a discipline's fundamental discursive protocols, to graduate students seeking professional authorization through the appropriation of more sophisticated disciplinary strategies, to scholars working to play a transformative role in their fields. Intended at the same time as much for the mythical general reader as for college and university faculty, graduate students, and undergraduates, including but not limited to those specializing in the particular fields represented, the essays cannot help but humble through their liberal arts character, which throws into relief the amateur status, in the full sense, of all readers intent on expanding their horizons beyond those most familiar, comfortable, and comforting. The project's founding premise, arguably the founding premise of the liberal arts as well of the research university, is that what most inspires and challenges our capacities as learners—as students taking four or five courses at a time know all too well—are the differences not only between and among but *within* particular disciplines, differences that manifest themselves perhaps above all in the writing that shapes and informs each field's self-understanding.

Part One

THE PHYSICAL SCIENCES

Writing Physics

N. DAVID MERMIN (Physics)

WHEN Jonathan Monroe invited me to contribute to this volume and the lecture series from which it derives, he provided a long list of questions that might be addressed. Many of them were autobiographical. Physics offers so few public opportunities to speak and write about yourself, that I found this impossible to resist. I'll begin with his opening question: What first drew you to your discipline?

What first drew me to my discipline was magic. It came in two varieties: relativity and quantum mechanics.

I know that the magic of relativity had grabbed me before I was sixteen, because I remember the first day of high-school physics. The teacher was a tight-lipped gentleman who, it was rumored, had risen to the rank of colonel in World War I. He liked to throw hard rubber erasers at people he thought were dozing.

"Physics," the Colonel told us, "is about laws that govern the behavior of matter. There is the law of the conservation of mass." My hand shot up. "Doesn't relativity say that mass is not conserved?" There was a long, terrifying silence. "I don't know anything about relativity," snarled the Colonel at last. "Do you?"

I never again inquired about anything not in the textbook, *Modern Physics* by Charles E. Dull.

So I knew something about relativity when I was sixteen. The magic of it was this: If you could move at 99.98 percent of the speed of light, then in a little over four years you could go four light-years, and get to the nearest star. But—here was the magic part—you would be only a month older when you got there.

Same thing on the way back. When you got home everybody would be eight years older, but you would have aged only two months. If you did it three or four times you could come back younger than your own kids!

Just as amazing, if, on the way out in your spacious mile-long rocket, you passed another one-miler on the homebound run and measured its length as it flashed past, you would find it to be only one foot long, and everybody in it, flattened to the thickness of sheets of paper. And, most mysterious of all, the occupants of the homebound rocket would find that you and your rocket were correspondingly squashed.

How could this be? How could each of two rockets be shorter than the other? I desperately wanted to understand.

Although I took a course in relativity in graduate school, I didn't understand until I arrived at Cornell in 1964 as an assistant professor of physics. I was given my first semester off from teaching, the better to prove my prowess as a hot-shot researcher. (A big mistake, since I was looking forward to teaching and, in my new environment, feeling distinctly unhot). In November, however, I was asked to give a substitute lecture in the big introductory physics course. I attended the lecture before mine. It was on relativistic length contraction and I didn't understand a word of it. Fortunately I had the weekend to think it over. I realized that the reason I didn't understand was that most of what the professor had said was wrong. So I figured out how to say it right, and began my lecture with a delicately worded "review" of what he had said. From then on I was hooked on the teaching of relativity.

The following semester the chair of my department decided that besides teaching a hot-shot graduate course, I should teach a course for high school teachers in a science-education program in Cornell's College of Agriculture. The course was supposed to be about a new set of teaching experiments. "Here," he said, handing me a key. "They're all in a filing cabinet on the third floor of Rockefeller Hall."

I climbed to the third floor and opened the cabinet. It contained what looked to me like a pile of undifferentiated junk. What to do? Fortunately the chair had put me on a committee to look into how to improve the teaching of high-school physics. So I came to the committee meeting with an agenda, inspired only in part by my run-in with the Colonel. After due consideration, we concluded that the most effective way to improve high-school physics was to incorporate relativity into the curriculum.

Thus empowered, I announced to my dozen high school teachers that I would provide keys to the cabinet for anybody who wanted to play with the experiments, but that I was going to teach them relativity. They were delighted. A month into the semester I received a letter from the Cornell Department of Science Education denouncing me for dereliction of duty;

I sent them back a copy of our committee report and never heard from them again.

That was in 1965. My lecture notes for the high school teachers became a book, from which I sporadically taught relativity to nonscientists at Cornell until about 1990. At that point I realized I didn't like the book any more. Part of this stemmed from the increasing discomfort I felt in having to pretend that I was the same person as the owner of the brash narrative voice from the pre-revolutionary side of the 1960s. More important, though, was my discovery, since my class with the high school teachers, that writing relativity wasn't nearly as easy as I had once thought, as successive generations of Cornell undergraduates were bringing vividly to my attention. Now I'm deep in the process of writing a competing book. I've learned a better way to do it.

As an indication of the challenge in writing relativity, consider this: Recently I wrote an article in *Physics Today* objecting to the way some scientists had attacked Bruno Latour, a famous authority on scientists and their ways, for writing nonsense about relativity. I pointed out (I thought uncontroversially) that at least some of what Latour had said was not only correct, but quite elegantly put: "Instead of considering instruments (rulers and clocks) as ways of representing abstract notions like space and time, Einstein takes the instruments to be what generates space and time. Instead of space and time being represented through the mediation of the instruments, it is space and time which have always been representing the humble and hidden practice of superimposing notches, hands, and coordinates." While Latour also seemed to say some rather silly things about relativity, this particular formulation is precisely to the point.

Yet *Physics Today* published three critical letters to the editor. Every one of them took up my quotation from Latour. The first said that statements like Latour's "are thick upon the ground." It took the phrases I praised to be banalities. The second said that Latour's phrases were mistranslations from Einstein's German. It took the phrases I praised to be wrong. The third said that "When Mermin praises Latour for asserting that in relativity 'Einstein takes the instruments to be what generate space and time,' the science wars have already been lost." It took my praise of Latour to be the end of civilization as we know it.

What makes writing relativity so tricky is this: Built into ordinary language—in its use of tenses, for example—are many implicit assumptions about the nature of temporal relations that we now know to be false. We have known since 1905 that when you say that two events in different places happen at the same time you are not referring to anything inherent in the events themselves. You are merely adopting a conventional way of locating them in time, that can differ from other equally valid conventional assignments of temporal order which do not have the events happening at the same time.

This error—the implicit assumption that the simultaneity of events has more than a conventional meaning—can infect statements that seem to have nothing to do with time. Detecting the hidden presence of time can be challenging. Suppose, for example, somebody who doesn't like to back up has a garage with doors at the front and the rear on a circular drive. Whether or not "the car is shut in the garage" can be a matter of convention. For implicit in being "shut in the garage" is that neither door is open. For the car to be shut in the garage, both doors must be closed at the same time. If "at the same time" is a matter of convention, then under appropriate conditions it can be a matter of convention whether the car was ever shut in the garage.

Time also makes an implicit appearance in the correct assertion that the mile-long rocket is only a foot long when moving, because the length of a moving rocket is the distance between two places. The first place is where its front end happens to be at some moment; the second place is where its rear end is, at the same time that its front end is in that first place. If "at the same time" is problematic, then so is the length of anything that moves.

Language evolved under an implicit set of assumptions about the nature of time that was beautifully and explicitly articulated by Newton: "Absolute, true, and mathematical time, of itself, and from its own nature, flows equably without relation to anything external. . . ." Lovely as it sounds, this is complete nonsense. Because, however, the Newtonian view of time is implicit in everyday language where it can corrupt apparently atemporal statements, to deal with relativity one must either critically reexamine ordinary language, or abandon it altogether.

Physicists traditionally take the latter course, replacing talk about space and time with a mathematical formalism that gets it right by producing a state of compact nonverbal comprehension. Good physicists figure out how to modify everyday language to bring it into correspondence with that abstract structure. The rest of them never take that important step and, like the professor I substituted for in 1964, they never really do understand exactly what they are talking about.

The most fascinating part of writing relativity is searching for ways to go directly to the necessary modifications of ordinary language, without passing through the intermediate nonverbal mathematical structure. This is essential if you want to have any hope of explaining relativity to nonspecialists. And my own view, not shared by all my colleagues, is that it's essential if you want to understand the subject yourself.

The other magic that first drew me to my discipline was quantum mechanics. When I was fourteen or fifteen I read a book by George Gamow, which I learned about from an editorial in *Astounding Science Fiction*. I've never been so excited by a book. It was my first exposure to the amazing facts of relativity. It also taught me some remarkable mathematics that I could actually see for myself made sense, which gave me confidence that the author could be right about the other things too. And it talked about quantum mechanics.

There was a car in a garage again. This time all the doors were shut all the time, so there was no possible ambiguity about "the car was in the garage." And yet, Gamow said, it was possible, without opening any doors, or damaging the car or the garage, that the car might subsequently appear outside the garage. (He was using this as a metaphor for the kind of radioactivity in which the nucleus of a heavy atom can shoot out a small fragment of itself, even though there is not enough energy for the fragment to penetrate the confining walls of the nucleus that contains it.)

Quantum mechanics is stranger than relativity. The strangeness comes again from the incompatability of ordinary language with the actual facts. But nobody has clearly identified the traps in ordinary language that make it so difficult to talk correctly about quantum phenomena, and nobody has come even close to finding a way to use ordinary language that eliminates the perplexities. As with relativity, physicists have discovered a mathematical formalism that gets it right, leading to a state of nonverbal comprehension. Nobody has figured out how do better than that, which makes trying to write about quantum mechanics without the mathematical formalism an exquisite challenge.

Suppose, for example, you have some stuff, and you put it into some kind of testing device that always responds by signaling Yes or No. Suppose when you test some particular stuff the device says Yes. You might be tempted to conclude that this was the kind of stuff that produces the answer Yes when tested, but that, of course, is more than you are entitled to say, since the response of the device might have little or nothing to do with the character of the stuff you just tested.

But surely you are entitled to conclude that this was not a specimen of a kind of stuff that must test No. After all if the stuff did require the answer to be No, the answer couldn't have been Yes. But it was Yes.

So it was a kind of stuff that doesn't have to test No.

Now suppose you worry about other things that might have happened to that particular stuff if you hadn't actually done that test. Since you actually did perform the test, you might think you've learned something about the stuff which could help you think about the possible results of other tests you might have performed but didn't.

Remarkably, however, if you make the hypothesis that it was a kind of stuff that doesn't have to test No, then there are circumstances under which you can deduce that if you had instead chosen to do a different kind of test the stuff could have behaved in a way that never happens when that different kind of test is actually done.

So even though the result was Yes when the stuff was tested, you have to conclude that if it hadn't actually been tested, it might have been the kind of stuff that has to test No. There's an additional assumption you have to make to get to this peculiar position: You have to assume that whatever character the stuff has can't be altered by a decision made by a friend of yours, who is off in the next county, out of contact with you and the stuff.

Some people conclude from this that the character of your own stuff can indeed be altered by decisions made by your faraway friend. This is called quantum nonlocality. Others, myself among them, conclude that it is treacherous to make judgments about the character of stuff, and extremely treacherous to reason from what actually happened to what might have happened but didn't.

It's fascinating to try to write about this. We've known ever since Bohr and Heisenberg pointed it out that you can get into trouble if you try to infer the existence of properties independent of the process by which those properties are said to be ascertained. But it's only through decades of trying to simplify and refine that kind of argumentation that we've come up with examples where you get into trouble by insisting that stuff that has just tested Yes, prior to the test could not have been the kind of stuff that must test No.

The very beautiful and concise mathematical language of quantum mechanics is designed to make it impossible to say things like the naughty things about tests I just said and, preferably, impossible even to think such thoughts. The mathematical language says that if you ask this particular question about that particular stuff then these are the possible answers and their likelihoods. It refuses to talk about what actually happens, beyond giving you the odds for the various possibilities. And it is utterly incapable of formulating questions about what would have happened under altered conditions, based on what actually did happen under actual conditions.

Language, on the other hand, is filled with talk about what might have happened but didn't. If only I hadn't turned left at Cayuga Street rather than Geneva, I would not have been sideswiped by the car pulling out from in front of the library. We've discovered that there are grave inadequacies built into such forms of expression. You can't deal with them until you've understood quantum mechanics. But you can't really have understood quantum mechanics until you are capable of dealing with them.

Many physicists would disagree, maintaining that the only legitimate questions are about the possible results of an experiment and the likelihood of getting each one of those results. Quantum mechanics unambiguously answers both kinds of questions, so there is no mystery about it. The puzzlement only arises when you try to combine what quantum mechanics tells you about the possible results of a group of mutually incompatible experiments. When you actually do any one such experiment you lose the ability to do any of the others. Why worry about what might have happened in the experiment you didn't do, if you no longer can do it? That's a question for philosophers, not physicists.

But most philosophers who do worry about quantum mechanics differ from the physicists who refuse to worry only because they worry and the physicists don't. The philosophers have, by and large, chosen to embrace nonlocality as a natural phenomenon, rather than homing in on what bad habits of thought and expression make so implausible an inference so hard to resist. Uncharacteristically for philosophers, they ought to be more worried about the nature of language, how it can trap us into formulating questions that have no sensible answers, and whether it is possible to restructure ordinary language in a way that liberates us from those built-in errors that make it so hard to think clearly about quantum physics. They ought, in short, to be worried about writing physics.

The challenge of expressing in ordinary language matters whose most natural representation is nonverbal operates on much less profound levels. At the insistence of the National Science Foundation, the Cornell Center for Materials Research has recently become interested in something called "outreach." Outreach means it's not enough to do research; you should also delight and instruct the general public outside the university. I'm sure that people in all disciplines enjoy doing that, but we scientists are the only ones who are now required to do it. That's fine in principle, but in practice the federal agencies have imposed so much paperwork on scientists for them to get research support that there is hardly time left for the research, let alone the outreach. Writing grant proposals and progress reports is the least edifying way of writing physics.

A column called "Ask a Scientist" has recently started in the *Ithaca Journal*. It is an example of outreach. If you are a Cornell scientist outreach can strike you at any time. It hit me in the following form: "Why is it that when I look at one side of a spoon I see my reflection right side up, and when I turn the spoon over I see my reflection upside down? Please answer by Wednesday in 250 words suitable for a ten-year-old."

This turned into an all-day challenge. Not knowing any conventional optics helped, because I first had to figure out for myself that the spoon behaved as advertised. I looked in a spoon to make sure. It did. Then I had to decide what I could take for granted: in this case, how flat mirrors behave. Then I had to find a concise way to express the simulation of a curved mirror by a collection of flat ones. Then I had to find a way to say this in a language of spoons, not mirrors, anticipating and thwarting every imaginable misreading. Here's the result:

"To make it easier to picture, think of an enormous spoon, about as big as your head, not counting the handle. You can understand how a curved mirror behaves by thinking of it as built up out of lots of little flat mirrors. So suppose the enormous spoon is a wooden one, made to reflect by gluing a lot of little flat mirrors to both its surfaces, like mosaic tiles on the inside and outside of a dome.

"Now imagine holding the spoon vertically some distance from your face, and looking directly into the bowl part of the spoon, with the middle of the bowl at the level of your eyes. As you lower your eyes toward the lower part of the bowl, the little mirrors that you see will tilt upwards, so you see in them the reflection of the upper part of your face. But as you raise your eyes toward the upper part of the bowl, the little mirrors that you see will tilt downwards, so you see in them the reflection of the lower part of your face. In other words, you see yourself upside down.

"On the other hand, if you turn the spoon so you're looking at the outside of its bowl, then as you lower your eyes the little mirrors that you see tilt downwards and you see a reflection of the lower part of your face, and as you raise your eyes the mirrors that you see tilt upwards and you see a reflection of the upper part. So reflected in that side, you look right-side up."

You may not think so, but that is serious writing. The agony of producing it was similar to what I endured trying to produce the disquisitions on relativistic and quantum physics in the earlier parts of this essay.

But it's not just quantum mechanics, relativity, and spoons that get me writing physics. I'm convinced that you don't understand the real significance of the research you've been struggling with for the past year until you begin to write about it. Only then do you realize that it is much more interesting (or, if you're unfortunate and uncommonly honest, much less interesting) than you'd thought. Only then do you really see how your work fits into or, if you are lucky, changes the character of the tradition out of which it grew.

All this requires time. You cannot go through such a ruminative process if you feel the urgent need to get your work out ahead of your competitors. Because my written physics has to be slow-aged before it's fit for consumption, I've always sought unexplored backwaters to work in, or obscure corners of otherwise fashionable enterprises. At my back I hate to hear the competition hurrying near.

I was talking to a younger colleague about this just a few weeks ago. He was worried that his most interesting work was peripheral to what most people were doing, and therefore failed to arouse their interest. I said that if he found it interesting that ought to be enough—that I'd managed to get through an entire career that way. "Ah," he said, "but you've survived by managing to write about it in a way that makes people think it's interesting, even though it isn't." I took that as a compliment. It may be an example of what Jonathan Monroe had in mind when he asked us whether we considered our writing to be at odds with our discipline.

There have also been times when my writing of physics has directly troubled the guardians of my discipline. I once sent a paper to *Physical Review Letters*, the world's top physics journal, with the title "Beware of two-dimensional lattices with 46–fold symmetry." On the form acknowledging receipt of the manuscript was added in handwriting: "We question the suitability of the title. It is catchy but doesn't convey much information."

Notice two things about this response:

The title is characterized as "catchy." In the context of the table of contents of *Physical Review Letters* it might indeed arrest the eye, but the problem is not that the title tries to catch the attention of potential readers. What is disturbing is its invocation of raw human emotion. Beware! Titles of physics papers rarely address the feelings their contents ought to inspire in the reader. The dominant tradition in late 20th-century scientific prose has been to produce something suitable for direct transmission from one computer to another, from which any trace of human origin has been purged, and in which any suggestion of the humanity of the author or the reader would be in bad taste.

Furthermore, the complaint that the title is uninformative is a lame excuse. Had it been (as it was in an earlier draft) "Uniqueness of two-dimensional lattices with n-fold symmetry for $n < 46$" it would have triggered no alarms. The actual title—"Beware of two-dimensional lattices with 46–fold symmetry"—is more informative. The acceptable one leaves open the question of whether we stopped at 46, because 45 is already quite large enough, because it just got too hard to press the frontier further at that point, or because 46 is truly exceptional. The word "beware" aptly conveys both the complacency appropriate to cases less than 46, and the trouble this can land you in if you blithely assume that 46–fold symmetry will be no different.

I decided not to respond to this provocation until the paper had been reviewed. Neither referee even mentioned the title, but in due course I received from the editors an unusual letter of acceptance:

"We have decided to publish the paper provided you submit an appropriate informative title. We find that your title is catchy, but not informative. We don't mind catchy titles if they are also informative."

I decided to call their bluff, and gave them an indisputably informative title that still began with the word "beware." To my surprise and to their credit, they gave up at that point. Until writing this essay I had assumed that mine was the only title in the physics literature containing the word "beware." But as a very minor instance of how you don't understand the physics until you start to write it, when I dialed in to INSPEC to check this assumption I found 131 scientific titles containing the word "Beware." It seems to be prevalent in the engineering literature, as in "Beware of pitfalls when applying variable-frequency drives;" "Beware of organic impurities in steam-power systems;" or "Beware the wiles of eddy-current testing for diffused metal coatings."

The only title I could find that sounded like physics was "Beware of surface tension." Nevertheless, all I can honestly claim is that mine is the only title with the word "beware" ever to appear in *Physical Review Letters*. If you're a physicist, you know that's distinction enough.

In his own contribution to the present volume, Roald Hoffman mentions his efforts to undermine this unfortunate convention that afflicts contemporary scientific literature—that objectivity requires inhumanity. While Roald has worked with a needle, my preferred instrument has been the sledgehammer. The editors at *Physical Review Letters* had already learned to be suspicious of me because several years earlier I had used their journal triumphantly to conclude a long-running effort to see if I could make the silly word "boojum" an internationally accepted technical term. To show you what I had to put up with in the early stages of that campaign, here is a letter a supportive colleague received from the editor of the *Journal of Low Temperature Physics*:

"I have just received the comments of our referee on your paper and I enclose a copy of them. As you will see, he considers that the paper should be published provided the word 'Boojum' be replaced with a suitable scientific word or phrase in the title, abstract, and text. I too as General Editor concur unreservedly in this requirement. If you are willing to make such changes, we shall be happy to publish the paper."

Eventually I prevailed in spite of such attitudes. There are two striking trophies of my victory. The first is the Russian "budzhum," which made its public debut in both the nominative plural (budzhumi), the instrumental singular (budzhumom) and the spectacular instrumental plural (budzhumami). The second is an issue of the *MRS Bulletin* ("Serving the International Materials Research Community"), which featured on its cover "Complex Materials: Boojums at Work." The indication of my total victory was that nowhere in the article itself was there even a hint of the origins of the term. My traces were entirely covered.

While I had INSPEC up I checked to see how my boojums were doing, and found some disturbing titles: "Boojums and the shapes of domains in monolayer films;" and "Domain morphology in a two-dimensional anisotropic mesophase: Cusps and boojum textures in a Langmuir monolayer."

As these examples make clear, my triumph was an empty one. The boojums have not loosened up the prose; on the contrary, the prose has tightened up the boojums.

I have resisted for most of my professional life the tradition of stodginess in contemporary scientific prose. It began with my first paper in *Physical Review*, which at that time had a rule against the first person singular. You could not say "I" in *Physical Review*. The editorial "we" was mandatory.

Since most physics papers have multiple authors the issue did not often arise, but I very much like to write papers by myself. It is not just pompous to make "we" the authorial voice in a single-author paper. It deprives you of an opportunity to distinguish gracefully between when you're speaking for yourself and when you have in mind both yourself and your reader. "I [the author] emphasize that with this approach we [any of us] can rapidly solve the problem."

With such examples, I was actually able to persuade *Physical Review* to allow me the use of the first person singular. This lasted for a year or two. Then they made a rule that single-author papers had to use the first person singular. "We" was banned unless there were two or more authors. So I had to go through the same thing all over again.

Once again they saw the point, but they continue to exhibit a peculiar nervousness about any sign of humanity in the authorial voice. I once sent them a paper in which I referred to "nature herself." On the proofs "herself" had been removed. Was this a new feminist sensitivity in the editorial office? No, there was an explanation: "Please note that the editor feels this wording to be more literal, and therefore preferable." Indeed, my attention was directed to another alteration made for the same reason. I had cited a "charming" mathematical monograph both because I felt the author deserved the praise and, more to the point, to indicate to my readers that unlike most such documents, this one was actually readable. Not allowed.

A special problem for the writing of physics is created by the predominance of multi-author papers. Research is usually a collaborative process and writing has, inevitably, become highly collaborative. Single-author papers are now rather rare, and papers can be seen whose list of authors constitutes a quarter of the entire text. This is unfortunate. It is hard to discern an authorial voice in such papers. It is now almost impossible to acquire a sense of a physicist's style from a perusal of his or her collected papers, since many people have never in their lives written a paper without co-authors.

This is a tough milieu for one who views the writing as a major component of the research. I once remarked in a *Physics Today* column that "my writing is a process that does not converge; I cannot read a page of my own prose without wanting to improve it. Therefore when I read proofs I ignore the manuscript except to check purely technical points. Proofreading offers one more shot at elusive perfection." An official of the American Physical Society, conjuring up visions of me systematically altering what had passed the scrutiny of peer review, asked whether I fussed that way with my technical articles. He was horrified when I told him that I fussed with them even more.

How can you do that when you collaborate? My solution has been to avoid collaboration. This is easier for a theorist than an experimentalist. With one important exception, my collaborators over the years have been almost exclusively my own graduate students. It's an agonizing process. They, of course, produce the first draft. For some years I would then return a second draft which bore little resemblance to what I had been handed. I recognized the ghastly pedagogy in this procedure, but indulged myself with the thought that they would surely learn much from the contrast between the two versions, and this would show up in the next first draft of the next joint project. And indeed, to some extent this worked. I was, however, brought up short by a student who, I discovered with mixed emotions, took writing as seriously as I did. She was enraged by my second draft. I behaved honorably after that, and we've been good friends ever since. But that paper is the only one on which my name appears, that feels like I had nothing to do with it, even though I remember participating actively in the analysis.

The striking exception to my inability to be a coauthor is my eight-year collaboration with Neil Ashcroft on our 800-page book on solid state physics. We have very different prose styles. Yet the book has a clear and distinctive uniform tone, which can't be identified as belonging to either of us. I think the reason this worked was that Neil knows solid state physics much better than I do. So he would produce the first drafts. Characteristically, I would not understand them. So I would try to make sense of what he was saying, and then produce my typical kind of irritating second draft. Neil, however, would now have to correct all my mistakes in a massively rewritten third draft. I would then have to root out any new obscurities he had introduced in a fourth draft. By this kind of tennis-playing, we would go through five or six drafts, and emerge with something that was clear, correct, and sounded like a human voice. That voice, however, was neither of ours.

Let me call your attention to another peculiarity about writing physics, pertinent to the lecture series at Cornell in which this essay was first presented. Humanists read papers. Physicists give talks. The tradition of talking informally is so strong that most physicists are shocked when they discover that people in other disciplines read their talks from a prepared text. My presentation for the Knight Distinguished Lecture Series was only the third or fourth time in my life that I've read a talk. Only sissies do that. Since the invention of the overhead projector, an exception to this rule has gradually emerged. It's OK to read your talk provided you write it on plastic and project it on a screen so everybody else can see what you're reading. With this compromise you get neither the precision of the written language, nor the spontaneity of informal speech. It's an art form that seems to have become particularly popular with university administrators.

In high school I took a test that was supposed to tell me what to do with my life. I think it was called the Kuder Preference Test. You were asked questions like "Would you rather spend an hour reading to an invalid or taking apart a clock?" You answered the questions by punching holes in an answer sheet with a pin.

They told me afterwards that the test showed that I had two great interests: science and writing. So, they said, I should aim to become the editor of a science journal.

Implicit in this recommendation is the distinction, remarked on in this volume by Jonathan Culler, between writing and writing up. Clearly the proprietors of the test knew that scientists produced papers, but evidently they thought that this was writing up—not writing. Writing was done in editorial offices; in laboratories you only wrote up.

But writing physics is different both from writing up physics and from the editorial refinement of written-up physics. While there has to be something there before the writing begins, that something only acquires its character and shape through writing. My transformation of the ordinary spoon into a mosaic dome is clearly not writing up physics. I like to think it is writing physics. The distinction between the two might shed some light on current debates in the "science wars" between physicists and social constructivists. The physicists believe that there is a clean distinction between objective truth and mere social convention. They view physics as a process of discovering and writing up objective truths. Social constructivists—at least the ones I find interesting—maintain that objective truth and social convention are so deeply entangled that it's impossible to separate the two. For them physics is not writing up. Physics is writing.

Who would have thought, before Einstein's 1905 paper, that simultaneity was a convention—not an objective fact—that clocks were not a useful invention for the recording of objective time, but that time itself was a useful invention for characterizing the correlations between objective clocks?

The issue in the debates of the "science wars" is not whether the physical can be disentangled from the social—the real, from the conventional—but whether their deep entanglement is trivial or profound—a fruitful or a sterile way of understanding the scientific process.

The great Russian physicist Lev Landau was said to have hated writing. He co-authored an extraordinary series of textbooks in collaboration with Evgenii Lifshitz, who did all the writing. From my perspective Lifshitz operated in a co-author's paradise. He was linked to nature through Landau, who was in deep nonverbal communion with her, but had no investment whatever in the process of articulating that communion.

It is said that even Landau's profound technical papers were actually written by Lifshitz. Many physicists look down on Lifshitz: Landau did the physics, Lifshitz wrote it up. I don't believe that for a minute. If Evgenii Lifshitz really wrote the amazing papers of Landau, he was doing physics of the highest order. Landau was not so much a co-author, as a natural phenomenon—an important component of the remarkable coherence of the physical world that Lifshitz wrote about so powerfully in the papers of Landau.

So the testers were right about my interests—just wrong about how I ought to exercise them. They ought to have said, "You like science and you like writing, so be a scientist. Go forth, young man, and write science."

Writing (and Drawing) Chemistry

Roald Hoffmann (Chemistry)

In the chemical profession our stock in trade is not the book, but the scientific (chemical) article, published in a periodical. I have written 450 of them in my years at Cornell University; my colleague Harold Scheraga has published over 1000. We have promoted an assistant professor to tenure at Cornell with 11 published papers, and we have not promoted one with over 80.

The Nature of the Beast

It is instructive to see the article untamed, roaming its range. For this I would like to begin with some pages from the chemical journal that is arguably the world's best (at least in inorganic and organic chemistry, not in physical chemistry or biochemistry); publication venues and their prestige carry much baggage of history and fashion. The journal is not an American one. It is *Angewandte Chemie*, published out of Germany, it appears simultaneously in German and English editions. Despite its name, the journal contains precious little applied chemistry.

Angewandte Chemie, under the inspired and proactive leadership of its editor, Peter Gölitz, has cultivated an effective mix of largely solicited review or feature articles, short highlights, and many "Communications." These are brief accounts of novel chemistry, presumably worthy of urgent publication. And publication, following review by one to three anonymous (to the author) referees, is certainly rapid. Several Communications in the Nov. 2, 1998 issue of the journal carry June submission dates; the latest is dated July 1, 1998. For my friends in the humanities (I'm there too; I have been waiting over two years for a paper to appear in the *Canadian Review of Comparative Literature*), all I can say is "It can be done."

Let us leaf (see figures 1–5) through some pages in the Nov. 2, 1998 issue of *Angewandte Chemie* which arrived in my mailbox the week of November 9. (The original lecture on which this text is based was presented on Nov. 16, 1998.)

From these five sequential pages, as well as perusal of a greater sample, one notes:

(1) The authorship is international.

(2) There are many authors per paper; one of the differences between the sciences and the humanities and arts (theater and film are exceptions), is that the sciences have mastered the ethics of collaboration.

(3) The usual scholarly apparatus is there: author affiliations, endnotes (often numerous), acknowledgments of granting agencies and individual assistance or discussion.

(4) An unusual feature, particular to *Angewandte Chemie*, is the mandatory inclusion at the end of any experimental paper of an experimental section, detailing procedures for at least part of the experiments carried out.

(5) Most striking is the remarkable density of graphic material, most of it quasi-iconic representations of microscopic molecular structure. It is this feature of chemistry—the high graphical content of the literature and the science—which led me to include the parenthetical clause in my title (see Hoffmann and Laszlo, 1991). I will return to it, for now I hope I have convinced you that it is not my stylistic prejudice when I say that it is impossible to write chemistry without drawing molecules.

I also note that while there are some graphs and plots of observables, these are relatively few. And still fewer equations. This is not physics.

Is what these figures present typical? Yes, it certainly is so, of the literature of organic, inorganic, and biological chemistry. Physical chemistry is quite different, for its literature (viewed phenomenologically) carries more equations, and fewer depictions of molecules.

CALIXARENES

Let us now zoom in on one article, and read it together. I do this for the ostensible reason of analyzing this contemporary text as a text. But I must also 'fess up; I do it because I will not pass up the chance of teaching any audience, including the audience of the present volume, some chemistry.

A New Motif for the Self-Assembly of [2]Pseudorotaxanes; 1,2-Bis(pyridinium)ethane Axles and [24]Crown-8 Ether Wheels**

Stephen J. Loeb* and James A. Wisner

The threading of the paraquat dication PQT²⁺ through the cavity of bis(paraphenylene)[34]crown-10 (BPP34C10) to form the [2]pseudorotaxane [(BPP34C10)(PQT)]²⁺ (1) was the genesis of a diverse range of molecules that contain mechanical linkages (rotaxanes, catenanes, molecular shuttles, and switches) derived from this basic interaction, and stands as a landmark discovery in the area of supramolecular chemistry (Scheme 1).[1] Many examples of rotaxanes have

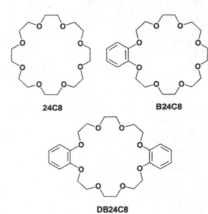

Scheme 1. Formation of the [2]pseudorotaxane 1 by insertion of the linear cationic axle PQT²⁺ through the cavity of the neutral crown ether wheel BPP34C10.

been reported involving π stacking between electron-rich and electron-poor aromatic rings,[2] hydrogen bonding between secondary dialkylammonium ions and crown ethers[3] or between amides and large ring lactams,[4] hydrophobic interactions within the cavity of a cyclodextrin,[5, 6] and metal–ligand interactions between transition metal ions and cyclic ligands.[7–9] In many of these systems the ion–dipole interaction between positively charged atoms of one component and the Lewis basic atoms of the other component makes a significant contribution to the binding. Although these electrostatic interactions are not directional and predictable in the same manner as hydrogen bonds or metal–ligand

[*] Prof. Dr. S. J. Loeb, J. A. Wisner
Department of Chemistry and Biochemistry
University of Windsor
Windsor, ON, N9B 3P4 (Canada)
Fax: (+1)519-973-7098
E-mail: loeb@uwindsor.ca

[**] Financial support for this work was provided by the Natural Sciences and Engineering Research Council of Canada.

bonds, they are nonetheless extremely important. For example, the PQT²⁺ ion in 1 is tilted away from perpendicular by 62° so as to maximize the N⁺···O interactions and also form weak CH···O hydrogen bonds along with the major π-stacking components.[1]

Herein, we present a new motif for the design of [2]pseudorotaxanes based on the simple concept of optimizing N⁺···O interactions between pyridinium ions and simple crown ethers.[10] The N⁺–N⁺ distance in PQT²⁺ is about 7.00 Å while in the isomeric 1,2-bis(pyridinium)ethane dication 2a it is only about 3.75 Å (Scheme 2). Although Stoddart et al. have reported that the interaction between dibenzylparaquat and DB24C8 is negligible,[11, 12] an examination of CPK and computer models suggested a good match between 2a (the "axle") and the 24-membered crown ethers (wheels) 24C8, B24C8, and DB24C8 (Scheme 3) that should

Scheme 2. Comparison of the intramolecular N⁺–N⁺ distances in the isomeric pyridinium ions PQT²⁺ and [pyCH₂CH₂py]²⁺ (2a).

Scheme 3. Formation of [2]pseudorotaxanes from 24C8, B24C8, and DB24C8.

optimize the N⁺···O interactions. Scheme 4 shows how two sets of N⁺···O interactions might be accompanied by a series of four C–H···O hydrogen bonds that are formed with alternate oxygen atoms in the crown ether. The question remains as to whether these interactions are sufficient to produce a stable [2]pseudorotaxane in the absence of the π-stacking interactions found in 1 and related molecules.

The addition of one equivalent of 24C8 to a solution of one equivalent of 2a(BF₄)₂ in MeCN gave the [2]pseudorotaxane 5a. An association constant K_a of 165 M⁻¹ was measured for this interaction by ¹H NMR titration in MeCN at 298 K. By variation of the substituent X on the pyridinium ring other axles can be incorporated and a more detailed understanding of the overall interaction can be obtained. The strength of the interaction can be controlled by varying X as shown in Table 1. In particular, the introduction of the electron-with-

FIGURE 1

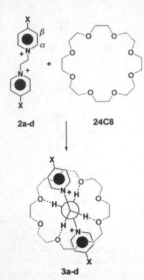

2a-d   24C8

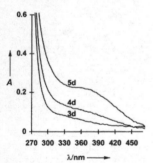

3a-d

Scheme 4. Newman projection along the C–C vector of the N⁺CH₂CH₂N⁺ portion of the dication [XpyCH₂-CH₂pyX]²⁺, **2a–d**, (X = H, Me, Ph, CO₂Et,). This combination of N⁺···O ion–dipole interactions and C–H···O hydrogen bonds might stabilize the formation of [2]pseudorotaxanes with 24C8.

drawing group CO₂Et results in the largest association constant for the interactions with each of the three crown ethers.

Incorporation of aromatic groups into the crown ether provides the possibility of π stacking between the pyridinium rings and the catechol rings of the crown ether. In the ¹H NMR spectra of the two pseudorotaxanes derived from **2a** (X = CO₂Et) with B24C8 (**4d**) and DB24C8 (**5d**) π stacking in solution is clearly evident: the signals for the β protons of the pyridine group shift upfield ($\delta = 8.56$, 8.36, and 8.14 for the pseudorotaxanes with 24C8, B24C8, and DB24C8, respectively). This trend is mirrored by a uniform increase in K_a from 320 to 740 to 1200 M⁻¹ and an increase in the intensity of a charge transfer absorption band at about 370 nm (Figure 1). In addition, **3d–5d** show significant downfield shifts ($\delta =$

0.20–0.31)for the α and NCH₂ protons, which is indicative of the formation of C–H···O hydrogen bonds to the oxygen atoms of the crown ether.

These results and the threading conformation proposed in Scheme 4 are supported by the solid-state structure of [(EtO₂CpyCH₂-CH₂pyCO₂Et)(DB24C8)]²⁺ (**5d**; py = C₅H₄N⁺).[13] Figures 2 and 3 show different views of the threading of the dicationic axle through the cavity of the DB24C8 macrocycle. The [2]pseudorotaxane is stabilized by 1) eight N⁺···O interactions (N–O 3.76–4.88 Å), 2) eight C–H···O hydrogen bonds (the four predicted ones between the bridging ethane unit and alternate ether oxygen atoms as well as four others between pyridinium hydrogen atoms and symmetry related O5 atom

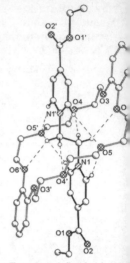

Figure 2. A ball-and-stick representation of the crystal structure **5d**, formed from [EtO₂CpyCH CH₂pyCO₂Et]²⁺ (**2d**) and DB24C

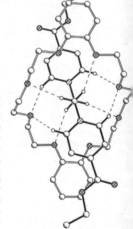

Figure 3. A ball-and-stick representation of the crystal structure of **5d**, shown along the C9–C9' bond. This view corresponds to the Newman projection show schematically in Scheme 4. N⁺–O distances: N1⁺–O3 4.88, N1⁺–O4 4.43, N1⁺–O5 3.76, N1⁺–O6 4.66 Å. C–H···O hydrogen bonds (lengths [Å] and angles [°]): H9A–O4' 2.54, H9B–O6' 2.66, H6A–O5 2.36, H7A–O5' 2.54; C9-H9A-O4' 165.0, C7-H7A-O5' 141.0, C6-H6A-O5 154.2, C9-H9B-O6' 150.0.

Figure 1. UV absorption spectra of **3d**, **4d**, and **5d**. The intensity of the charge-transfer band in the region 270–470 nm increases with increased capacity for π-stacking interactions.

Table 1. Association constants (K_a) and free energies of complexation (ΔG) for **3a–d**, **4a–d**, and **5a–d** formed from [X-pyCH₂CH₂py-X]²⁺, **2a–d**, an 24C8, B24C8, or DB24C8 in MeCN at 298 K.[a]

| X | 24C8 | | B24C8 | | DB24C8 | |
	K_a [M⁻¹]	$-\Delta G$ [kJ mol⁻¹]	K_a [M⁻¹]	$-\Delta G$ [kJ mol⁻¹]	K_a [M⁻¹]	$-\Delta G$ [kJ mol⁻¹]
H (**a**)	165	12.7	195	13.1	180	12.9
Me (**b**)	105	11.6	205	13.2	230	13.5
Ph[b] (**c**)	160	12.6	300	14.2	320	14.3
CO₂Et[b] (**d**)	320	14.3	740	16.4	1200	17.6

[a] Sample concentrations 2.0 × 10⁻³–5.0 × 10⁻³ M. [b] Chemical exchange was slow on the NMR time scale and peaks were observed for both complexed an uncomplexed species. K_a was determined by integration from a 1:1 mixture. All other K_a values were determined by NMR titration experiments by using th program EQNMR.[16] Estimated errors: < 10 % for K_a > 100.

FIGURE 2

(C–O 2.36–2.66 Å), and 3) π-stacking interactions between the electron-rich catechol rings of the crown ether and the electron-poor aromatic rings and ester group of the pyridinium salt.

The new binding motif for the formation of [2]pseudorotaxanes presented herein demonstrates for the first time that simple crown ethers can be used to form [2]pseudorotaxanes. The ability to easily tune the interaction strength and the availability of these simple components bodes well for the extension of this motif to more complex supramolecular systems with interlocked [n]rotaxanes and [n]catenanes.

Experimental Section

All pyridinium bromide salts were prepared by the literature method.[14] The BF_4^- salts were precipitated from water by the addition of $NaBF_4$ or NH_4BF_4 and recrystallized before use. DB24C8 was purchased from Aldrich and used as received. B24C8 and 24C8 were prepared by literature methods.[15] In a typical experiment, [2]pseudorotaxanes were formed in solution by mixing equimolar solutions of $2a(BF_4)_2$–$d(BF_4)_2$ and crown ether in MeCN. Typical data for [2]pseudorotaxanes in which $X = CO_2Et$: **3d**: ^1H NMR (300 MHz, CD_3CN, 298 K): $\delta = 9.27$ (d, 4H, $J = 5.3$ Hz; α-pyH), 8.56 (d, 4H, $J = 5.3$ Hz; β-pyH), 5.40 (s, 4H; NCH_2), 4.50 (q, 4H, $J = 7.1$ Hz; $C(O)OCH_2$), 3.50 (s, 32H; OCH_2), 1.44 (t, 6H, $J = 7.1$ Hz; CH_3); ES-MS m/z (%): 770 (5) [$M - BF_4$]$^+$, 341 (100) [$M - 2BF_4$]$^{2+}$. **4d**: ^1H NMR (300 MHz, CD_3CN, 298 K): $\delta = 9.24$ (d, 4H, $J = 6.4$ Hz; α-pyH), 8.36 (d, 4H, $J = 6.4$ Hz; β-pyH), 6.80 (m, 4H; Ar), 5.46 (s, 4H; NCH_2), 4.47 (q, 4H, $J = 7.1$ Hz; $C(O)OCH_2$), 4.02 (m, 4H; $ArOCH_2$), 3.94 (m, 4H; OCH_2), 4.83 (m, 8H; OCH_2), 3.63 (m, 4H; OCH_2), 3.43 (m, 4H; OCH_2), 3.18 (m, 4H; OCH_2), 1.44 (t, 6H, $J = 7.1$ Hz; CH_3); ES-MS m/z (%): 818 (7) [$M - BF_4$]$^+$, 365 (100) [$M - 2BF_4$]$^{2+}$. **5d**: ^1H NMR (300 MHz, CD_3CN, 298 K): $\delta = 9.24$ (d, 4H, $J = 6.7$ Hz; α-pyH), 8.14 (d, 4H, $J = 6.7$ Hz; β-pyH), 6.74 (m, 8H; Ar), 5.58 (s, 4H; NCH_2), 4.40 (q, 4H, $J = 7.1$ Hz; $C(O)OCH_2$), 4.00 (m, 24H; OCH_2) 1.44 (t, 6H, $J = 7.1$ Hz; CH_3); ES-MS m/z (%): 865 (12) [$M - BF_4$]$^+$, 389 (100) [$M - 2BF_4$]$^{2+}$.

Received: April 28, 1998 [Z 11791 IE]
German version: *Angew. Chem.* **1998**, *110*, 3010–3013

Keywords: crown compounds · rotaxanes · self-assembly · supramolecular chemistry

[1] B. L. Allwood, N. Spencer, H. Shahriari-Zavareh, J. F. Stoddart, D. J. Williams, *J. Chem. Soc. Chem. Commun.* **1987**, 1064–1066;

[2] D. Philp, J. F. Stoddart, *Angew. Chem.* **1996**, *108*, 1242–1286; *Angew. Chem. Int. Ed. Engl.* **1996**, *35*, 1154–1196, and references therein.

[3] P. R. Ashton, P. T. Glink, J. F. Stoddart, P. A. Tasker, A. J. P. White, D. J. Williams, *Chem. Eur. J.* **1996**, *2*, 729–736.

[4] R. Jäger, F. Vögtle, *Angew. Chem.* **1997**, *109*, 966–980; *Angew. Chem. Int. Ed. Engl.* **1997**, *36*, 930–944, and references therein.

[5] A. P. Lyon, D. H. Macartney, *Inorg. Chem.* **1997**, *36*, 729–736, and references therein.

[6] D. B. Amabilino, P. R. Ashton, S. E. Boyd, M. Gómez-López, W. Hayes, J. F. Stoddart, *J. Org. Chem.* **1997**, *62*, 3062–3075.

[7] H. Sleiman, P. N. W. Baxter, J.-M. Lehn, K. Airola, K. Rissanen, *Inorg. Chem.* **1997**, *36*, 4734–4742.

[8] P. Gaviña, J.-P. Sauvage, *Tetrahedron Lett.* **1997**, *38*, 3521–3524.

[9] M. Fujita, F. Ibukuro, H. Seki, O. Kamo, M. Imanari, K. Ogura, *J. Am. Chem. Soc.* **1996**, *118*, 899–900, and references therein.

[10] For a recent example of host–guest interactions between crown ethers and pyridinium compounds, see M. Lämsä, J. Huuskonen, K. Rissanen, J. Pursiainen, *Chem. Eur. J.* **1998**, *4*, 84–92.

[11] M.-V. Martínez-Díaz, N. Spencer, J. F. Stoddart, *Angew. Chem.* **1997**, *109*, 1991–1994; *Angew. Chem. Int. Ed. Engl.* **1997**, *36*, 1904–1907.

[12] For an example of a pseudorotaxane involving DB24C8 and a paraquat type molecule, see P. R. Ashton, S. J. Langford, N. Spencer,

J. F. Stoddart, A. J. P. White, D. J. Williams, *Chem. Commun.* **1996**, 1387–1388.

[13] Crystal structure data for **5d**(BF_4)$_2$: monoclinic, space group $P2_1/c$, $a = 13.2421(4)$, $b = 15.7037(5)$, $c = 12.1739(4)$ Å, $\beta = 94.909(1)°$, $V = 2522.3(1)$ Å^3, $Z = 2$, $\rho_{calcd} = 1.308$ g cm^{-3}, $2\theta_{max} = 45.0°$, Mo$_{K\alpha}$ radiation ($\lambda = 0.71073$ Å), $T = 296$ K. A pale yellow crystal with dimensions $0.2 \times 0.2 \times 0.3$ mm was grown by vapor diffusion of isopropyl ether into a solution of **5d** in MeCN and mounted on a fibre. The 3280 unique reflections ($R_{int} = 0.0715$) were integrated from frame data obtained from programmed hemisphere scan routine on a Siemens SMART CCD diffractometer. Decay ($<1\%$) was monitored by 50 standard data frames measured at the beginning and end of data collection. Systematic absences in the diffraction data and determined unit-cell parameters were consistent with the space group $P2_1/c$. Lorentzian-polarization correction and semi-empirical absorption correction, based on redundant data at varying effective azimuthal angles, were applied to the data ($\mu = 0.112$ cm^{-1}, min./max. transmission $= 0.221/0.492$). The structure was solved by direct methods, with Fourier syntheses, and refined with full-matrix least-squares methods against $|F^2|$ data to give $R(F) = 0.0815$, $wR(F^2) = 0.2271$, $GOF = 1.033$, $N_o/N_v = 3275/354$. All non-hydrogen atoms were refined anisotropically. Hydrogen atoms were treated as idealized contributions. Scattering factors and anomalous dispersion coefficients are contained in the SHELXTL 5.03 program library (Sheldrick, G. M., Madison, WI). Crystallographic data (excluding structure factors) for the structure reported in this paper have been deposited with the Cambridge Crystallographic Data Centre as supplementary publication no. CCDC-101459. Copies of the data can be obtained free of charge on application to CCDC, 12 Union Road, Cambridge CB2 1EZ, UK (fax: (+44) 1223-336-033; e-mail: deposit@ccdc.cam.a-c.uk).

[14] M. I. Attalla, N. S. McAlpine, L. A. Summers, *Z. Naturforsch. B* **1984**, *39*, 74–78.

[15] C. J. Pedersen, *J. Am. Chem. Soc.* **1967**, *89*, 7017–7036.

[16] J. Hynes, *J. Chem. Soc. Dalton Trans.* **1993**, 311–312.

[Te$_6$N$_8$(TeCl$_4$)$_4$]—Tellurium Nitride Stabilized by Tellurium Tetrachloride

Werner Massa, Carsten Lau, Michael Möhlen, Bernhard Neumüller, and Kurt Dehnicke*

Exactly 100 years ago tellurium nitride was first obtained by the reaction of tellurium tetrabromide with liquid ammonia.[1] The composition TeN was ascribed to this yellow, extremely poorly soluble, and highly exlosive substance. Considering the analogy to the crystallographically well characterized homologues S_4N_4[2] and Se_4N_4,[3] this assignment has not been entirely ruled out to this day.[4] However, later analytical work made the composition Te_3N_4 with tetravalent tellurium probable.[5–7] The tellurium compounds with nitride functionalities which were characterized in recent years also derive from tellurium(+IV). Among these are the complexes of type **1** with $X = Cl$[8] and F,[9] which correspond to the structure motif **A** with pyramidal nitride functionality, and the nitride

[*] Prof. Dr. K. Dehnicke, Prof. Dr. W. Massa, Dr. C. Lau, Dr. M. Möhlen, Priv.-Doz. Dr. B. Neumüller
Fachbereich Chemie der Universität
Hans-Meerwein-Strasse, D-35032 Marburg (Germany)
Fax: (+49) 6421-28-8917

FIGURE 3

halides **2**[10] and **3**[11] with the structure motif **B** and trigonal-planar nitride functionality, which is also realized in **4** with the structure motif **C**.

N[Te(NSN)X]₃ **1**   [Te₄N₂Cl₈](AsF₆)₂ **2**   Te₁₁N₆Cl₂₆ **4**
(X = F,Cl)
                  [Te₃N₂Cl₅(SbCl₅)]SbCl₆ **3**

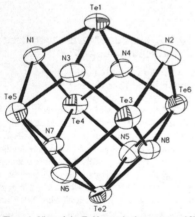

A   **B**   **C**

We now found a method of approach to tellurium nitride stabilized by TeCl₄ molecules in the reaction of tellurium tetrachloride with tris(trimethylsilyl)amine in THF [Eq. (1)]. This tellurium nitride can be obtained in more than 80% yield.

$$10\,TeCl_4 \;+\; 8\,N(SiMe_3)_3 \;\xrightarrow{THF}\; \underset{\textbf{5}}{[Te_6N_8(TeCl_4)_4]} \;+\; 24\,ClSiMe_3 \qquad (1)$$

Compound **5** forms pale yellow, moisture-sensitive, non-explosive crystals. According to the crystal structure analysis[13] these crystals still contain 7.5 equivalents of THF per formula unit, four of which enter into weak bonding interactions with the atoms Te1 and Te2. With 271.3 pm their Te–O distances agree with the Te–O bond lengths of 273.1 pm in [TeCl₄(OPCl₃)]₂.[16] The core of the structure of [**5**·4THF]·3.5THF consists of the rhombic dodecahedral unit Te₆N₈, in which the tellurium atoms form the corners of a distorted octahedron and the nitrogen atoms occupy the faces of the octahedron as μ_3 ligands (Figure 1). Four of these

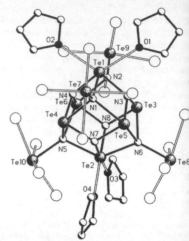

Figure 2. Molecular structure of [**5**·4THF] in the crystal. In the disordered TeCl₄ groups at Te(8–10) only the more strongly occupied orientations are shown. Selected average bond lengths [pm] and angles [°] (standard deviations taken from the mean of the single values): Te(1–6)–N(1,2,5,6) 228.5(6), Te(7–10)–N(1,2,5,6) 204.0(6), Te(1–6)–N(3,4,7,8) 201.3(6), Te(1,2)–O(1–4) 271.3(8), Te–Cl 251.6(4); Te-N(1,2,5,6)-Te 95.5(2), Te-N(3,4,7,8)-Te 114.4(2), Te-N(1,2,5,6)-Te(7–10) 121.0(2).

nitrogen atoms are coordinated with TeCl₄ molecules, the chlorine atoms of which adjust themselves well to the shape of the Te₆N₈ core due to the steric effect of the free electron pair at the tellurium atom (Figure 2). At the same time, with 304–331 pm the distances of the chlorine ligands of the TeCl₄ molecules to the Te atoms of the core which are not

Figure 1. View of the Te₆N₈ core in the structure of [**5**·4THF]·3.5THF. Displacement ellipsoids are at the 30% probability level at 223 K.

coordinated with THF are clearly below the van der Waals sum of radii (381 pm). Since the shielding of the Te₆N₈ core obtained thereby is not yet perfect, the tellurium atoms Te1 and Te2 which are facing each other are solvated by THF molecules. This results in Te₆N₈ molecules which are isolated from one another in the crystal lattice because of their jacket and thus lose their explosive character. Upon heating under argon **5**·7.5THF loses tetrahydrofuran at 83°C. From 141°C onwards **5** is intrinsically unstable with dinitrogen evolution and blackening under separation of tellurium beginning. At 168°C, finally, TeCl₄ can be observed as yellow sublimate.

The TeCl₄ molecules bonded to the nitrogen atoms N(1,2,5,6) cause not only a restriction of the Te-N-Te bond angles of the Te₆N₈ skeleton from 114.4° to 95.5° at N(3,4,7,8) but also a stretching of the affected Te–N bonds of the Te₆N₈ core to 228.5 pm on average; all the other Te–N distances are only 201.3 pm. As a result, the latter are only a bit shorter than the Te–N bonds of the nitride functionality in the molecular complex **1** with 203.1 pm for X = F[9] and 206.1 pm for X = Cl.[8] Almost the same length is also shown by the Te–N bonds of the TeCl₄ molecules which are connected to the Te₆N₈ skeleton (av 204.0 pm). Te–N bonds which are a little shorter with an approximate length of 198 pm were observed in the cationic complexes **2** and **3**.[10, 11] In all cases these distances approximately meet the value of 199 pm for Te–N single bonds.[17] An approximately planar surrounding of the tellurium atoms by the four chlorine atoms as given in **5** is also observed in the polymeric structure of phenyltellurium trichloride.[18]

In THF **5** shows dynamic behavior in the ¹²⁵Te NMR spectrum. Only two signals of different intensities are observed at δ = 716 for the coordinated TeCl₄ molecules

FIGURE 4

and at $\delta = 567$ for the tellurium atoms of the Te_6N_8 core. This is in accord with the idea of a synchronized change of location for the four $TeCl_4$ molecules on the Te_6N_8 surface. Detachment of the $TeCl_4$ molecules does not take place in this process; the ^{125}Te NMR signal of $TeCl_4$ in THF is at $\delta = 1036$.[19] Because of their disorder behavior the change of location of the $TeCl_4$ molecules is also indicated in the crystalline state, even at 223 K. In contrast, the THF molecules which are only loosely bonded are subject to quick exchange according to the ^1H NMR spectrum.

Received: May 20, 1998 [Z 11886 IE]
German version: Angew. Chem. 1998, 110, 3008–3010

Keywords: nitride · nitrogen · tellurium

[1] R. Metzner, Ann. Chim. Phys. 1898, 15, 250.

[2] B. D. Sharma, J. Donohue, Acta Crystallogr. 1963, 16, 891; M. L. DeLucia, P. Coppens, Inorg. Chem. 1978, 17, 2336.

[3] H. Bärnighausen, T. von Volkmann, J. Jander, Acta Crystallogr. 1966, 21, 571; H. Folkerts, B. Neumüller, K. Dehnicke, Z. Anorg. Allg. Chem. 1994, 620, 1011.

[4] H. Garcia-Fernandez, Bull. Soc. Chim. Fr. 1973, 1210; see also N. Wiberg, Holleman-Wiberg, Lehrbuch der Anorganischen Chemie, 101st ed., de Gruyter, Berlin, 1995.

[5] W. Strecker, W. Ebert, Chem. Ber. 1925, 58, 2527.

[6] C. Mahr, Dissertation, Universität Marburg, 1928.

[7] O. Schmitz-DuMont, B. Ross, Angew. Chem. 1967, 79, 1061; Angew. Chem. Int. Ed. Engl. 1967, 6, 1071.

[8] H. W. Roesky, J. Münzenberg, M. Noltemeyer, Angew. Chem. 1990, 102, 73; Angew. Chem. Int. Ed. Engl. 1990, 29, 61.

[9] J. Münzenberg, H. W. Roesky, S. Besser, R. Herbst-Irmer, G. M. Sheldrick, Inorg. Chem. 1992, 31, 2986.

[10] J. Passmore, G. Schatte, T. S. Cameron, J. Chem. Soc. Chem. Commun. 1995, 2311.

[11] C. Lau, H. Krautscheid, B. Neumüller, K. Dehnicke, Z. Anorg. Allg. Chem. 1997, 623, 1375.

[12] C. Lau, B. Neumüller, K. Dehnicke, Z. Anorg. Allg. Chem. 1996, 622, 739.

[13] Crystal structure determination of [5·4THF]·3.5THF ($C_{30}H_{60}Cl_{16}N_8O_{7.5}Te_{10}$, $M_r = 2496.06$): A colorless crystal (ca. $0.54 \times 0.54 \times 0.45$ mm) was analyzed with an area detector system (IPDS, Stoe) at $-50\,°C$ with Mo$_{K\alpha}$ radiation ($\lambda = 71.069$ pm, graphite monochromator). Unit cell monoclinic, $a = 2291.7(2)$, $b = 1222.7(1)$, $c = 5356.0(5)$ pm, $\beta = 101.74(1)°$; $V = 14694 \times 10^{-30}$ m^3, space group $I2/a$, $Z = 8$, $\rho_{calcd} = 2.257$ Mg m^{-3}, μ(Mo$_{K\alpha}$) = 4.53 mm^{-1}, $F(000) = 9184$. Because of reduced intensity at increasing diffraction angle, data were only collected up to $\theta = 24°$, $\Phi = 0 - 250°$, $\Delta\Phi = 1°$, $t = 1$ min per record. Of 55355 reflections collected, 11290 were independent ($R_{int} = 0.060$) and 7648 observed ($I \geq 2\sigma(I)$). Measurement at even lower temperature was not possible, since a phase transition apparently occurs at approximately 220 K. Below this temperature diffuse streaks occur along the nevertheless very long c axis with maxima corresponding to a double superstructure. Semiempirical absorption corrections (from equivalent reflections) were carried out, and the structure was solved by direct methods and refined against all F^2 data[14] by full matrix. The $TeCl_4$ molecules bonded to the Te_6N_8 core showed strong disorder. Three of them had to be described by split atom models, which in two cases showed also a shift component in addition to a rotational component. All atoms, just as those of the core, could be refined with individual anisotropic displacement parameters. The four THF molecules coordinated at the core could be refined without using split positions, but with large anisotropic displacement parameters. The 3.5 THF molecules per molecule additionally fitted into gaps of the packing, one of which was situated on a twofold axis, and showed very strong motion and/or disorder. A model refined with split positions for two THF molecules converged at $wR_2 = 0.1182$ (all reflections) and $R = 0.0404$ (observed reflections).

Because of the less than satisfactory possibility of describing the electron density blurred over this solvent range, its contribution to the structure factors was calculated by way of Back-Fourier transformation[15] and subtracted from the data set. Thereafter, the main structure [5·4THF] could be refined with clearly improved accuracy ($wR_2 = 0.0901$, $R = 0.0348$, residual electron density $0.95/-0.79$ e Å^{-3}). The geometrical details documented here refer to this refinement. The structure determined at 223 K has the character of a high-temperature form in which the solvate molecules and $TeCl_4$ groups show high mobility or disorder. As documented in the quite physically meaningful shapes of displacement ellipsoids ($U_{eq} = 0.054 - 0.083$ Å^2) of all atoms of the Te_6N_8 core, its orientation is not noticeably involved. Thus, no significant influence on the geometry is expected. Crystallographic data (excluding structure factors) for the structure reported in this paper (those obtained by Back-Fourier transformation as well as those obtained according to the disorder model) have been deposited with the Cambridge Crystallographic Data Centre as supplementary publication no. CCDC-101663 and CCDC-101664. Copies of the data can be obtained free of charge on application to CCDC, 12 Union Road, Cambridge CB2 1EZ, UK (fax: (+44) 1223-336-033; e-mail: deposit@ccdc.cam.ac.uk).

[14] G. M. Sheldrick, SHELXTL 5.03, Siemens Analytical X-ray Instruments, Inc., Madison, WI (USA), 1996.

[15] P. van der Sluis, A. L. Spek, Acta Crystallogr. Sect. A 1990, 46, 194–201.

[16] K. Gretenkord, E. Lührs, B. Krebs, zitiert in B. Krebs, F.-P. Ahlers, Adv. Inorg. Chem. 1990, 35, 235.

[17] J. P. Johnson, G. K. McLean, J. Passmore, P. S. White, Can. J. Chem. 1989, 67, 1687.

[18] F. W. B. Einstein, T. Jones, Acta Crystallogr. Sect. B 1982, 38, 617.

[19] C. Lau, Dissertation, Universität Marburg, 1997.

Langmuir – Blodgett Films of Single-Molecule Nanomagnets**

Miguel Clemente-León, Hélène Soyer, Eugenio Coronado,* Christophe Mingotaud,* Carlos J. Gómez-García, and Pierre Delhaès

The discovery that individual molecules can act as magnets of nanometer size is a very recent one.[1, 2] The most thoroughly studied single-molecule magnets are the mixed-valence manganese clusters $[Mn_{12}O_{12}(carboxylate)_{16}]$ (carboxylate = acetate,[1, 3] propionate,[4] benzoate,[5] and 4-methylbenzoate[6]), referred to here as Mn_{12}. The current excitement for this kind of magnetic cluster is primarily due to

[*] Prof. Dr. E. Coronado, M. Clemente-León, Dr. C. J. Gómez-García
Dept. Química Inorgánica. Univ. de Valencia
Dr. Moliner 50, E-46100 Burjasot (Spain)
Fax: (+34) 96-3864322
E-mail: eugenio.coronado@uv.es

Dr. C. Mingotaud, H. Soyer, Dr. P. Delhaès
Centre de Recherche Paul Pascal – CNRS
Avenue A. Schweitzer, F-33600 Pessac (France)
Fax: (+33) 556845600
E-mail: mingotaud@axpp.crpp.u-bordeaux.fr

[**] This work was supported by the Ministerio de Educación y Cultura (Grant No. MAT98-0880) and the EU. M.C.-L. thanks the Generalitat Valenciana for a predoctoral fellowship. We thank the Spanish CICYT and the Generalitat Valenciana for the financial support to purchase the SQUID magnetometer.

FIGURE 5

The paper is "Directed Positioning of Organometallic Fragments inside a Calix[4]arene Cavity," by Catherine Wieser-Jeunesse, Dominique Matt and André De Cian (see figures 6–9), all from the Université Louis Pasteur, located on rue Blaise Pascal in multicultural Strasbourg, Alsace, France.

The article is about three pages long. Almost one page contains experimental detail. Half a page is the endnote apparatus. The body of the article is then about one and a half printed pages, of which roughly a third consists of graphical material: three schemes and a figure.

Let us begin to read the article. To a lay audience, the title is almost comprehensible ("organometallic" being an understandable subject area construction, metals + organic), except for "Calix[4]arene." It is clear that this is a name of a molecule or class of molecules. But what molecules? Our entrance to this small garden of molecular delights is barred (temporarily) by a cognitive disjunction, an angel bearing the awesome sword of nomenclature. Is "calixarene" some systematic scientific name? It couldn't be that calyxes of flowers, or chalices (à la the holy grail) sneak into the chemists' world?

Have no fear. Does it make you feel better when I tell you that half the physical chemists in the world also don't know what a calixarene is?

"Calix[4]arene" is indeed a descriptive, so-called "trivial" name for a class of molecules. The representative of interest to the authors is drawn out in Scheme 1 of the Wieser-Jeunesse, Matt, and De Cian paper (see Figure 10 = Scheme 1). It consists of four (that's the "4" in calix[4]arene) six-carbon benzene rings, which are also called arenes. Each of the four bears an oxygen atom, which is actually almost the only atom whose symbol is explicitly given. And hanging off the four oxygens is a little tail, reconstructed by the chemist from the part iconic, part symbolic, zigzag as a $CH_2CH_2CH_3$ or "n-propyl" group. The four arene rings are linked by another zig (a CH_2 group) into a ring. For all the world, the core of the molecule looks like a square of Balkan dancers, tripping lightly, yet energetically on the molecular scene.

And why "calix"? Precisely because it looked like a chalice to David Gutsche, the maker of the first representative of this class (Nickon and Silversmith, 1987). You wouldn't want to see its systematic official name, and neither would 99.999% of chemists. Calix[4]arene serves just fine. And yes, there are calix[5]arenes . . .

Let us begin with the rather long first paragraph of the paper:

A major attraction of cone-shaped calix[4]arenes concerns the presence of a macrocyclic cavity defined by four symmetrically sited phenoxy rings.[1] To date, exploitation of such organized structures has mostly relied on converg-

spectroscopy of ^{15}N-labeled calmodulin. Measurements were made at 15 °C on a Varian Inova 500 MHz NMR spectrometer, and the protein concentration was 1 mM in H_2O/D_2O (9/1) at pH 6.8. Figure 2 displays a small region of ^{15}N–^1H correlation spectra of calmodulin. Figure 2a shows the conventional HSQC spectrum obtained without the use of

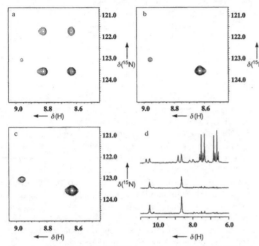

Figure 2. Contour plots of ^{15}N–^1H correlation spectra of ^{15}N-labeled calmodulin. a) Conventional HSQC spectrum, obtained without decoupling during the t_1 and t_2 periods. b) Spectrum recorded in a conventional TROSY experiment.[4] c) Spectrum recorded in a sensitivity-enhanced TROSY experiment (see text). d) One-dimensional cross sections from the spectra a–c at $\delta(^{15}N) = 123.6$ (from top to bottom). The peaks between 6 and 8 ppm in the HSQC cross section correspond to the cross-peak multiplets at the ^{15}N frequency ($\omega_N - \pi^1 J_{NH}$), which is not observed by TROSY experiments. Spectra b and c, which were recorded and processed with the same parameters, have been scaled to the same noise level. The spacing factor between two consecutive contour lines is 1.2.

decoupling during the t_1 and t_2 periods. It is notable that even at 500 MHz there are significant differences in line width between the four individual multiplets. Figures 2b and 2c are taken from spectra recorded in conventional and sensitivity-enhanced TROSY experiments, respectively. Comparison of Figures 2b and 2c, as well as all other correlation peaks (not shown here), shows that a uniform enhancement in sensitivity of all peaks by a factor of $\sqrt{2}$ was achieved without introducing any artifacts.

The introduction of the TROSY experiment makes NMR spectroscopy a promising technique for studying the structure and function of larger biomolecules. We have improved the sensitivity of the original 2D TROSY experiment by a factor of $\sqrt{2}$ by using different phase cycling and data-processing schemes. This improvement will doubtless have widespread practical application in high-field NMR studies of large proteins.

Received: June 19, 1998 [Z 12014 IE]
German version: Angew. Chem. 1998, 110, 3019–3021

Keywords: NMR spectroscopy · proteins

[1] a) G. Wagner, J. Biomol. NMR 1993, 3, 375–385; b) D. Nietlispach, R. T. Clower, R. W. Broadhurst, Y. Ito, J. Keller, M. Kelly, J. Ashurst, H. Oschkinat, P. J. Domaille, E. D. Laue, J. Am. Chem. Soc. 1996, 118, 407–415.

[2] a) H. M. McConnell, J. Chem. Phys. 1956, 25, 709–715; b) R. R. Vold, R. L. Vold, Prog. NMR Spectrosc. 1978, 12, 79–133; c) M. Goldman, J. Magn. Reson. 1984, 60, 437–452; d) S. Wimperis, G. Bodenhausen, Mol. Phys. 1989, 66, 897–919; e) J. Boyd, U. Hommel, I. D. Campbell, Chem. Phys. Lett. 1990, 175, 477–482.

[3] a) L. E. Kay, L. K. Nicholson, F. Delaglio, A. Bax, D. A. Torchia, J. Magn. Reson. 1992, 97, 359–375; b) A. G. Palmer, N. J. Skelton, W. J. Chazin, P. E. Wright, M. Rance, Mol. Phys. 1992, 75, 699–711; c) N. Tjandra, A. Szabo, A. Bax, J. Am. Chem. Soc. 1996, 118, 6986–6991.

[4] K. Pervushin, R. Riek, G. Wider, K. Wuthrich, Proc. Natl. Acad. Sci. USA 1997, 94, 12366–12371.

[5] a) A. G. Palmer III, J. Cavanagh, P. E.Wright, M. Rance, J. Magn. Reson. 1991, 93, 151–170; b) J. Cavanagh, M. Rance, J. Magn. Reson. 1990, 88, 72–85; c) L. E. Kay, P. Keifer, T. Saarinen, J. Am. Chem. Soc. 1992, 114, 10663–10665; d) J. Schleucher, M. Sattler, C. Griesinger, Angew. Chem. 1993, 105, 1518–1521; Angew. Chem. Int. Ed. Engl. 1993, 32, 1489–1491.

[6] a) R. R. Ernst, G. Bodenhausen, A. Wokaun, The Principles of Nuclear Magnetic Resonance in One and Two Dimensions, Clarendon, Oxford, 1987; b) O. W. Sorensen, G. W. Eich, M. H. Levitt, G. Bodenhausen, R. R. Ernst, Prog. NMR Spectrosc. 1983, 16, 163–192.

[7] D. I. States, R. A. Haberkorn, D. J. Buben, J. Magn. Reson. 1982, 93, 151.

[8] Note added in proof: A reviewer's comments alerted us to a difference between Varian and Bruker spectrometers, which requires that the y-axis receiver phases be inverted. It is also necessary to invert the y-axis pulse phases. In the pulse sequence of Figure 1, the particular phase cycling means that only the phase of the second 90° ^1H pulse needs to be considered. For optimal sensitivity, the phase of this pulse should be $-y$ for Varian and $+y$ for Bruker. If this phase is inverted then the "steady-state" enhancement, described by Pervushin et al. (J. Am. Chem. Soc. 1998, 120, 6394–6400) after this manuscript was submitted, will be lost. The sensitivity enhancement presented in this work is independent of the phase of this pulse and a $\sqrt{2}$ enhancement is gained over the corresponding TROSY experiment that has the same phase for this pulse.

Directed Positioning of Organometallic Fragments Inside a Calix[4]arene Cavity

Catherine Wieser-Jeunesse, Dominique Matt,* and André De Cian

A major attraction of cone-shaped calix[4]arenes concerns the presence of a macrocyclic cavity defined by four symmetrically sited phenoxy rings.[1] To date, exploitation of such organized structures has mostly relied on converging π systems on the inner side that facilitate weak binding of various substrates,[2] including certain metal cations.[3] Surprisingly, despite increasing interest in the application of calixarenes as ligands in transition metal chemistry,[4] the

[*] Dr. D. Matt, Dr. C. Wieser-Jeunesse
Université Louis Pasteur, UMR 7513 CNRS
Groupe de Chimie Inorganique Moléculaire
1 rue Blaise Pascal, F-67008 Strasbourg Cedex (France)
Fax: (+33) 3-88-617852
E-mail: dmatt@chimie.u-strasbg.fr
Dr. A. De Cian
Université Louis Pasteur, UMR 7513 CNRS
Laboratoire de Cristallochimie et Chimie Structurale
4 rue Blaise Pascal, F-67008 Strasbourg Cedex (France)

Angew. Chem. Int. Ed. 1998, 37, No. 20   © WILEY-VCH Verlag GmbH, D-69451 Weinheim, 1998   1433-7851/98/3720-2861 $ 17.50+.50/0   2861

FIGURE 6

interior of the cavity has not been used to entrap or confine reactive fragments bound to transition metal ions.[5] Such architectures could possess the capability to promote metal-centered reactions that are sterically constrained, thereby allowing combined shape control and regioselectivity.[6] Furthermore, it is likely that the cavity walls will afford protection of highly reactive "M–R" units against undesired side reactions. We now report the first calix[4]arenes with organometallic fragments positioned inside the larger opening of the cavity.

Our approach to the construction of such systems exploits the coordinative properties of the hemispherical ligand 3, a calix[4]arene bearing two P^{III} centers located on distal p-carbon atoms of the upper rim. Diphosphane 3 was conveniently prepared in two steps from 1[7] by using well-established procedures:[8] diphosphorylation of 1 with Ph₂POEt/NiBr₂ resulted in formation of the di(phosphane oxide) 2, which was then quantitatively reduced with PhSiH₃ to afford 3 (Scheme 1).

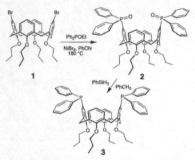

Scheme 1. Synthesis of the hemispherical ligand 3 in two steps.

Diphosphane 3 seems to be an ideal scaffold on which to assemble *trans*-chelate complexes: for example it reacts with one equivalent of AgBF₄ to form complex 4. The FAB mass spectrum of 4 exhibits an intense signal at m/z 1069.6 with the appropriate isotopic profile for the $(4 - BF_4)^+$ ion. NMR data collected for 4 show the molecule to possesses C_2 symmetry,

with the chemical shift found for the ^{31}P NMR signal being exactly as expected for the assigned structure.[9]

The above studies serve to indicate, not unsurprisingly, that the phosphane groups remain readily accessible for complexation with Ag⁺ ions; more challenging targets were then sought. Treatment of 3 with $[PtH(thf)(PPh_3)_2]^+$ in refluxing THF afforded the platinum(II) complex 5 quantitatively. As for 4, the ^{1}H and ^{13}C NMR data indicate an apparent C_2-symmetry for the calixarene skeleton. Furthermore, the ^{31}P NMR spectrum unambiguously establishes the *trans*-spanning behavior of the diphosphane as well as the presence of two types of phosphorus atoms (the phosphorus atoms on the calixarene appear as a doublet with ^{195}Pt satellites at $\delta = 15.0$; $J(P,P') = 20$ Hz, $J(P,Pt) = 2706$ Hz). The bulky PPh₃ ligand, positioned *trans* to the hydride ligand, forces the Pt–H bond to point inside the calixarene cavity. The signal for the hydride atoms appears approximately 1.3 ppm upfield with respect to the related $[PtH(PPh_3)_3]^+$ ion,[10] thus reflecting the high shielding effect of the two phenoxy rings that border the hydride atom. In contrast to other complexes of the type $[PtH(PPh_3)(\overset{\frown}{P\,P})]^+$ that contain a *trans*-spanning diphosphane,[11] complex 5 is inert towards *cis/trans* isomerization in solution. Since only the *trans* isomer has the necessary stereochemical features to position the hydride atom group inside the cavity, the reluctance to isomerize attests to the stability of the inclusion complex.

With the aim to entrap larger metallo-fragments inside the cavity, a solution of 3 in THF was treated with the cationic alkylpalladium complex $[PdMe(cod)(thf)]BF_4$ (cod = cyclooctadiene). Subsequent addition of pyridine resulted in the quantitative formation of complex 6. Characteristic features of the ^{1}H NMR spectrum are the presence of a triplet for the methyl group at $\delta = -0.79$, a solitary AB quartet for the ArCH_2Ar bridges, and a virtual triplet for four $(o\text{-}P)$–ArH hydrogen atoms ($|^3J(PH) + {}^5J(PH)| = 9$ Hz). In the ^{31}P NMR spectrum the phosphorus atoms appear as a singlet at $\delta = 27.0$. Two-dimensional NOESY spectra (500 MHz) indicate that the methyl hydrogen atoms lie in close proximity to the phenolic CH bonds of the two phosphorus-substituted phenoxy rings. Taking into account that the bulky pyridine ligand does not allow gyroscopic spinning of the pyridine-Pd-Me fragment around the P–P axis, these findings clearly establish that the methyl group is locked inside the cavity.

A further illustration of the unique complexing properties of calixarene 3 concerns the positioning of octahedral metal centers at the entrance of the cavity. Treatment of commercial ruthenium trichloride with carbon monoxide in boiling ethoxyethanol followed by the addition of 3 afforded the Ru^{II} complex 7 in high yield (Scheme 2). The *cis* arrangement of the two carbonyl units was inferred from the infrared spectrum, which showed two absorption bands in the CO region ($\tilde{v} = 2072(s)$ and $1995(s)$ cm^{-1}). Complex 7 slowly isomerizes in 1,2-dichloroethane into the *trans,trans,trans* isomer 8 ($\tilde{v}(C{\equiv}O) = 1924(s)$ cm^{-1}). The *trans*-spanning behavior of the diphosphane was confirmed by an X-ray diffraction study (Figure 1). The most remarkable feature of this structure is the entrapment of one metal carbonyl unit inside the calixarene cavity, the CO ligand being exactly intercalated

FIGURE 7

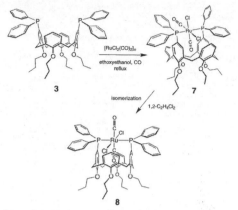

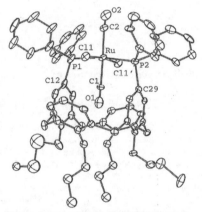

Scheme 2. Positioning of octahedral ruthenium units at the mouth of calixarene **3**.

Figure 1. Structure of complex **8** (ORTEP). Selected bond lengths [pm] and angles [°]: Ru–P1 240.9(5), Ru–P2 240.3(5), Ru–Cl 196(2), Ru–C2 188(2), Ru–Cl 241.0(3), P1–Cl2 182(2), P2–C29 184(1); P1-Ru-P2 172.2(3), Cl-Ru-Cl 171.9(2), Ru-P(1)-C(12) 106.6(5), Ru-P(2)-C(29) 107.2(5). The molecule possesses a mirror plane containing the phosphorus and ruthenium atoms. Each carbon atom of the propyl groups that are linked to the OArP rings are disordered over two positions.

between the two bordering P-substituted phenyl rings. The distance between these planes and the CO ligand axis is rather short (about 2.75 Å), thus suggesting a bonding interaction between the sandwiched CO and the two PPh rings. The relatively low $\bar{\nu}$(CO) frequency (1924(s) cm^{-1} compared with 1998 cm^{-1} for *trans,trans,trans*-[RuCl$_2$(CO)$_2$(PPh$_3$)$_2$][12]) supports this assumption.

Experimental Section

All reactions were carried out in dry solvents under purified nitrogen.

2: Yield: 82%; m.p. >280°C; ^{1}H NMR (300 MHz, CDCl$_3$, 25°C): $\delta =$ 7.76–7.69 and 7.54–7.48 (20H, PPh$_2$), 7.40 (d, 4H, m-H of OArP, ^3J(P,H) = 12 Hz), 6.24 and 6.02 (AB$_2$ spin system, 6H, m- and p of OAr, ^3J = 7.5 Hz), 4.42 and 3.12 (AB spin sytem, 8H, ArCH$_2$Ar, ^2J(A,B) = 13 Hz), 4.08 (pseudo t, 4H, OCH$_2$, $^3J \approx$ 8 Hz), 3.60 (t, 4H, OCH$_2$, $^3J =$ 8 Hz), 1.94 (m, 4H, OCH$_2$CH$_2$), 1.82 (m, 4H, OCH$_2$CH$_2$), 1.06 (t, CH$_3$, $^3J =$ 8 Hz), 0.90 (t, CH$_3$, $^3J =$ 8 Hz); ^{13}C{^{1}H} NMR (50 MHz, CDCl$_3$, 25°C): $\delta =$ 161.52 and 155.12 (2s, arom. C$_q$–O), 137.67–122.31 (arom. C atoms), 77.14 and 76.74 (2s, OCH$_2$), 30.96 (s, ArCH$_2$), 23.51 and 23.17 (2s, CH$_2$CH$_3$), 10.84 and 9.86 (2s, CH$_3$); ^{31}P{^{1}H} NMR (121 MHz, CDCl$_3$, 25°C): $\delta =$ 29.4 (s, PPh$_2$); elemental analyses calcd for C$_{64}$H$_{66}$O$_6$P$_2$·0.5 CHCl$_3$ (993.18 + 59.69): C 73.58, H 6.37; found: C 74.00, H 6.37.

3: Yield: 75%; m.p. 230–233°C; ^{1}H NMR (300 MHz, CDCl$_3$, 25°C): $\delta =$ 7.37–7.33 (20H, PPh$_2$), 7.06 (d, 4H, m-H of OArP, ^3J(P,H) = 8 Hz), 6.29 and 6.11 (AB$_2$ spin system, 6H, m and p-H of OAr, $^3J =$ 8 Hz), 4.41 and 3.06 (AB spin system, 8H, ArCH$_2$Ar, ^2J(A,B) = 13 Hz), 4.03 (pseudo t, 4H, OCH$_2$, $^3J \approx$ 8 Hz), 3.63 (t, 4H, OCH$_2$, $^3J =$ 8 Hz), 2.00 (m, 4H, OCH$_2$CH$_2$), 1.81 (m, 4H, OCH$_2$CH$_2$), 1.06 (t, CH$_3$, $^3J =$ 7.5 Hz), 0.91 (t, CH$_3$, $^3J =$ 7.5 Hz); ^{13}C{^{1}H} NMR (50 MHz, CDCl$_3$, 25°C): $\delta =$ 159.80 and 155.10 (2s, arom. C$_q$–O), 137.25-122.02 (arom. C atoms), 77.00 and 76.60 (2s, OCH$_2$), 30.94 (s, ArCH$_2$Ar), 23.51 and 23.15 (2s, CH$_2$CH$_3$), 10.82 and 9.93 (2s, CH$_3$); ^{31}P{^{1}H} NMR (121 MHz, CDCl$_3$, 25°C): $\delta = -6.4$ (s, PPh$_2$); elemental analyses calcd for C$_{64}$H$_{66}$O$_4$P$_2$ (961.18): C 79.98, H 6.92; found: C 80.18, H 6.74.

4: Yield: 80%; m.p. 187–190°C (decomp); ^{1}H NMR (300 MHz, CDCl$_3$, 25°C): $\delta =$ 7.43-7.37 (24H, arom. H), 6.82 (s, 4H, m-H of OArP), 6.18 (t of B$_2$A spin system, 2H, p-H of OAr, $^3J =$ 8 Hz), 4.40 and 3.05 (AB spin system, 8H, ArCH$_2$Ar, ^2J(A,B) = 13 Hz), 4.01 (pseudo t, 4H, OCH$_2$, $^3J \approx$ 8 Hz), 3.70 (t, 4H, OCH$_2$, $^3J =$ 8 Hz), 1.98 (m, 4H, OCH$_2$CH$_2$), 1.89 (m, 4H, OCH$_2$CH$_2$), 1.09 (t, CH$_3$, $^3J =$ 7.5 Hz), 0.83 (t, CH$_3$, $^3J =$ 7.5 Hz); ^{13}C{^{1}H} NMR (50 MHz, CDCl$_3$, 25°C): $\delta =$ 157.18 and 156.85 (2s, arom. C$_q$–O), 136.09-123.02 (arom. C atoms), 77.64 and 76.59 (2s, OCH$_2$), 30.85 (s, ArCH$_2$Ar), 23.91 and 23.57 (2s, CH$_2$CH$_3$), 10.79 and 9.80 (2s, CH$_3$); ^{31}P{^{1}H} NMR (121 MHz, CDCl$_3$, 25°C): $\delta =$ 10.4 (two d, PPh$_2$, J(^{107}Ag,P) = 503 Hz, J(^{109}Ag,P) = 580 Hz); MS (FAB): m/z calcd for C$_{64}$H$_{66}$O$_4$P$_2$Ag [M – BF$_4$]: 1069; found 1069.6; elemental analyses calcd for C$_{64}$H$_{66}$BF$_4$O$_4$P$_2$Ag (1155.86): C 66.51, H 5.76; found: C 66.66, H 5.43.

5: Yield: 73%; m.p. 226–230°C; ^{1}H NMR (300 MHz, CDCl$_3$, 25°C): $\delta =$ 7.42–7.02 and 6.87 (43H, arom. H), 6.24 (t of B$_2$A spin system, 2H, p-H of OAr, ^3J(A,B) = 6 Hz), 4.44 and 3.09 (AB spin sytem, 8H, ArCH$_2$Ar, ^2J(A,B) = 13 Hz), 4.04 (pseudo t, 4H, OCH$_2$, $^3J \approx$ 6 Hz), 3.69 (t, 4H, OCH$_2$, $^3J =$ 7 Hz), 1.97 (m, 4H, OCH$_2$CH$_2$), 1.89 (m, 4H, OCH$_2$CH$_2$), 1.10 (t, CH$_3$, $^3J =$ 9 Hz), 0.92 (t, CH$_3$, $^3J =$ 7 Hz), – 6.93 (dt with Pt satellites, 1H, PtH, ^2J(H,P$_{cis}$) = 17 Hz, ^2J(H,P$_{trans}$) = 167 Hz); ^{13}C{^{1}H} NMR (50 MHz, CDCl$_3$, 25°C): $\delta =$ 157.39 and 156.70 (2s, arom.C$_q$–O), 136.40–122.43 (arom. C atoms), 77.90 and 76.65 (2s, OCH$_2$), 30.93 (s, ArCH$_2$), 23.51 and 22.94 (2s, CH$_2$CH$_3$), 10.74 and 9.77 (2s, CH$_2$CH$_3$); ^{31}P{^{1}H} NMR (121 MHz, CDCl$_3$, 25°C): $\delta =$ 24.2 (t with Pt satellites, PPh$_3$, ^2J(P,P') = 20 Hz, J(P,Pt) = 2120 Hz), 15.0 (d, PPh$_2$, ^2J(P,P') = 20, J(P,Pt) = 2706 Hz). MS (FAB): m/z calcd for C$_{82}$H$_{82}$O$_4$P$_3$Pt [M – BF$_4$]: 1418.5; found: 1418.8 (expected isotopic profile); elemental analyses calcd for C$_{82}$H$_{82}$ BF$_4$O$_4$P$_3$Pt (1506.38): C 65.38, H 5.49; found: C 65.18, H 5.43.

6: Yield: 81%; m.p. 163–166°C (decomp); ^{1}H NMR (300 MHz, CD$_2$Cl$_2$, 25°C): $\delta =$ 7.79 (d, 2H, o-H of pyridine), 7.52 (t, 1H, p-H of pyridine, $^3J =$ 5 Hz), 7.32–7.24 (20H, PPh$_2$), 7.06–7.00 (m, 6H, m- and p-H of OAr), 6.79 (m br, 2H, m-H of pyridine), 6.62 (virtual t, 4H, AA'XX'A''A''' spin system (X = P), 4H, m-H of OArP, |^3J(P,H)+^5J(P',H)| = 9 Hz), 4.56 and 3.24 (AB spin sytem, 8H, ArCH$_2$Ar, ^2J(A,B) = 13 Hz), 4.15 (pseudo t, 4H, OCH$_2$, $^3J \approx$ 8 Hz), 3.81 (t, 4H, OCH$_2$, $^3J =$ 7 Hz), 2.06 (m, 4H, OCH$_2$CH$_2$), 1.97 (m, 4H, OCH$_2$CH$_2$), 1.15 (t, CH$_3$, $^3J =$ 7 Hz), 0.96 (t, CH$_3$, $^3J =$ 7 Hz), – 0.79 (s, 3H, Pd-CH$_3$, J(P,H) = 6 Hz); ^{13}C{^{1}H} NMR (CD$_2$Cl$_2$, 50 MHz, 25°C): $\delta =$ 157.95 and 157.59 (2s, arom. C$_q$–O), 151.66–121.56 (arom. C atoms), 78.32 and 77.08 (2s, OCH$_2$), 31.32 (s, ArCH$_2$Ar), 23.98 (s, CH$_2$CH$_3$), 11.00 and 9.98 (2s, CH$_3$); ^{31}P{^{1}H} NMR (CD$_2$Cl$_2$, 121 MHz, 25°C): $\delta =$ 27.0 (s, PPh$_2$) MS (FAB): m/z calcd for C$_{65}$H$_{69}$O$_4$P$_2$Pd [M – pyridine – BF$_4$]: 1081; found: 1081.1 (expected isotopic profile); elemental analyses calcd for C$_{70}$H$_{74}$BF$_4$NO$_4$P$_2$Pd (1248.53): C 67.34, H 5.95, N 1.12; found: C 67.41, H 6.10, N 0.93.

7 : Yield: 84%; m.p. >280°C; IR (KBr): $\bar{\nu}$(C≡O) = 2072(s) and 1995(s) cm^{-1}; ^{1}H NMR (500 MHz, CD$_2$Cl$_2$, 25°C): $\delta =$ 8.31–8.28 and 7.36–7.34 (20H, PPh$_2$), 6.82 (virtual t, 4H, m-H of OArP), 6.81 and 6.65 (B$_2$A spin system, 6H, m- and p-H of OAr, ^3J(A,B) = 6 Hz), 4.47 and 3.19 (AB spin sytem, 8H, ArCH$_2$Ar, ^2J(A,B) = 13 Hz), 3.99 (pseudo t, 4H,

FIGURE 8

COMMUNICATIONS

OCH_2, $^3J \approx 8$ Hz), 3.78 (t, 4H, OCH_2, $^3J = 7$ Hz), 2.02 (m, 4H, OCH_2CH_2), 1.94 (m, 4H, OCH_2CH_2), 1.11 (t, CH_3, $^3J = 7.5$ Hz), 0.91 (t, CH_3, $^3J = 9$ Hz); $^{13}C\{^1H\}$ NMR (75 MHz, CD_2Cl_2, 25°C): $\delta = 158.48$ and 157.75 (2s, arom.C_q–O), 135.02–123.95 (arom. C atoms), 78.47 and 76.79 (2s, OCH_2), 31.09 (s, $ArCH_2$), 23.95 and 23.51 (2s, CH_2CH_3), 11.05 and 10.01 (2s, CH_2CH_3), C≡O not detected; $^{31}P\{^1H\}$ NMR (121 MHz, CD_2Cl_2, 25°C): $\delta = 12.9$ (s, PPh_2); MS (FAB): m/z calcd for $C_{65}H_{66}ClO_5P_2Ru$ $[M - Cl - (CO)]$: 1125; found: 1125.5 (expected isotopic profile); elemental analyses calcd for $C_{66}H_{66}Cl_2O_6P_2Ru$ (1189.18): C 66.66, H 5.59; found: C 66.54, H 5.63.

8: Yield: 95%; IR (KBr): $\tilde{v}(C≡O) = 1924(s)$ cm^{-1}; ^1H NMR (500 MHz, CD_2Cl_2, 25°C): $\delta = 7.91–7.89$ and 7.37–7.35 (20H, PPh_2), 6.86 and 6.67 (B_2A spin system, 6H, m- and p-H of OAr, $^3J = 7.5$ Hz), 6.75 (virtual t $ABXX'A'B'$ spin system, 4H, m-H of OArP, $^3J(A,X) \approx ^3J(B,X) \approx 5$ Hz), 4.51 and 3.22 (AB spin sytem, 8H, $ArCH_2Ar$, $^2J(A,B) = 13$ Hz), 4.14 (pseudo t, 4H, OCH_2, $^3J \approx 8$ Hz), 3.79 (t, 4H, OCH_2, $^3J = 7$ Hz), 2.01 (m, 4H, OCH_2CH_2), 1.95 (m, 4H, OCH_2CH_2), 1.13 (t, CH_3, $^3J = 7.5$ Hz), 0.90 (t, CH_3, $^3J = 9$ Hz); $^{31}P\{^1H\}$ NMR (121 MHz, CD_2Cl_2, 25°C): $\delta = 42.4$ (s, PPh_2). Crystal data for $8 \cdot C_2H_4Cl_2$: $M_r = 1288.14$, orthorhombic, space group $Pbcm$, $a = 19.4779(6)$, $b = 17.7412(3)$, $c = 17.2124(5)$ Å, $V = 5947.5(5)$ Å^3, $Z = 4$, $\rho_{calcd} = 1.44$ g cm^{-3}, Mo$_{K\alpha}$ radiation ($\lambda = 0.71073$ Å), $\mu = 0.544$ mm^{-1}. Data were collected on a Kappa CCD Enraf Nonius system at 173 K. The structure was solved by direct methods and refined on F_o^2 by full-matrix least squares. All non-hydrogen atoms were refined anisotropically. $R1 = 0.089$ and $wR2 = 0.117$ for 3296 data with $I > 3\sigma(I)$. Crystallographic data (excluding structure factors) for the structure reported in this paper have been deposited with the Cambridge Crystallographic Data Centre as supplementary publication no. CCDC-101566. Copies of the data can be obtained free of charge on application to CCDC, 12 Union Road, Cambridge CB21EZ, UK (fax: (+44)1223-336-033; e-mail: deposit@ccdc.cam.ac.uk).

Received: May 8, 1998 [Z11832IE]
German version: *Angew. Chem.* 1998, *110*, 3027–3030

Keywords: calixarenes · intercalation · phosphanes · supramolecular chemistry

[1] For example, see "Calixarenes": C. D. Gutsche in *Monographs in Supramolecular Chemistry, Vol. 1* (Ed.: J. F. Stoddart), Royal Society of Chemistry, Cambridge, 1989; V. Böhmer, *Angew. Chem.* 1995, *107*, 785–818; *Angew. Chem. Int. Ed. Engl.* 1995, *34*, 713–745; M. A. van Wageningen, E. Snip, W. Verboom, D. N. Reinhoudt, H. Boerrigter, *Liebigs Ann.* 1997, 2235–2245.

[2] For example, see R. Ungaro, A. Pochini, G. Andreeti, P. Domiano, *J. Chem. Soc. Perkin Trans. 2* 1985, 197–201; W. Xu, R. J. Puddephatt, L. Manojlovic-Muir, K. W. Muir, C. S. Frampton, *J. Incl. Phenom.* 1994, *19*, 277–290; V. C. Gibson, C. Redshaw, W. Clegg, M. R. J. Elsegood, *J. Chem. Soc. Chem. Commun.* 1995, 2371–2372; J. L. Atwood, K. T. Holman, J. W. Steed, *Chem. Commun.* 1996, 1401–1407; P. D. Beer, M. G. B. Drew, P. B. Leeson, M. I. Ogden, *Inorg. Chim. Acta* 1996, *246*, 133–141; C. L. Raston, J. L. Atwood, P. J. Nichols, I. B. N. Sudria, *Chem. Commun.* 1996, 2615–2616; R. Abidi, M. V. Baker, J. M. Harrowfield, D. S.-C. Ho, W. R. Richmond, B. W. Skelton, A. H. White, A. Varnek, G. Wipff, *Inorg. Chim. Acta* 1996, *246*, 275–286; A. Ikeda, Y. Suzuki, M. Yoshimura, S. Shinkai, *Tetrahedron* 1998, *54*, 2497–2508.

[3] A. Ikeda, S. Shinkai, *J. Am. Chem. Soc.* 1994, *116*, 3102–3110.

[4] D. V. Khasnis, J. M. Burton, J. D. McNeil, H. Zhang, M. Lattman, *Phosphorus Sulfur Silicon* 1993, *75*, 253–256; C. Dieleman, C. Loeber, D. Matt, A. De Cian, J. Fischer, *J. Chem. Soc. Dalton Trans.* 1995, 3097–3100; D. M. Roundhill, *Progr. Inorg. Chem.* 1995, *43*, 533–592; I. Neda, H.-J. Plinta, R. Sonnenburg, A. Fischer, P. G. Jones, R. Schmutzler, *Chem. Ber.* 1995, *128*, 267–273; B. R. Cameron, S. J. Loeb, *Chem. Commun.* 1996, 2003–2004; C. Loeber, D. Matt, P. Briard, D. Grandjean, *J. Chem. Soc. Dalton Trans.* 1996, 513–524; C. Wieser, D. Matt, J. Fischer, A. Harriman, *J. Chem. Soc. Dalton Trans.* 1997, 2391–2402; M. Giusti, E. Solari, L. Giannini, C. Floriani, A. Chiesi-Villa, C. Rizzoli, *Organometallics* 1997, *16*, 5610–5612; A. Zanotti-Gerosa, E. Solari, L. Giannini, C. Floriani, A. Chiesi-Villa, C. Rizzoli, *Chem. Commun.* 1997, 183–184; C. Wieser, D. B. Dieleman, D. Matt, *Coord. Chem. Rev.* 1997, *165*, 93–161.

[5] A homooxacalix[4]arene-Eu complex containing a coordinated acetone molecule that is located inside the cavity has been reported: Z. Asfari, J. M. Harrowfield, M. I. Ogden, J. Vicens, A. H. White, *Angew. Chem.* 1991, *103*, 887–889; *Angew. Chem. Int. Ed. Engl.* 1991, *30*, 854–856.

[6] H. K. A. C. Coolen, P. W. N. M. van Leeuwen, R. J. M. Nolte, *Angew. Chem.* 1992, *104*, 906–909; *Angew. Chem. Int. Ed. Engl.* 1992, *31*, 905–907; M. T. Reetz, S. R. Waldvogel, *Angew. Chem.* 1997, *109*, 870–873; *Angew. Chem. Int. Ed. Engl.* 1997, *36*, 865–867; K. Goto, R. Okazaki, *Liebigs Ann.* 1997, 2393–2407.

[7] M. Larsen, M. Jørgensen, *J. Org. Chem.* 1996, *61*, 6651–6655.

[8] V. I. Kalchenko, L. I. Atamas, V. V. Pirozhenko, L. N. Markovsky, *Zh. Obshch. Khim.* 1992, *62*, 2623–2625; S. Ozegowski, B. Costisella, J. Gloede, *Phosphorus Sulfur Silicon.* 1996, *119*, 209–223; C. Loeber, C. Wieser, D. Matt, A. De Cian, J. Fischer, L. Toupet, *Bull. Soc. Chim. Fr.* 1995, *132*, 166–177.

[9] M. Camalli, F. Caruso, S. Chaloupka, P. N. Kapoor, P. S. Pregosin, L. M. Venanzi, *Helv. Chim. Acta* 1984, *67*, 1603–1611.

[10] K. Thomas, J. T. Dumler, B. W. Renoe, C. J. Nyman, D. M. Roundhill, *Inorg. Chem.* 1972, *11*, 1795–1799.

[11] G. Bracher, D. M. Grove, L. M. Venanzi, F. Bachechi, P. Mura, L. Zambonelli, *Helv. Chim. Acta* 1980, *63*, 2519–2530.

[12] R. Vac, J. H. Nelson, E. B. Milosavljević, L. Solujić, *Inorg. Chem.* 1989, *28*, 3831–3836.

A New Radical Allylation Reaction of Dithiocarbonates**

Béatrice Sire, Stéphanie Seguin, and Samir Z. Zard*

In contrast to radical cyclizations, which have practically revolutionized the construction of polycyclic systems, intermolecular radical additions to olefins have had a comparatively limited impact on organic synthesis.[1] This is chiefly because of the difficulty in avoiding competing bimolecular side reactions which, in the case of intramolecular processes, can usually be controlled by the use of high dilution techniques (e.g. slow, syringe pump addition of one of the reagents). With stannane-based reactions, for example, the difficulty lies in preventing premature hydrogen atom transfer to the radical before it adds to the olefin. One special exception is the allylation reaction with allyltriorganotin.[2] In this case, the allyl transfer step is the one that regenerates the stannyl radical to propagate the chain and, even if this step is not very fast by radical reaction standards,[3] there are no other major competing pathways. This fairly general and quite useful intermolecular C–C bond forming procedure unfortunately uses tin and therefore suffers from the same drawbacks as other tin-based systems: high cost and difficulty in removing toxic organotin contaminants.[4] These are serious

[*] Dr. S. Z. Zard,[+] Dr B. Quiclet-Sire, S. Seguin
Institut de Chimie des Substances Naturelles
91198 Gif-Sur-Yvette (France)
Fax: (+33)1-69-07-72-47

[+] Further address:
Laboratoire de Synthèse Organique associé au CNRS
Ecole Polytechnique, 91128 Palaiseau Cedex (France)
Fax: (+33)1-69-33-30-10

[**] We wish to thank Thi-My Ly for preparing compound 1e.

FIGURE 9

FIGURE 10

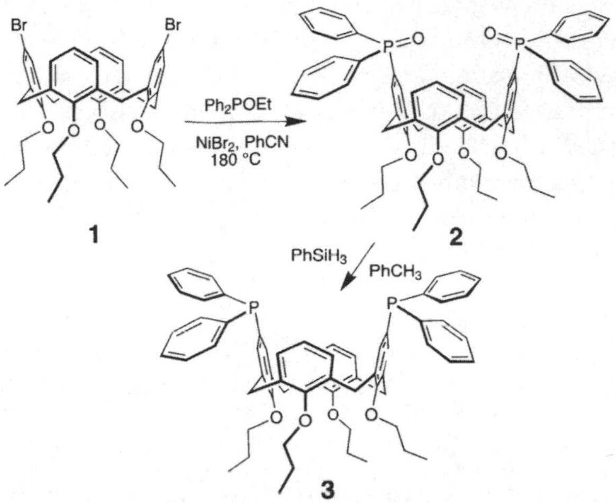

Scheme 1. Synthesis of the hemispherical ligand **3** in two steps.

ing π systems on the inner side that facilitate weak binding of various substrates,[2] including certain metal cations.[3]1

To make sense of the words we need to look at the picture, Scheme 1, again. The beetle quadrille is sort of cone-shaped. "Phenoxy" is a chemical word for the combination of an oxygen with an arene ring; the same grouping plays a role in molecules as diverse (and as common) as vanillin, aspirin, and mescalin. "Macrocyclic" is a fancy word for "big ring." The addiction to Latinate expressions to express learnedness has not vanished, even if chemists in general know precious little Latin.

In the second sentence of the introductory paragraph there is some delimitation of the current interest in the molecule that is central to this study, the rhetorical intent clear, to provide a space for the raison-d'être of this study. The "π-systems" referred to are the electrons cruising above and below the face of the six-carbon arene rings that make up the calixarene; there is a long, long history both of the importance of this subset of electrons, and their tangible involvement in the stability of that ring. If you want to know more, a combination of a dose of Pynchon's *Gravity's Rainbow* and an organic chemistry course by one of my colleagues will help. Wieser-Jeunesse, Matt, and De Cian say that others have been playing with these electrons, using them to bind weakly to metal cations (positive ions).

---

1. The bracketed numbers are the endnote references in the original text.

The background to all this work is a desire to achieve control (shall we malign that obsession as male, when a woman is one of the co-authors of this work?) over the way molecules react and their structures. The thinking is geometrical, almost billiard ball-like, on the microscopic level. Molecules are an in-between land, yes—they are quantum objects, and yet, in so many heuristically useful ways, they are also little structures, to be ingeniously assembled, disassembled, constructed. The architectonic thinking is very clear in this paragraph.

The authors continue:

> Surprisingly, despite increasing interest in the application of calixarenes as ligands in transition metal chemistry [4] the interior of the cavity has not been used to entrap or confine reactive fragments bound to transition metal ions.[5]

Here there is a reaching out to another type of chemistry (inorganic chemistry, which studies metal ions), and a furthering of the rhetorical strategy. There is no doubt that the authors will provide us with the utility lacking in the previous work:

> Such architectures could possess the capability to promote metal-centered reactions that are sterically constrained, thereby allowing combined shape control and regioselectivity.[6]

We see more geometrical descriptors, further aspirations to control, just a little more jargon. The paragraph ends with the claim of this paper very clearly announced:

> We now report the first calix[4]arenes with organometallic fragments positioned inside the larger opening of the cavity.

I would characterize the jargon as moderate at this level, and the claims actually not exaggerated. The rhetorical posture is—to me—acceptable.

The authors next get down to business:

> Our approach to the construction of such systems exploits the coordinative properties of the hemispherical ligand **3**, a calix[4]arene bearing two P^{III} centers located on distal p-carbon atoms of the upper rim. Diphosphane **3** was conveniently prepared in two steps from **1**[7] by using well-established procedures:[8] diphosphorylation of **1** with $Ph_2POEt/NiBr_2$ resulted in formation of the di(phosphane oxide) **2**, which was then quantitatively reduced with $PhSiH_3$ to afford **3** (Scheme 1).

What Wieser-Jeunesse, Matt, and De Cian are doing is pretty easy to describe. They take the calixarene (they don't tell us in what quantity) 1,[2] which has two bromine atoms at the top of two of the four arene rings, and using these bromide handles, change them to more complicated groupings containing a phosphorus and an oxygen, then remove an oxygen. The experimental section does not actually give details of the synthesis, but provides the physical proof for the structure of compounds/molecules 2 and 3. Real substances are manipulated, many physical transformations made, much labor, real work. None of that is detailed here. The authors speak, as chemists today do, of molecules that they do not see, but for which they have excellent indirect evidence (knowing without seeing, wonderful stuff!). Elsewhere, Emily Grosholz and I have written of this incredible process, and the way that the chemists' necessity to move simultaneously in macroscopic and microscopic worlds forces chemists to use a mixture of symbolic and iconic representation of compounds/molecules (Grosholz and Hoffmann, 2000).

Making molecule 3 is the necessary preparation—the remainder of this excellent paper uses 3 to do everything the authors set out claims to:

> Diphosphane 3 seems to be an ideal scaffold on which to assemble *trans*-chelate complexes: for example it reacts with one equivalent of $AgBF_4$ to form complex 4. The FAB mass spectrum of 4 exhibits an intense signal at m/z 1069.6 with the appropriate isotopic profile for the $(3-BF_4)^+$ ion. NMR data collected for 4 show the molecule to possess C2 symmetry, with the chemical shift found for the ^{31}P NMR signal being exactly as expected for the assigned structure.[9]

As Wieser-Jeunesse, Matt, and De Cian say in the first sentence, the "diphosphane" is designed to, and does, clasp pretty much any metal ion, and silver in particular. This is shown in their molecular structure 4, reproduced in Figure 11.

The next part of the paper is interesting, for it begins with a sentence that for a chemical paper is relatively uncommon:

> The above studies serve to indicate, not unsurprisingly, that the phosphane groups remain readily accessible for complexation with Ag^+ ions; more challenging targets were then sought.

2. It is chemical custom to refer to molecular structures by boldface numbers. This is done both by the authors of the paper studied and by me, using the same numbers. The structures are defined in the figures.

FIGURE 11

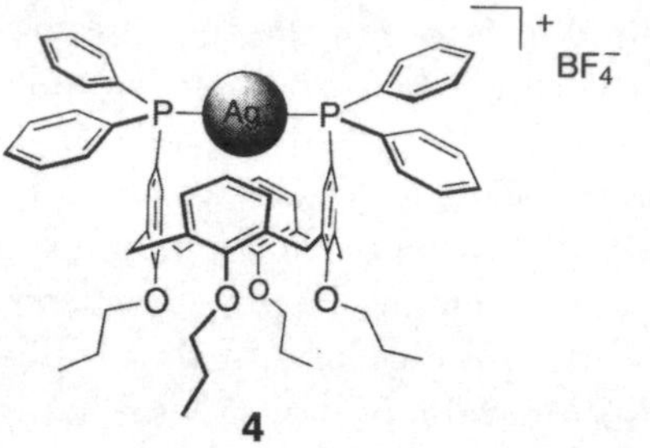

This says: "that was easy; let's try for something harder." Do you think they will fail?

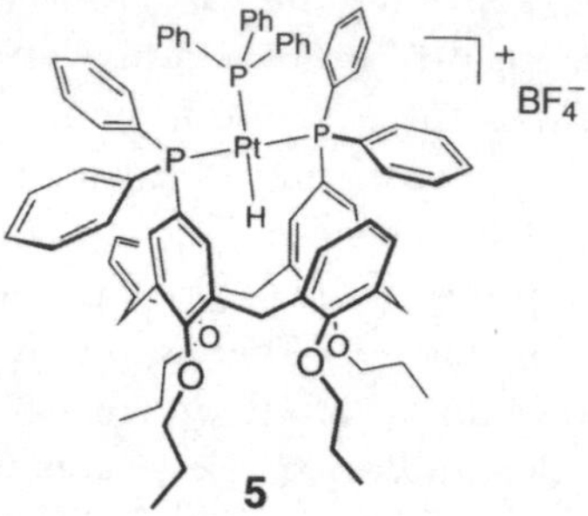

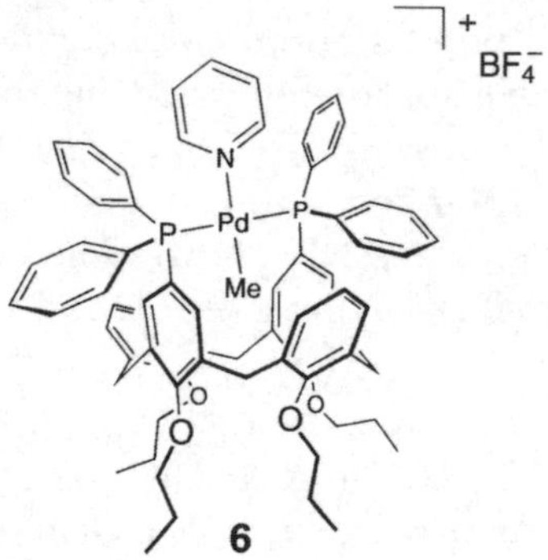

Let me next sketch in sparse detail the subsequent neat chemistry Wieser-Jeunesse, Matt, and De Cian carried out. Using instead of a silver compound a platinum one, they get a platinum-containing unit bound in between the phosphoruses. But now that platinum unit is not "naked," like the silver was, but carries a hydrogen poking into the cavity of the chalice—which doesn't have all that much room for extra atoms. The hydrogen senses the constrained environment; signals from within tell us it is there and nowhere else. That's the NMR (nuclear magnetic resonance) spectroscopy referred to in the paper; in a fit of creative euphemism our fearful society has renamed the technique in its medical incarnation as MRI.

The alternative, given the desire of the platinum to have a square-planar environment, would have been to poke the much bigger PPh_3 (Ph is an abbreviation for phenyl, or a C_6H_5 benzene) group inside.

Incidentally, "Given the desire . . ." refers to my métier, for as a theoretical chemist I would like to think of myself as a delineator of desire. Of course, the desire (to be in one geometry or another) is there, whether I am there or not. What I do is teach people, by telling plausible stories, why a molecule takes on one shape and not another. Politician, priest, storyteller, arbiter of molecular desire—that's what I am. At least one day a week.

Wieser-Jeunesse, Matt, and De Cian then tuck in a palladium, with a still bulkier "Me" (that is a piece of colloquial notation for the CH $_3$ grouping of atoms) group on the inside, **6** (see Fig. 11). It is only contemplating my imminent departure for Lacoste, Provence, to live, perchance to write, for a month in the shadow of the ancestral château of the Marquis de Sade, which leads me to muse about the fact that Wieser-Jeunesse, Matt, and De Cian don't stop there. They want to test the limits, ring the changes, see how much that constrained chalice space will take. All the ways of its bonding . . .

In their Scheme 2 (Fig. 12 here) you see the realized plan: even a locally octahedral ruthenium atom can be lured to bind in the cavity of the calixarene (the structure, determined with X-ray crystallography, is shown in their article).

FIGURE 12

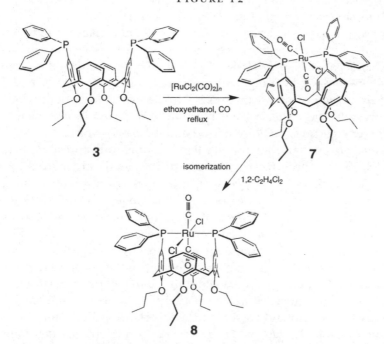

Scheme 2. Positioning of octahedral ruthenium units at the mouth of calixarene **3**.

One carbon monoxide "ligand" on the ruthenium, the one poking into the cavity, is much affected. Wieser-Jeunesse, Matt, and De Cian claim bonding; I actually would disagree, for theoretical reasons. This is my only disagreement with their lovely work.

On this note the paper ends, quite abruptly. I might add that this excellent research caught not only my eye, but that of the editors of the periodical, who feature its climactic synthesis in a separate graphic (Fig. 13) on the cover of that issue of *Angewandte Chemie*.

THE WAY IT IS TOLD

You open an issue of a modern chemical periodical, and you see more of what I have shown you. Riches upon riches: reports of new discoveries, marvelous molecules, unmakeable, unthinkable yesterday—made today, reproducibly, with ease. The chemist reads of the incredible properties of novel high temperature superconductors, organic ferromagnets, and supercritical solvents. New techniques of measurement, quickly equipped with acronyms—EXAFS, INEPT, COCONOESY—allow you to puzzle out the structure of what you make more expeditiously. Information just flows. It's chemistry—communicated, exciting, alive.

I have shown to you an article reporting excellent chemistry, and a well written one. I assure you that it is given to me and my colleagues to read much that is palpably worse. How tired I am of seeing articles that begin with "The structure, bonding, and spectroscopy of molecules of type X have been subjects of intense interest.[a-z]"! In the vast majority of the chemical literature I see a ritual product, at times stultifying in its sameness. There is general use of the third person and the passive voice. Few overtly expressed personal motivations, and few accounts of historical development, are to be found. Here and there in the neutered language one glimpses stated claims of achievement or priority—"a novel metabolite," "the first synthesis," "a general strategy," "parameter-free calculations." But these are more in the service of hype than elegance. On studying many papers one finds a mind-deadening similarity. In this land of the new! Nevertheless, one also sees here and there style—a distinctive, connected scientific/written/graphic way of looking at the chemical universe.

There is much more to say, both about the history of the journal article, and the essentially chemical nature of the process of representation of molecules (Hoffmann and Laszlo, 1991) The rhetorical structure of the chemical article is also fascinating—elsewhere, I have argued that much more goes on in that article than one imagines at first sight; that what goes on is a kind of dialectical struggle between what a chemist imagines

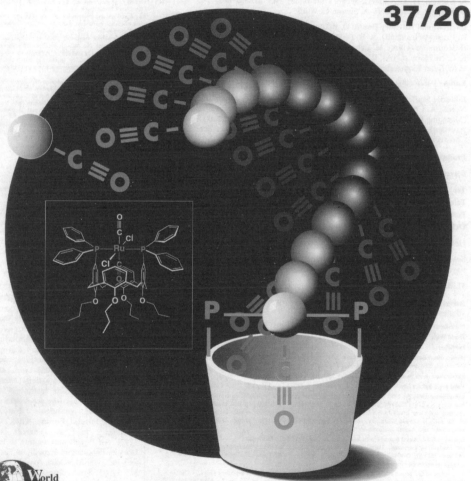

D 3461

ANGEWANDTE
CHEMIE
INTERNATIONAL EDITION

A Journal of the
Gesellschaft
Deutscher Chemiker

1998
37/20

World Wide Web

http://www.wiley-vch.de/
home/angewandte/

WILEY-VCH

ACIEF5 37 (20) 2743–2906 (1998) · ISSN 1433–7851 · Vol. 37 · No. 20 · November 2, 1998

FIGURE 13

should be said (the paradigm, the normative) and what he or she must say to convince others of his argument or achievement. That struggle endows the most innocent-looking article with a lot of suppressed tension (see chapters 17 and 18 in Hoffmann, 1995).

What Is to Be Done?

I love this complex molecular science. I know that its richness was created by human beings. So I'm unhappy to see their humanity suppressed in the way they express themselves in print. The periodical article system of transmitting new knowledge has worked remarkably well for two centuries or more. But I think there are real dangers implicit in its current canonical form.

One danger, specific to the scientific article, is that by dehumanizing our mode of communication, by removing emotion, motivation, the occasionally irrational, we may in fact have done much more than chase away the Naturphilosophen of the early nineteenth century. One hundred and fifty years down the line what we have created is a mechanical, ritualized product that 5×10^5 times per year propagates the notion that scientists are dry and insensitive, that they respond only to wriggles in a spectrum. The public at large types us by the nature of our product. How can it do otherwise, when we do not make a sufficient effort to explain to the public what it is that we really do in our jargon-barricaded world?

What is to be done? I would argue for a general humanization of the publication process. The community should relax those strictures, editorial or self-imposed, on portraying in words, in a primary scientific paper, motivation, whether personal and scientific, emotion, historicity, even some of the irrational. So what if it takes a little more space? As it is, we can keep up with the chemical literature, and tell the mass of hack work from what is truly innovative, without much trouble. And we recognize hype ever so easily. The humanizing words will not mislead; they may actually encourage us to read more carefully the substance of what is said. I would plead for a valuation and teaching of style, in the written and spoken language of one's own country, as well as in English. I think chemistry has much to gain from reviving the personal, the emotional, the stylistic core of the struggle to discover and create the molecular world.

Follow Your Own Advice

Nice words in that plea for humanizing the scientific article—who could argue with them? Well, the young assistant professor trying to carve out a career niche, anxious to have people see and value his or her research as it is published in the literature—is he or she likely to follow this advice? And risk losing it at the gate, so to speak, as conservative editors and reviewers, intent to find something moderately intelligent to say, look askance at modernities of style, colloquialisms, not to speak of worse deviances from the ossified standard?

It would take a very, very courageous young colleague to do so. He or she should turn the question around and ask me: "Do you, Roald, even as you are in a much more privileged position than I am (he doesn't realize that my papers are for various reasons criticized more vehemently than his), do you follow your preaching?"

Yes, and no; sadly, mostly no. I write papers that generally look like the ones you've seen (well, maybe a little prettier); Figure 14 shows a page from a recent paper (Merschrod, Tang, and Hoffmann, 1998). Note the blend of graphic and text, the desperate aspiration to a *Gesamtkunstwerk*: I do cultivate a certain style with cognitive and literary features; the components of that style on the chemical, cognitive side are:

(a) an in-depth examination of many compounds, attention to the literature;

(b) lots of carefully designed drawings, of molecules and orbitals;

(c) a suppresion of results produced by the computer in favor of qualitative explanations; and

(d) a mixture of rationalization and prediction.

As literary devices, I use

(a) a generally discursive style, with occasional repetitions and rehearsals, and lots of those drawings, too; and

(b) colloquial language where I can, trying to have the paper read the way a seminar sounds. This is a device whose purpose is to make the reader feel comfortable with inherently complex material.

All these devices—the pedagogic style, repetition, colloquial language— are guaranteed to cause trouble with reviewers and editors. So I struggle, to this day, 450 papers down the line. Here is an example of a recent (1997) review of one of my papers, reacting to style more than content:

> The theoretical data in this paper is of value and definitely deserves publication. But the paper, which is extremely well-written and beautifully presented, is far too long as a vehicle to transmit the essential data which it includes. The elegant diagrams and discursive style are highly desirable at the

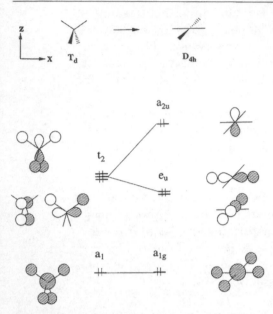

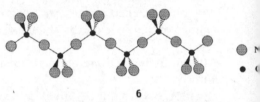

5

some Ni-Ni bonding in departing from the squar planar structure.

A similar situation should also arise in the ez tended structure. Using the tetrahedral buildir block shown at the right of **5**, we can construct one-dimensional extended structure **6** (one of mar possibilities). In hypothetical structure **6**, we keep the Ni-C bond lengths the same as in **2**. The resultin Ni-Ni separation is 3.04 Å.

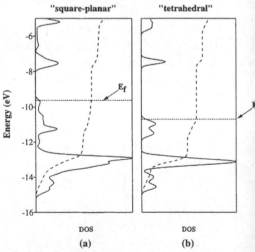

6

Fig. 4. Schematic orbital correlation diagram for the occupied molecular orbitals of CH_4 in T_d (left) and D_{4h} (right) geometries.

planar counterpart. The origin of the stability difference may be seen for CH_4 in Fig. 4. In a tetrahedral geometry, the t_2 orbitals form three C-H σ bonds, while in the square-planar conformation, the t_2 orbitals split into a bonding e_u set of orbitals and a high-lying a_{2u} orbital.

The latter is non-bonding, while the strength of the C-H bonding in the e_u orbitals of the D_{4h} geometry is almost a third smaller than that in the t_2 orbitals in the T_d geometry (as measured by computed overlap populations). The result is a net loss of C-H bonding in the planar geometry as compared to the tetrahedral one. We decided to look at a tetrahedral alternative for the $(Ni_4C)^{4-}$ molecular cluster, to see whether there was any factor discriminating against it. On going from a square planar $(Ni_4C)^{4-}$ model to a tetrahedral one (**5**, keeping Ni-C bond lengths constant; the computational details are not shown here), the three highest occupied orbitals in Fig. 1 become a totally bonding t_2 set. The Ni-C bonds are strengthened in the tetrahedral geometry of Ni_4C^{4-}, just as they are in the case of CH_4. Tetrahedral Ni_4C^{4-} is computed as 1.15 eV more stable than the D_{4h} form. There appears to be nothing wrong with this structure, though one loses

How do the energetics of the tetrahedral alterna tive compare to those of the planar geometry in th extended systems? The unit cell of **6** is $[Ni_6C_2]^{8-}$ containing twice as many atoms as in **2**. The e tended Hückel calculation indicates that hypothe

Fig. 5. Total DOS plots of (a) the "square-planar" structur (**2**) and (b) the "tetrahedral" one (**6**). The horizontal dott line denotes the Fermi level.

FIGURE 14

level of a postgraduate thesis, but for publication in the open literature the manuscript needs to be greatly condensed, in particular to meet the current standards of the journal.

The editor, a friend, commenting on my remonstration says:

> Roald, I believe referee D was not criticizing your paper because it is peda-gogical. He was complimenting it. I think he was trying to say that in his opin-ion, although the paper is very well written, it is suitable for a more special-ized journal.

The paper was rejected, and found a home in another journal.
Basta!
Often I and my coworkers write papers the way the system wants us to write them. Here's an example from the beginning of one (Landrum, Hoffmann, Evers, and Boysen, 1998):

> The TiNiSi (or Co_2Si) structure type (space group Pnma, Pearson symbol oP12) is a lower symmetry relative of the $CeCu_2$ structure (space group Imma). In a previous publication, we presented a detailed analysis of the bonding in the $CeCu_2$ structure type.[1] While $CeCu_2$ is quite a common structure, with 81 known examples as of 1991,[2] the TiNiSi structure type is even more versatile; 495 manifestations are reported in the same publica-tion. There are strong similarities between the two structure types. Both TiNiSi and $CeCu_2$ have three-dimensional four-connected (3D4C) anionic networks with cations sitting in large channels. Both networks can be viewed as being composed of two-dimensional sheets of edge sharing six-membered rings similar to those in black phosphorus running perpendicu-lar. . . .

Sometimes, my students and I manage to do better (Landrum and Hoff-mann, 1998). Here is an example:

> The more crystal structures we know, the clearer it becomes that in the solid state there are many contacts in the range between a bond and a van der Waals interaction. N. W. Alcock introduced the useful term "secondary bonding" for these, and formulated a set of rules for their occurrence and directionality.[1]
>
> For electron-rich main-group systems there are two popular ways to ad-dress in a qualitative way the electronic structure of secondary bonded species—either as a manifestation of hypervalence (electron-rich three-center or multicenter bonding [2]) or as directional donor-acceptor bond-ing.[3] We feel these approaches are in fact equivalent, though we doubt that

the number of energetic electrons expended on the demerits of one or the other chemical views is exhausted.

More of my papers are of the first variety, I must admit.

There is another reason why I do not write in a radically different style. As a theoretician I am in the business of shaping (in a very minor way) a worldview of chemistry. I am after the mind of the chemist. Not the mind of my fellow theoreticians; they're too smart, and besides they have their own spiritual wares to peddle. Not my older experimentalist colleagues, for they are often set in ways of thinking that work perfectly well for them. My audience is very clearly in sight—I write for the senior graduate student, for the young assistant professor. Their minds are open; if it is useful, they will take up a new way of thinking.

For my audience, writing in an entirely offbeat way, inventing batteries of neologisms, claiming that the patently derivative is entirely new by . . . rephrasing the problem—all of these are doomed strategies. The way to introduce the new is in small steps, in a sequence of minor seductions of ever-thirsty mind. So, on stylistic matters, or inventing new words, I go easy. I use familiar concepts, comfortable phrases to introduce a new way of looking at the world. Just here and there I sneak in a word, a phrase that shocks the reader into the realization that he or she is empowered to see things in a different light.

I write, I draw, chemistry . . . so as to teach.

BIBLIOGRAPHY

Grosholz, Emily, and Roald Hoffmann. 2000. "How Symbolic and Iconic Languages Bridge the Two Worlds of the Chemist: A Case Study from Contemporary Bioorganic Chemistry." In *Minds and Molecules: New Philosophical Perspectives in Chemistry*, edited by Nalini Bhushan and Stuart Rosenfeld. Oxford: Oxford University Press.

Hoffmann, Roald. 1995. *The Same and Not the Same.* New York: Columbia University Press.

Hoffmann, Roald, and Pierre Laszlo. 1991. "Representation in Chemistry." *Angewandte Chemie, International Edition English* 30:1–16.

Landrum, Gregory A., and Roald Hoffmann. 1998. "Secondary Bonding between Chalcogens or Pnicogens and Halogens." *Angewandte Chemie* International Edition 37: 1887–90.

Landrum, Gregory A.; Roald Hoffmann; Jürgen Evers; and Hans Boysen. 1998. "The TiNiSi Family of Compounds: Structure and Bonding." *Inorganic Chemistry* 37: 5754–63.

Merschrod, Erika; S. Huang Tang, and Roald Hoffmann. 1998. "Bonding in an Unusual Nickel Carbide." *Zeitschrift für Naturforschung* 53b: 322–32.

Nickon, Alex, and Ernest F. Silversmith. 1987. *Organic Chemistry, the Name Game.* New York: Pergamon Press.

Wieser-Jeunesse, Catherine, Dominique Matt, and André De Cian. 1998. "Directed Positioning of Organometallic Fragments inside a Calix[4]arene Cavity." *Angewandte Chemie* International Edition 110: 2861–64.

Writing Women into Science

Margaret W. Rossiter
(Science and Technology Studies)

My twin brother Charles and I were born in July 1944, a direct result of the U.S. Army's housing policy for married officers during World War II. Our parents had known each other since the 1920s, when they both were students at Malden High School in Malden, Massachusetts, and both graduated from Harvard and Radcliffe Colleges in 1934. They did not marry, however, until three weeks after Pearl Harbor, when my father learned that he was in the Army "for the duration" and that the Army subsidized married officers' housing off-base. They, and eventually we, lived on or near military bases in the U.S., then moved back to Malden, where my father was a history teacher at Malden High School. In 1951 we all moved to Melrose, the next city north of Boston, where my parents had designed a modern ranch house. At this writing my widowed mother is still there.

History of Science in the Suburbs

I first came across the history of science as a teenager. The high school science textbooks of the time often had a sidebar, where, after explaining Newton's Law or Gay-Lussac's experiments, the author elaborated on who this person had been. I always found this "humanizing of science" more interesting that the actual science, for in lab sections we could rarely get the actual experiments to come out "right."

Another place in the suburbs to learn about the history of science was the public library. The one in Melrose, still there but since remodeled, had a rather good selection of books on science and society, especially the history of science. These were such staples as *Men of Mathematics*, by E. T. Bell, *The Music of the Spheres* by Guy Murchie, and other works. Then there were writings connected with science education in the late 1950s. Unbeknownst to me then, a lot of the works I was reading were an outgrowth of Sputnik and probably designed to inspire me to want to become a physicist. That did not take, although I took a lot of science courses, but indirectly it led me to the related and then still embryonic field of the history of science. Among the books I read then were a series of paperbacks, put out by the Educational Services Incorporated of Newton, Massachusetts, and marked with a small circle on the cover and on the spine, on sale in bookstores at malls and in larger bookstores in Cambridge or Boston. These were under two hundred pages, and easy to read. They were biographies, usually, of great white male scientists of past centuries. As I learned much later, they were close to the state of the art of history of science as it was then written. I devoured them, but still did not know that the history of science was a subject anywhere. Besides this reading my parents took me to relevant public lectures in Boston, such as the Ford Hall Forum and the Lowell Lectures. The latter even included a set of lectures, given at the Boston Public Library, by Harvard Professor I. Bernard Cohen on the history of science. And so, when in the spring of 1962 I was publicized in the *Boston Globe* for being one of thirty or so National Merit Scholars around Greater Boston, the reporter could say not only that I liked to read but also that I preferred the history of science and in particular the seventeenth and eighteenth centuries. That was about all there was then.

College Concentration—Dropping Out of Science

At Radcliffe College, where I had been accepted early decision in the fall of 1961 for the class of 1966, I initially intended to major in mathematics. But after about a month in the very high-powered introductory Mathematics 11 I gave up that idea. Somehow I could not understand why anyone would want to prove a theorem that had already been proven by so many others, as was stressed in class and in the problem sets. But Chemistry 1 enchanted me, partly in retrospect because of a very good, even kindly, teacher named Harry Sisler, who was visiting Harvard from the University of Florida. He made chemistry seem beautiful, as in a sense it was. The fact that the air, solids, and water were all made up of molecules intrigued me. The textbook was also user-friendly—enough information, but not too much. And there was a rather nice lab man who took pity on me when he realized that indeed, unlike everyone else, I had not already studied chemistry in high school. Another lab man also used me as a guinea pig for a new textbook along more theoretical lines (molecular orbitals) that he was writing. I was flattered, but in retrospect I suppose his thinking was that if I could understand it, then anyone could. My lack of previous training, even for Chemistry 1, also meant that in sections, when the TA asked someone to explain why we could not have fractional valence (the prevailing view then) I thought maybe we could. (This impossibility has since been achieved.) So I became a chemistry major for a while.

I also recall reading an article in *Isis* that freshman year, my only year on top of a bunk bed, and reading about the business meetings of the History of Science Society, with Marie Boas (later Hall), A. Rupert Hall, and various others.

But organic chemistry sophomore year with Louis Fieser convinced me that chemistry wasn't beautiful anymore. The labs had the unexpected advantage of allowing one to arrange her own time—setting up and letting a slow process run while doing something else. But in the lectures it became clear that we were merely learning lots of ways to turn substance A into Q, via a long alphabet of of tricks and turns. Chemistry was no longer beautiful, just a bunch of gimmicks, whereas medieval history with Giles Constable, which met at the same time in another building, was again a source of beauty. Just why had the Roman Empire fallen in 476? There seemed to be many possible reasons. So I dropped Chem 20 at mid-year (the head TA said I would always regret it, but I never have). That spring I also took Everett Mendelsohn's General Education course Soc. Sci. 119, the Social Implications of Modern Science, and I recall jumping up and down at the bookstore when I ran into someone I knew from my Math 1a section. I had found what I wanted to read more and more about. So somewhere along the line, I found "History and Science" as a major.[1] (At which point my former freshman adviser at Radcliffe said "I predicted this," as indeed I was, unbeknownst to me, in the doctoral study she was doing on female science dropouts.) But reading about science was much more interesting than actually doing it myself.

After sophomore year (1964) I had a pleasant summer job, paid by an NSF grant to Prof. I. B. Cohen, and supervised by George Basalla. We were given access to a room in Littauer Hall that held so many books on science policy and sociology of science that I wished I could be locked in and left to read it all—I remember especially Anne Roe's *Making of a Sci-*

1. Joy Harvey, "History of Science, History and Science, and Natural Sciences: Undergraduate Teaching of the History of Science at Harvard, 1938–1970," in *Catching Up with the Vision: Essays on the Occasion of the 75th Anniversary of the Founding of the History of Science Society,* ed. Margaret W. Rossiter, issued as supplement to *Isis* 90 (1999): S-270–94.

entist. When the NSF program officer came to see what we were doing, he was displeased that I was not more of what was called an "internalist." During the remaining few weeks that summer I went to England and Paris with my mother, seeking out Newton's birthplace in Woolsthorpe, near Colchester, among many other historic sights.

In sophomore tutorial we read such classic works as Thomas S. Kuhn's *Structure of Scientific Revolutions,* in the original yellow paperback put out by the Encyclopedia for Unified Science. We were told by the tutors not to believe it. Another tutor asked what I was interested in—there was the seventeenth century and the nineteenth century and not much else. (This has since changed dramatically.) Because I kept asking, "What happened after Copernicus?" I was sent off to a tutor who worked on biology in the nineteenth century.

Somewhere along the line I read Dirk Struik's *Yankee Science in the Making,* which came out in paperback with a marvelous pink cover. Reading it was very exciting, especially as it was mostly about New England, where I had grown up. (Years later I met Struik and complimented him on it, and he agreed that it was a very good book.) Another time, perhaps junior year, I had an hour to kill between classes over in the Divinity Avenue area of the Harvard campus. It was too far to go to the Coop and so I wandered through the University Museum. (Serendipity is important.) At its bookstore I bought an intriguing little book by Edward Lurie on the history of the Museum of Comparative Zoology that must have been recently published. So the next year when it was time to pick a thesis topic I chose American science, especially the role of Louis Agassiz in the Lawrence Scientific School (LSS), and then spent many hours in the Harvard University Archives, then on the sixth floor of Widener Library. Doing research was great fun, for as I read more and more I found I had to keep refining my hypothesis (that Louis Agassiz had not dominated the LSS, as everyone said, for he never came to its meetings) and so it remained challenging to the end. Nevertheless the finished product was marred by a bad typist, who finished too late to correct her many errors.

Graduate Study

During senior year I had pneumonia in the fall term. This, in retrospect, had two consequences. One was that I missed all the department's presentations on what (other) graduate schools were offering in the history of science. Thus I had to track down such information myself. I sent for lots of catalogs, read them thoroughly, and applied to two programs—Wisconsin and Penn. Both accepted me, but when I went to visit them I was impressed with neither. Penn seemed to have only part-time students then, which wasn't quite my idea of graduate school, and so I accepted Wisconsin.

The other consequence of my illness was that I was exhausted by the time that summer came and had taken no steps to find a job. (I may also have forfeited my chance to return to the American Automobile Association in Boston where I had spent four previous summers.) Thus I went over to the Radcliffe Appointment Bureau to see what I could find. As luck would have it there was a little sign—"history of science job at the Smithsonian, history of science background preferred." Jean Wallace, a fellow history and science major, had gotten married in June, left for California, and so turned down a summer job that the department had arranged for her earlier. This vacancy was a godsend. I got the job immediately, called a dorm-mate from Moors Hall who was living in Washington, D. C., for the summer, and became a historian of American science at the Smithsonian Archives. Sam Surratt, then archivist, had hired Michele Aldrich, then a grad student at the University of Texas, and me to go over to the National Museum of Natural History with clipboard in hand to describe what written materials each division held. This was part of a plan to start a central archive by gaining control of old and endangered written materials dispersed among the various divisions of the Museum. I was mildly aware of these tensions but had a marvelous time, spending a week each in the Fish Division, the Bird Division, the Reptiles, and so on. (I especially remember Reptiles, as it had a live Gila monster in a cage near the old papers.) Perhaps more importantly, I met persons who were doing the history of American science—Suratt was a long-term Berkeley grad student of A. Hunter Dupree; Nathan Reingold was there, just starting up his Joseph Henry Papers project; and Michele was writing her dissertation on the history of the New York State Geological Survey. They all wondered why if I wanted to do American science I was going to Wisconsin, when the obvious place was the history department at Berkeley, where Dupree, author of several works, was a professor, though it was rumored that he had been unhappy there of late.

All this was useful later that year when I got to Wisconsin and realized that Robert Siegfried's promises that the History of Science Department would soon be doing more in American science were not even close to being fulfilled. Nevertheless I signed up for four courses and dug in. One, given by another department, was on the history of higher education in Europe and America. It was outstanding, as was one in the spring on American intellectual history. But the history of science courses in the department were disappointing, and I complained a lot to some of the older students, who kept advising that if I disliked it so much I should take a year off. I thought that would only penalize me, when the department was the problem. But I learned a valuable lesson in trying to cope with the situation. I decided that I should try to transfer out of Wisconsin, preferably to Berkeley, and, assuming that this would be successful, I should put my year at Wisconsin to its best use. I should try to learn as much as possible this year on my own, because the next school would expect that I had learned something. So I spent a lot of time in the library, reading books from the newly-acquired shelf and in the Graduate Reading Room, especially in the Q section (history of science in the Library of Congress classification system). I assumed that the books there were important and I should be knowledgeable about them, even if my courses were not assigning them. It did not take a genius to figure out what the major books were and get busy. In retrospect this is good advice for anyone in graduate school—figure out what you ought to be learning and do it on your own.

Eventually I got accepted at both Yale and Berkeley (but not Harvard, where someone remembered me as a "troublemaker"[2]). My father gave me two hundred dollars to fly out to Berkeley and meet this professor so as not to make another mistake. I did, and discovered that Dupree would be on leave the next year (1967–68) and then be moving to Brown University. He recommended that I accept the Yale fellowship (from the U.S. Public Health Service for four years at about two hundred dollars a month) and we would work out something from there. So I did, and later that summer (from a second stint at the Smithsonian) officially withdrew from Wisconsin, where I had earned an M.A. in the spring.

Yale had no courses on the history of American science either, but it admitted it and allowed me to sign up for independent study. I also took a course with George Wilson Pierson on "Tocqueville's America," the very subject of an immense book of his. This was a terrifying course, partly because the class was small and I was the only woman there (where, as he put it, we were to "separate the men from the boys")—and partly because he was a stern and aloof person who had various reasons for disliking the faculty of the history of science department. But by then I had explored the dimly-lit Yale University Archives (Beinecke Library was not yet built) and wrote my course paper on Benjamin Silliman's lectures at the Lowell Institute in Boston in 1840. Pierson was evidently greatly impressed (but

2. In the spring of my senior year, the *Harvard Crimson* asked several upperclassmen what advice they had for freshmen picking majors. I said that in History and Science there were ways around the written rules, which required all the general examinations of a history major. This provoked a stern "letter to the editor" by Prof. Mendelsohn. I wondered why he was so upset and denying current practice. I later learned that the committee that ran the major was about to be voted departmental status. Evidently my well-intentioned revelation had attracted the attention of the powers that were.

being laconic did not say much then—though he did much later in a 1974 letter to Henry Guerlac that I subsequently came across in the Cornell archives), and this paper became my first article when published in 1971 in the *New England Quarterly.*[3]

After this I had to choose a thesis topic. Several of the professors in the Yale department who were foreigners and/or whose field was "the exact sciences in antiquity" used to needle me that nothing of consequence had happened in America before 1933, when Albert Einstein arrived. I used to counter with the possibility of a biography of James Dwight Dana, one of Yale's great nineteenth-century scientists, whose home was a block away on Hillhouse Avenue. With this in mind I took a pleasant undergraduate course in mineralogy, a bit of a hassle since Yale College was not yet coed. But before getting on to my orals I had to learn enough German to pass the language exams. I decided that it would be cheaper to spend the summer in Munich (where there were four marks to the dollar then) than it would be to take a language course at the Yale summer school. This idea became even more financially advantageous when the professors said that if I would agree to attend the international congress of the history of science in Paris the next summer (1968) I could have my fellowship over the entire summer. So I went and had a marvelous time taking the course and various side trips outside Munich. Upon returning to New Haven I decided that Dana was a dreary topic after all, as he was sick so much of the time, but I was by then interested in Americans who had studied in Germany in the nineteenth century. There were a great many of them, but those in chemistry were of particular interest, as many had studied in Justus Liebig in Giessen, which I had visited. A lot of them had sent letters home, which were still available in various manuscript repositories. So the American students of Justus Liebig seemed like a good topic, especially as Frederic Holmes, the chair of my committee, had written on Liebig, and Hunter Dupree, also on the committee, was an Americanist. But Holmes was skeptical that there was enough written on the history of American agriculture to justify limiting it to the history of agricultural chemistry. I convinced him that this was indeed a well-worked area—the many students of Prof. Paul Gates at Cornell would alone fill nearly a shelf of books about agriculture in New York State.

But an intellectual problem developed shortly thereafter. Why, if New York agriculture was booming, as it seemed to be after the construction of the Erie Canal (1817–25), would anyone send their son at great expense

3. Margaret W. Rossiter, "Benjamin Silliman and the Lowell Institute: The Popularization of Science in Nineteenth-Century America," *New England Quarterly* 44 (1971): 602–26.

to Germany to study how to farm differently? The whole justification of my dissertation—that a problem with New York agriculture inspired many young men to go to Giessen to study agricultural chemistry with Liebig— seemed to be falling apart. But then one afternoon I stopped by the periodical room in Sterling Library to waste a little time and my hand fell on a recent issue of *New York History*. Lo and behold it contained an article by Paul Gates about the great fear in upstate New York after the opening of the canal. It revealed that although statistics for New York agriculture showed increased economic activity after completion of the canal, there was also new competition from Ohio, Wisconsin, and the Midwest, whose products were also being shipped to New York City on the canal. Thus a substantial farmer might indeed be worried about the future. Delighted, I raced back to my chapter. Another lucky bit of serendipity also occurred one day in the library when I ran into George Pierson. He asked about my thesis topic and then gave me the invaluable news that the John Pitkin Norton Papers had recently been deposited there by a descendant but had not yet been catalogued! They became the basis of at least two chapters. It was a great rush to finish the thesis in the spring of 1971, because both of my parents were sick and in different hospitals in the Boston area. Pierson later said my dissertation would have won the John Addison Porter Prize at Yale (which he had won years before), if it had been submitted to the right committee in time.

One of the other important events of my graduate years was a big meeting in the spring of 1970 on the history of American science, perhaps the first ever, run by George Daniels at Northwestern University. There I met Stanley Guralnick, who was working with Charles Rosenberg at Penn, and especially Sally Gregory Kohlstedt from Illinois, the only other woman present, who became a lifelong friend, advisor, and supporter.

POSTDOCTORAL FELLOWSHIPS

Not knowing in my last year (1970–71) what the future would hold, although the older students were getting good jobs, and encouraged by the Yale professors (one of whom was on the selection committee) I had applied for an NSF postdoctoral fellowship to work more with Hunter Dupree at Brown. I got it, but for various reasons never did move to Brown. I stayed in New Haven, used more Yale collections that were being arranged, and went to see the professor once a month. As the fellowship provided a $1,000 research stipend, I went to the international congress of the history of science in Moscow and Leningrad in August 1971 with a group of about 23 fellow Americans, one of whom was Melvin Kranzberg and another John Beer. This was a great experience and my second exposure to the international aspects of the history of science.

As that year wore on and it turned out that there would be no job for me, I ran into George Pierson again at the Yale Library, where he had an office. He inquired how I was faring and then sent a letter to the Charles Warren Center at Harvard for me. As a result I got one of their fellowships and had a marvelous year there, as the youngest, a kind of kid sister, to about ten other Fellows, who gave me further clues on how the academic world ran. That year the Center moved into Robinson Hall, a stone's throw from Widener Library. There could be no better place to study American history.

During that year each Fellow had to give a talk to the rest of the group. It turned out that I was to be the first, as I was (again) the only female. Meanwhile my interests were changing—with tremendous career consequences. When applying I had said that I wanted to study the professionalization of American science and get to the twentieth century, which hardly anyone did then. To prepare for this, once accepted, I skimmed the first edition of the reference work, the *American Men of Science* (1906), while intermittently watching the 1972 Olympics on television. As I flipped through, noting which men were the important ones (those with long entries), I also noticed some women (with very short entries). One of those persons sharing our summer house (an architectural showpiece designed by architect Segei Chermayeff) was a Wellesley graduate (Cynthia Thompson), who recommended that I keep track of these women. I did so, and by the time I had to give my talk at the Warren Center I had a lot of data. Not knowing anything about the Center's past, I decided to present my material on these women scientists. (A sign of how unusual it was for a women's history paper to be presented then and there was that Professor Kitty Preyer of Wellesley, a former Fellow, made it a point to come to the talk, even though her own field was legal history.)

Before long I sent the completed manuscript off to *Scientific American* and *Science*, both of which promptly rejected it. Dismayed, I surveyed other suitable journals in Widener Library's periodical room and settled on the *American Scientist*. (Nathan Reingold said to add twice as many footnotes and send it to *Isis*, but that was not the audience I wished to reach.) I was lucky that ecologist G. Evelyn Hutchinson of Yale turned out to be a reader. (He later told me his hobby was reading autobiographies of British women botanists!) One virtue of publishing in the *American Scientist* was a chance to include some pictures, and the archivist at Mount Holyoke was very helpful—women in bustles doing chemical experiments epitomized well what I was talking about. The article appeared in June 1974, and before long I had over two hundred reprint requests.[4] This is, of course, unusual for a historian. Some people wrote me about their grand-mother who had earned a doctorate in the 1890s, and others reported their own bit of history, as when they had done something important in World War II or were the first to earn a certain degree at a certain place. So I had to decide whether to pursue this topic further or not. George Pierson said no, one article was enough. It would please my "tribe," but if I ever wanted to get an academic job I should get back to more main-stream topics. I thought this was prudent advice. I could keep on doing the history of agricultural science, as indeed I was anyway, having become typecast by my dissertation topic and invited to some prestigious meetings on the history of learning run by the American Academy of Arts and Sci-ences. But there was no guarantee of a job in the history of agriculture, should one come along. Nevertheless, no other topic was quite so com-pelling as learning more about American women scientists.

PH.D. GLUT AND REAGANOMICS

One of my Yale professors, Derek J. de Solla Price, used to give us grad students very good advice in an informal way, offhandedly, over at 56 Hillhouse Avenue, one of the two centers for the combined Department of the History of Science and Medicine. One of his gems was that one should apply for all sorts of things, because even if one did not get this, one might get something else, as the people on that committee were also on lots of others and this could have beneficial consequences.

I had sent my essay on Benjamin Silliman to the Schuman Prize Com-mittee of the History of Science Society. It did not win, but it impressed the committee chairman, John Heilbron of Berkeley, whose department it turned out had some vacancies in the history of science—one because Dupree had left in 1968 and one longstanding one in the history of biol-ogy. In any case they needed a one-year replacement and seemed con-vinced that I could do the job. When some other prospects fizzled, I de-cided this was my best bet and flew out to Berkeley, after a summer (Watergate summer) in New York arranging the Charles F. Chandler Pa-pers at Columbia and living at the Rockefeller University dorms. My dis-sertation was also accepted that summer for publication by Yale University Press, whose staff had at first complained that it had no time to read about the history of manure.

4. Margaret W. Rossiter, "Women Scientists in America before 1920," *American Scientist* 62 (1974): 312–23.

The year (1973–74) passed pleasantly and quickly, but before long I was unemployed—just when the *American Scientist* article came out. I had a very nice apartment and so it seemed best just to sit still and get on with my projects in Berkeley. Surely there would be a job the next year. Besides, in 1974 Gerald Ford was running for election and there was such a recession that he extended the unemployment benefits, for which I was eligible, to a full year. Thus I could pay the rent, revise my dissertation, work on the agricultural papers I had been invited to prepare, and, having met and been encouraged by Ronald Overmann of the NSF, send off a grant proposal to him to support a project on still more women scientists. It was a productive year, but NSF had trouble finding people to read my proposal. Evidently they sent it to established women scientists, of whom there were a few then, and they said there was nothing to study and I should not stir up trouble by trying to find it. At the end of the year (spring 1975) Berkeley rehired me with great lukewarmness for its continuing vacancy in the history of biology. (By then governor Ronald Reagan had cut the university's budget so much that the position in the history of American science had disappeared.)

The job market did not improve, nor did my prospects within it, despite the publication of my dissertation in 1975.[5] I continued with my research on women scientists and decided to write a whole book on the subject, starting in the beginning, whenever that was, and getting up to the recent past. This of course would not take long, as Nathan Reingold and others kept assuring me, since there was probably just one archival collection (the Frances Densmore Papers at the National Anthropological Archives in Washington, D.C.) that he knew of. But the more one digs the more she finds, and Berkeley's decentralized libraries and helpful librarians greatly aided my task. I divided in order to conquer. I would start out by focussing on one field, such as geology, and then walk down the hill to the Earth Sciences Library, trying to predict what I might want to find. Were there ever any women geologists? If so where would their obituaries be? Was this indexed? Had there ever been an association of women geologists? If so did it have a history that might be in the card catalog or in some major bibliography? I also picked up other clues. At a party I met Bob Seidel's then-wife, a librarian, who asked if I had ever heard of the *Biography Index*. No, I hadn't, but it was a very helpful tool, as I learned when I went through about twelve volumes of it. Over the years and on the basis of a lot of exploratory work like this and some grant renewals (once NSF

5. Margaret W. Rossiter, *The Emergence of Agricultural Science: Justus Liebig and the Americans, 1840–1880* (New Haven: Yale University Press, 1975).

did see fit to fund me), my manuscript grew rather long. In fact, it got to be too long.

What, for example, had started out as a general introductory chapter on "Entering the Profession" split into four separate chapters, as my examples kept proliferating. As they did I learned to distinguish between degree-earning and job-holding, two things that early items on women scientists, like newspaper clippings with the headline "woman in science," conflated. These writings were, despite their titles, usually about the first women to earn degrees and not about those holding jobs, a key difference, then as well as in the 1970s. In fact there were so few items at all on employment that it would be more accurate to say there was general silence. Nevertheless I needed a chapter on employment, even if it would cover such familiar topics as the women astronomers at the Harvard College Observatory, about whom a certain amount had been written; Ellen Richards and the early home economists, who had also been described; and a smattering of botanists and such in the federal government. None of this seemed to show any of the great archival breakthroughs that some of the other chapters did. But then one day as I walked down to campus from my nice apartment in the Berkeley Hills, it dawned on me—that was *all* that they were employed to do. In fact amidst all the glorification of the pioneers, there was a kind of undiscussed silence about the overt segregation that was going on: they were assistants in some places, like observatories and government agencies, with no chances for advancement, or employed in home economics or child psychology or maybe botany, all of which might be construed as feminine. So I featured the term "women's work" in science and coined the terms "hierarchical segregation" and "territorial segregation" to explain these two different but related phenomena. That chapter, which had been so particularly hard to write, turned out to be the most innovative in the whole book and later an article in *Isis*.[6] It also led to a Guggenheim Fellowship in 1981.

At some point in the late 1970s Berkeley's John Heilbron, who may have been reading my proposals to NSF as a member of its advisory panel on the history and philosophy of science (as it was called then), recommended that I split my project in two. If one is trying to live on grants and grant renewals, he warned, it is good to have some finite product once in a while. This was news to me and very reasonable advice. In the course of

6. Margaret W. Rossiter, " 'Women's Work' in Science, 1880–1910," *Isis* 71 (1980): 381–98. A picture from this article appeared on the cover of that issue of *Isis*, thus attracting worldwide attention to the political acceptance of the topic. I learned this at the next international congress in Bucharest, Romania, in 1981, where several of us started an International Commission on the History of Women in Science, Technology, and Medicine.

a van ride up to the University of California at Davis to read a dissertation there, I pondered the pros and cons of splitting the whole, in its then current state, into two. I had one volume to about 1940 for sure, but for the rest I had only a puny amount. But I decided that I needed to finish off the pre-1940 period. Even this took a few more years. Meanwhile, finding a publisher proved both easy and hard. Henry Tom, then at the University of Chicago Press but later at the Johns Hopkins University Press, was always very encouraging and took me out for coffee at the annual history meetings. Unlike many others he thought my project was feasible and would take about six years. Meanwhile some other people told me that this manuscript would surely interest a commercial publisher, but none of those approached was ever even slightly interested. (In particular Sheldon Meyer at Oxford University Press turned my proposal down in the late 1970s, on the grounds that the history of American science was of no interest and that of women scientists even less so. A few years later in 1981 when I got a Guggenheim and all the attendant publicity, he wrote me to get in touch about a contract. I dug out the previous letter and sent him back a copy, with some acerbic remarks as well as my compliments on his promotion to senior editor.) In 1982 the first volume came out, published in the end by Johns Hopkins University Press. At the last minute its index caused problems, as its length outgrew the press's specifications. The editor threatened to cut it drastically, but I heatedly resisted, because my research had been so dependent on others' indexes that listed even the obscure people. After all women were (at most) back then footnotes in the saga of the great men of science.

The timing of the book's publication was better than expected. I recall on a visit to the Johns Hopkins University Press that the managing editor took me aside and squeezed my arm, exclaiming with delight that she thought this one might sell, as indeed it has. At one point when my mother asked when it might be reviewed in the *New York Times*, someone at the Press told me that, you know, it was probably "not a *New York Times* book." But then the next week it was, when Alice Kimball Smith, a surprising choice because though a historian she had not worked on women in science or the period before 1940, reviewed it rather favorably in the Sunday *New York Times*. I am happy to report that it went into paperback in 1984, is still in print in 2000, and is occasionally referred to as a classic.[7]

Meanwhile I still did not have a job, and Ronald Overmann, who had been running the NSF Program in the History and Philosophy of Science since the early seventies, was ready for a year of leave. He had meant to go

---

7. Margaret W. Rossiter, *Women Scientists in America: Struggles and Strategies to 1940* (Baltimore: Johns Hopkins University Press, 1982; paperback reprint, 1984).

in 1981–82, but President Ronald Reagan and Budget Director David Stockman had that year cut the social sciences appropriation at NSF in half. (Interestingly we historians of science were the only social scientists to mount much of a protest.) When Overmann did go on leave in 1982–83, I was asked to fill in for him. At first I was reluctant to leave my pressing research—the second volume beckoned—but it eventually dawned on me that if I turned down the government people who were giving me grants and trying to help me, they might be insulted. I accepted finally and had a most tumultuous and interesting year, greatly aided by two wonderful assistants, Michelle Graves and Bonney Sheahan. It was an instructive experience to be at the interface of my fellow researchers and the government bureaucracy. I met some very nice people I never would have met otherwise, and I kept myself sane by spending each Saturday at the manuscript division of the Library of Congress reading my way through one part (that on organizations) of the immense (1700 boxes!) Margaret Mead Papers.

I had expected to return to Berkeley and kept my apartment while I was away, but in June 1983 Barbara Rosenkrantz surprised me by inviting me to come to Harvard as a visiting lecturer for a year to fill in for Everett Mendelsohn, who would be on leave, and to teach a course on the history of women in science. The salary was low, but each time I said "no" it went up a bit. Eventually it (there were no benefits) got close to the 9-month equivalent of my government job and I accepted. I had fun creating two upper level seminars: one on American science since 1945 (which was the basis of my *Osiris* 1 piece in 1985[8]) and another on women in science.

But soon that too ended and I was back to volume 2, but now on the east coast and nearer my parents. My father was ill with diabetes and hemochromatosis, from which he died in 1986. The American Academy of Arts and Sciences, which had been administering my grants for years, gave me an office in its new building in Norton's Woods just off the Harvard campus and I pressed on. In the fall of 1985, realizing that my Harvard library card was not as infinitely renewable as my Berkeley one had been, I began to realize that I would have to move on. I knew about the NSF's Visiting Professorships for Women Program (VPW), especially as I had been on the NSF Director's Committee on Equal Opportunities in Science and Technology for two years (just before and just after my stint on the NSF payroll). I figured that I ought to apply for a visiting post somewhere before Ronald Reagan cut this budget too. So I skimmed my History of Science Society newsletters and decided on Cornell University,

8. Margaret W. Rossiter, "Science and Public Policy since World War II," *Osiris* 1 (1985): 273–94.

where L. Pearce Williams had recently started a graduate program in the history and philosophy of science. Though I did not know him, it seemed better to be located where the field was growing than where it was not. It also helped that some people at Cornell might care about the history of agricultural science and that, after I had given a lecture there a year or two before on women and science, some graduate students had been interested enough to start a club for women scientists. The outside referees seemed to think that Cornell was a great place for me, even though, as I later learned, few in Cornell's History Department, where I was given a temporary office, would have agreed had they been consulted. Though the NSF gave me just one year's worth of money, Will Provine, Cornell's renowned historian of biology, convinced the vice president for research to waive the overhead, and I was able to stay two years. In all my years around academia I have heard of only one other case like this anywhere.

CORNELL UNIVERSITY

In my first two years at Cornell (1986–88) I had some very wonderful graduate students—M. Susan Lindee, Betty Smocovitis, and Patrick Munday, who was even working on Liebig! As before I kept busy on my chapters, which were growing more numerous and longer, and was delighted with the fantastic Cornell libraries and librarians. I applied for and got a Rockefeller Foundation fellowship in gender roles (one of that program's last). I expected to use this when the NSF's VPW ended, but L. Pearce Williams got Cornell's agriculture dean (David Call) to agree to pay half my salary for three years. Eventually, after cancelling four appointments in the summer of 1988, Gregory Chester, dean of the Arts College, agreed to pay the other half. (I am told that Joan Jacobs Brumberg, then head of Women's Studies, had kept my case before Dean Chester.)

Then a year later in July 1989 I got one of those phone calls from the John D. and Catherine T. MacArthur Foundation that changed my career. I was astonished, though one or two people had told me over the years that they had written letters for me, and I knew from the early 1980s that they had been under pressure to give some of their grants to women. The *Ithaca Journal* put me on the front page, but all its reporters could conclude was that I hoped to be able to stay at Cornell as part of a new department on the history of science that might someday be created. I was later told that many scholars had been asked to write in and evaluate me for some sort of long-term position at Cornell, but that the administration's answer was negative. I was in the strange situation that many thought that I deserved an endowed chair, but there was no way to give me tenure, a lesser reward, since I was not in a department. The version I got was "no tenure without an outside offer." In the spring of 1990 that became a reality when I got an offer from the University of Georgia to be its Callaway Professor of History with a substantial research budget. No one at Cornell seemed able to do much about meeting the offer. Then at the last minute and seemingly inadvertently Patricia Carey Stewart, the longtime vice chairman of the Cornell board of trustees, wrote to congratulate me on the MacArthur Fellowship. Cornell does not have many, and one previous winner had left. She hoped that I was enjoying Cornell. I replied that, alas, I was on the verge of leaving (and enclosed a copy of Georgia's offer letter) and hoped that the University would treat its next MacArthur Fellow better. Evidently she did something, for within a few weeks the Arts College deans were eager to talk to me and offer a raise, a computer, and an endowed chair in three years. They had even figured out how to create a new department, something that had not happened in twenty or more years (since computer science and comparative literature in the 1960s). The then-provost Mal Nesheim was also eager to see me. At our meeting he guaranteed me tenure, saying that though it would take the Arts College a while to get committees together and vote on this (indeed it took about a year), whatever they voted I would get tenure, since he could overrule them! I was impressed and accepted on the spot. (People later told me I should have gotten his promise in writing.) But I realized then that if I accepted right away I could get back to my chapters that very afternoon and would not have to think about real estate in Athens, Georgia, where I now had many friends. A week later we were discussing a new department, which became a reality in July 1991 after the required two votes of the Arts College faculty.

Meanwhile I was eager to finish my sequel, especially since I was aware of the many historians of science before me who had promised one that they never finished. My volume two on the period 1940–72 finally came out in 1995,[9] stalled by about a year by Henry Tom's desire to get for it one of the last of the book subsidies from the National Endowment for the Humanities, whose budget was being reduced. This meant I would not have to cut the extensive notes and could even include an extended bibliographic essay, which I hope has helped other scholars trying to work on the immense post–World War II period. The reception of this volume eventually exceeded all my expectations by being awarded both the HSS's

9. Margaret W. Rossiter *Women Scientists in America: Before Affirmative Action, 1940–1972* (Baltimore: Johns Hopkins University Press, 1995; paperback reprint, 1997).

History of Women in Science Prize and its coveted Pfizer Prize, something I had not thought possible. Times had evidently changed, since the earlier volume had not won any Society prize (though it had won the Berkshire Prize for the best book by a woman historian in 1983).[10]

Since then I have continued to teach a course on the history of women in science, responding to the wealth of new work coming out. It is astonishing to remember how little there used to be. (When in the spring of 1972 someone had asked me for a complete bibliography of the subject I had been able to list only half a page of items.) In fact I find my 1982 book cast in the new role of "first footnote." Since then many scholars have located archival collections, as family papers, and written whole essays on people that I just listed in a chart or referred to in passing. Frequently these authors start out with a reference to my first volume, saying back in 1982 Margaret Rossiter mentioned this woman, and now I have written a whole essay on her. One never knows when writing a survey of an undeveloped field (and I used to wonder about this) whether one is opening up a new area for further work or whether one is exhausting a thin terrain so totally that other scholars will be discouraged for decades to come. Now we have a whole genre of reference books devoted to women in science, and scholars outside the United States are deploring the lack of similar volumes for their own countries and citing my books as models they ought to be pursuing. In some ways we are creating a new specialty within the ever-growing history of science.

Over the years my agriculture course has evolved from about ten students sitting around a table and discussing readings to lectures with about sixty. At one point a friendly assistant dean in the College of Agriculture and Life Sciences allowed it to meet the humanities requirement for that College's students and I have had many of them since. It is a pleasant change to get away from the women sometimes (hardly any of whom worked in agricultural science) and think about New York State, the Erie Canal, and such. Yet the literature on this topic is still so thin that it is hard to find enough books for the students to read, and those that one does find tend to go out of print. Perhaps this topic too will blossom, as there seem to be growing numbers of junior scholars entering the area and there are abundant research materials at Cornell.

Since 1994 I have also been the editor of *Isis*, the main journal of the history of science, that I read as a freshman on the top bunk back in

10. When for three years in a row my book did not win any prize from the HSS, members of its Women's Committee decided to start a new prize that would honor work on the history of women in science. They got the Council to approve it and even raised sufficient funds to endow it. The prize has been awarded every year since 1987, alternating between an article in the even-numbered years and a book in the odd-numbered.

Moors Hall. About 1992 the leaders of the Women's Committee of the HSS, of which I have been a member since its start, felt that it was time that a woman was editor of the journal. My arm was bent to apply. I was not at all clear about what an editor did, but Cornell agreed to contribute a bit, and I have enjoyed the experience of helping the mostly younger authors find their way into print. Occasionally we get essays on women or gender and science, and in fact *Isis* has for decades led the way with this, so much so that the University of Chicago Press last year published an anthology of seventeen major articles on this subject.[11] Part of the editor's job is to serve on the HSS Council and Executive Committee, where I have for seven years been the only woman. In a sense, after an unusual career as first an insider at two major graduate programs and then a long stint on the periphery, I have become a member of the establishment.

One big task recently has been preparing a special issue of *Isis* to commemorate the 75th anniversary of the founding of the Society in 1924.[12] My plans for this grew out of the opening in the last few years of several relevant manuscript collections, including the Henry Guerlac Papers at Cornell, and a fellowship at the Institute for Advanced Study in 1996–97. Going through these collections has been instructive, for occasionally I find a letter about myself and I am reminded how unprepared the Society or the field was for a young female Americanist troublemaker back around 1970.

At this writing I have plans (and cartons of notes and clippings) to write a third volume on the women scientists of the period since 1972, when "everything" happened, getting perhaps as far as 1995 or so when Newt Gingrich and others started talking about the end of affirmative action. It is both familiar and uncomfortable to look with historical eyes at a period I lived through. Right now I have all I can do to get to the various archives as they become available. Some are immense; some are restricted; most are unprocessed. God willing, I will find a way to write these chapters too.

In retrospect, the field of the history of science has broadened a lot in the last thirty to fifty years from the biographies of great white male European men and "the exact sciences in antiquity" to a wealth of more "relevant," as we used to say around 1970, and controversial topics, as the twentieth century, the United States, and social history, including even women and gender. These were unimaginable back then. The history of science is no longer just inspirational reading for future, active, or retired scientists or science enthusiasts. It now has links to government policy, business his-

11. Sally Gregory Kohlstedt, ed., *History of Women in the Sciences: Readings from* Isis (Chicago: University of Chicago Press, 1999).

12. See note 1.

tory, and the history of technology, and current events. I had a part in broadening and remaking the field and persisted despite a lot of discouragement. Then slowly during the 1980s, as new resources became available, persons inside the field and at various institutions began to make room for me. Now I am part of the central governing body of this transformed field and wish the Society were doing more to help today's even more numerous postdoctoral fellows on whom the field's future depends.

I also wonder where the field would be if some of us had not persevered. And why should what I have done been such a struggle? What I was doing, was not so outrageous, and a lot of people, some in key places, were, though I did not know it at the time, pulling for me. Yet as L. Pearce Williams has told me, it was nip and tuck all the way even at Cornell University.

Part Two

THE SOCIAL SCIENCES

Writing Politics

ISAAC KRAMNICK (Government)

WRITING has helped shape my sense of self. Thus, when I address the questions set by Jonathan Monroe for these reflections—"how I myself became a writer; how my discipline and writing in my discipline has evolved over the past century; how my writing relates to these dominant models in my discipline"—I enter terrain where my own personal narrative of self-formation looms as large a theme as the relationship of my writing to the practices and self-understanding of others who write on politics.

OUR WRITER AS A YOUNG MAN

The first thing I ever wrote longer than a book report or a fan letter to Ted Williams was in the eleventh grade; it was a five-page attack on communism that I wrote to get into Massachusetts Boy's State, run by the American Legion. The year was 1954 and I lived in a small rural town, 25 miles from Boston, a quite unusual town. The population was about 2500, mainly small chicken and cow farmers and workers in the town's shoe factory. The town had one school building for all the grades and my graduating class had nineteen people. But most atypical was my more immediate context. There were some 40 Jewish families in the town, mainly farmers, and my particular extended family was the most religiously observant of the lot. The several generations of uncles and nephews had built a family synagogue, a small wooden structure that could have been in a Polish shtetl but for its being in a green cow pasture.

Those who have learned about growing up in American-Jewish life after World War II from Saul Bellow, Philip Roth, or Bernard Malamud, will quickly see the anomaly of my childhood. These rural Jews were deeply religious in a literalist traditional way. Hardworking and hard-praying, they were non-intellectual, even anti-intellectual; there were no books at home and my cousins and I were not encouraged to read or to learn. We were encouraged only to perform dutifully the hundreds of prayers, rituals and ceremonies of orthodox Jewry. Only one of my fifteen cousins went to college, and, of course, he went to the new Jewish university nearby, Brandeis. Learning was, in fact, suspect in the family, because its skepticism invariably threatened the rote religious performances which marked you as truly good and virtuous.

If their disdain for learning is not a dramatic enough departure from the stereotypical rendition of growing up Jewish in America, let me add that my extended family were also Republicans—small farmers utterly untouched by the union movement and urban Jewish socialism. They were profoundly conservative and on what was then the right wing of the Republican party, which in the specific terms of the 1950s meant you were for Senator Robert Taft, because Eisenhower was much too liberal.

Which brings me back to 1954, the eleventh grade and my first serious piece of writing: my rousing indictment of the evils of communism, which would have made Senator McCarthy proud—a copy of which, in fact, the local American Legion Post proudly sent to the then governor of Massachusetts, Christian Herter. My debut essay was, of course, hardly mine, since for me as for most American high school kids in the 1950s, writing a long report or essay meant copying out and stringing together whole sentences and paragraphs plagiarized from encyclopedias. I think we were in fact taught that it was a sign of good writing if you copied from several different encyclopedias. I, of course, had no encyclopedias at home, but more strategically minded than most of my classmates I went to the next, slightly wealthier, town's library, thinking its encyclopedias were probably better.

This is how I acquired what I call my "imitative" voice in writing. If you are initiated into writing by the laborious copying of text from encyclopedias, your prose tends to be simple, direct, and uncomplicated. It tends to be accessible to ordinary nonspecialist readers, and I like to think that that is still true of my writing 45 years later.

Then, of course, came college, and then graduate school, both of which place tremendous obstacles in the path of anyone who would write simple and accessible scholarly prose. I'll return to this in a moment, but let me comment on my experience of writing at college.

I had to choose between attending Brandeis (then six years old) and Harvard (then 319 years old). My entire Jewish family and my high school teachers, virtually all Catholics, urged me to go to Brandeis. Their opinions were the same: if I went to Harvard I would become an atheist and a communist. This was 1955, remember. I chose Harvard not from conviction or respect for its longevity but because their scholarship was $100 more than Brandeis for the same tuition of $800 a year.

Harvard was hell. I stood out like a sore thumb; there weren't too many awkward, rural, anti-intellectual, religious, Republican Jews on campus. I wore plaid shirts and had not read Henry Adams, Albert Camus, or J. D. Salinger. Particularly painful was learning how to write academic prose. College professors, I discovered, frowned upon papers that reproduced encyclopedia text, even if paraphrased; moreover, I realized my freshman year that there were no findable encyclopedia entries that read "Plato, Locke, and Marx on private property." I have vague memories of writing papers like that in my first two years, papers where writing meant if not stringing together what different encyclopedias wrote, then reorganizing the professors' lecture notes in light of as many other secondary renderings of Plato or Locke or Marx you could find.

I do remember vividly, however, the first serious piece of writing I ever did, and with which I am still pleased. I was a junior in 1958 and a student in Arthur Schlesinger Jr's. large lecture course on American intellectual history. (He is still writing books and essays at age 84.) A twenty-page paper was required, and from the list of topics provided I chose to write a paper on Whitaker Chambers, the editor of *Time* Magazine (and more famously the accuser of Alger Hiss), who in his book *Witness* had described his early commitment to communism, his abandonment of it, and then his fierce religiously based anti-communism. Schlesinger had not lectured on Chambers and the book was too new to have created a stir or secondary literature. The encyclopedia cut-and-paste approach to writing the paper wouldn't work. All I could do was read his book. I did and I can remember still the excitement I felt as I outlined the argument for my paper. (I always do elaborate time-consuming outlines before I write, and then comes the feverish joyful exhaustion of writing it out in a virtually complete first draft.) The thrill in 1958 was that it was my argument, not the clever or thoughtful play with and reconstruction of others' arguments. What I wrote about in that paper is by now a tired academic cliché, and even then such arguments were being made by others, but I was on my own and I was convinced that Chambers, a very intelligent and sensitive person, had become a communist for the very reasons he would ultimately leave the party and become a religious anti-communist zealot: the quest for an all-encompassing set of beliefs whose doctrinal simplicity and intolerance provided certainty. In later years I would realize that my own personal crisis of religious and political belief which, true to the predictions of my family and high school teachers, did take place at Harvard, must have made possible my sensitivity to these issues in Chambers, and helped shape whatever insights the paper contained. The TA liked the paper and showed it to Professor Schlesinger, who commended me as well.

This writing experience, the Whitaker Chambers paper, changed my life, and it changed my sense of self. I was still shy and utterly consumed with feelings of inferiority alongside my classmates from Exeter, Choate, Groton, Boston Latin, Stuyvesant, Horace Mann, Newton, and Shaker Heights; I still seldom spoke in class, for fear of saying something silly or dumb that would bring laughter from classmates or teachers. But I discovered that writing was a safer way to assert one's self, to confront others, to put oneself forward. Writing was private; I did it alone; my writing was read when I wasn't there and couldn't hear or see the reaction. I was less immediately exposed in writing; the potential ridicule was distanced. Writing, then, forged my academic identity and my understanding of intellectual inquiry—not classroom or seminar discussions, or late night bull sessions with friends. I never then and seldom now conceive of the life of the mind as verbal agon; I am a disputatious and sometimes controversial scholar, but I assert myself principally in the relative safety of writing, not in conference panels or roundtables. This dimension of writing—its privacy—I suggest to theorists of writing, may be central to understanding the role and significance of writing for many people. It certainly is in my case.

In asserting myself in this way, through writing, at Harvard, I did well. I succeeded. Professors liked my writing and I got good grades (though I seldom spoke in class). I put myself forward in writing; and doing it well and being noticed, validated, literally seemed to give value to myself. Two particular Harvard professors reinforced and solidified my sense of self that began to emerge in the initiation ritual that writing the Whitaker Chambers paper turned out to be.

My mentors and role models, Judith Shklar and Stanley Hoffman, were then young assistant professors in their late twenties, and both would go on to distinguished careers at Harvard and as internationally renowned writers on politics. They were both Europeans who had escaped fascism as children and they were in love with the American dream. I was the beneficiary of their ardor, since I seemed to them proof that anyone, even an unsophisticated Jewish country bumpkin, could make it at Harvard. They became my guides on my journey to the new world of ideas. They were also important in my development as a writer. Identifying so strongly, as they did, with American ideals, they self-consciously wrote like Americans, their writing style crisp, simple, and straightforward. They used neither social science jargon nor obscure esoteric abstraction and obfuscation. Just as I had begun writing by imitating encyclopedia style (actually copying it) I now imitated my two mentors and self-consciously sought to write just like they did—and I think I still do.

College ended for me with my being totally preoccupied with writing. My senior year was absorbed in writing an honors thesis on William God-win's political thought. My memories of that last year in college always re-turn to the solitude of writing. The thesis was well received and my teach-ers told me that I should go to graduate school, so I did. Once again, writing was defining who I was.

In graduate school at Harvard I still seldom spoke in seminars and to the extent that I competed in the marketplace of ideas it was through writ-ing. I remember each unpleasant year of graduate school only through that year's seminar papers. The miserable experience that is graduate school culminated in a Ph.D. dissertation on Bolingbroke's political thought, the Bolingbroke who was the St. John that Alexander Pope tries to awaken in the opening lines of his *Essay on Man.* When it was done, much to my utter amazement, it was championed by the eminent Ameri-can historian Bernard Bailyn, who had been trying to understand why American revolutionaries so often cited the English Tory Bolingbroke and who found his explanation in my manuscript. He helped get the dis-sertation published, and it would make my career and reputation. Yet again writing crucially shaped the patterns of my life.

Over the years colleagues and graduate students have noted what a savvy and strategic choice I made for a Ph.D. topic. I immediately disabuse them of such a heroic reading of our writer by telling them the truth of how, in fact, I came to write on Bolingbroke. Judith Shklar, still my men-tor in graduate school, called me into her office in my third year. "Time to think about your dissertation," she said. "Let's explore the possibilities. I suggest a person; the boundaries of the research are clearer. You know the 17th and 18th centuries best; you're horrible in any language but Eng-lish; and it should be someone not often written about, who you can make important—who needs another thesis on Hobbes, Locke or Hume?" She finally paused and then said, "How about Bolingbroke?" I then spoke for the first time. "Who's he?" I asked. "That proves my point. Make him well known—that's your dissertation topic," she pronounced. So much for in-spired choice. And so much for our writer as a young man. Let me turn now to my confrontation with political science, a not-so-epic struggle.

OUR WRITER CONFRONTS POLITICAL SCIENCE

At Harvard I was a student in the government department, just as I now teach at Cornell in the government department. The vast majority of other such departments in American colleges and universities are, of course, called "political science" with the exception of the few, like that at Princeton, that are called politics departments. Behind these different department names—government, politics, and political science—lies a long story, which I will abbreviate for you.

The study of politics and the discussion of political issues in the 19th-century American college took place in courses labeled "moral philosophy" or "moral science." These courses could be usually found in departments of rhetoric and English literature, or in theology or classics departments, because the texts read by students were classical and early modern works, generally accepted as models of rhetoric or moral inspiration. In these courses, often taught by the college or university president, students usually read the great political writers in Western culture: Plato, Aristotle, Cicero, Aquinas, Machiavelli, Locke, Rousseau, and Burke. Courses in "moral philosophy" dealt with political life, but usually in the service of larger normative concerns. Establishing God's moral and virtuous order in America required the cultivation in 19th-century college students of a firm sense of citizenship, duty, and obligation, all in the service of the invariant moral standards summed up as God's natural law.

All-important in undermining "moral philosophy" at the center of the academic study of politics was Darwinism and the prestige of science in America after the Civil War, and hence the emergence of political science. Columbia University was at the vanguard. In the 1860s it was the home of Francis Lieber, the first professor in America of political science. Cornell, at its origins a hotbed of secular scientific enthusiasm, quickly followed; one of its original six instructional divisions in 1868 was called the "Department of History, Social, and Political Science." In 1880, Columbia established the School of Political Science, and in 1888 that school started publishing the *Political Science Quarterly*. The creation of this new learned discipline was codified in 1903 with the founding of the American Political Science Association. The spirit and mood behind the establishment of this discipline is reflected in Columbia University's announcement that its School of Political Science was "dedicated to scientific scholarship" which would foster "the progressive development of truth" as a replacement for traditional beliefs based on religious authority.[1]

What the founders of political science in the early 20th century meant by making political studies more scientific was summed up by James Bryce, the fourth president of the American Political Science Association. He urged its members to turn away from "philosophical generalizations"

---

1. John Burgess, *Reminiscences of An American Scholar* (New York: Columbia University Press, 1934), 203.

about politics and away from Hegelian inquiry into metaphysical "abstractions" like "sovereignty," "law" and "the state." Bryce urged his colleagues to "stick close to the facts," to engage in empirical research "to see what forms the state has taken and which have proved best, what powers governments have enjoyed and how those powers have worked."[2]

These early political scientists were part of the general embrace of science and expertise during the Progressive Era that links empiricism to social improvement and political reform. Early conferences on the science of politics saw political science serving larger objectives outside the university in public life. Academic political science would, it was believed, improve the quality of American politics writ large. As one of its early practitioners put it,

> Unless a higher degree of science can be brought into the operations of government, civilization is in the very gravest peril from the caprice of ignorance and passion. . . . The whole scheme of governmental activity requires a body of scientific political principles for even reasonable efficiency and success. It is the function of political science to provide this science of politics.[3]

Political science's birth, then, is an expression of the pragmatic revolt against Hegelian abstraction. It's the mood of John Dewey and the early Walter Lippman calling for the application of what they called "organized intelligence," and "scientific expertise" to politics in order to produce what they labeled with the name "public policies." America should, as these early fans of science put it, apply the same scientific methods to the management of society that worked so well in taming the natural world. Since this plea for a scientific management of society does not today seem to be intuitively an idea on the left, it bears repeating that these early political scientists in the first decades of the 20th century were overwhelmingly progressives opposed to the domination of American politics by businessmen and bosses. The New School for Social Research, established in these years, is a monument to the left-progressive faith in the scientific study of society, developing rational expert practitioners who would reform America. The founding of *The New Republic* by Cornell's Willard Straight is also a part of this story, for it rapidly became the most important public and nonacademic vehicle for essays illustrating this marriage of reform and the new empirical approach to politics.

This political science, born in the early 20th century, represented what

2. James Bryce, "The Relations of Political Science to History and Practice," *American Political Science Review* (February 1909): 4.

3. "Reports of the National Conference on the Science of Politics," *American Political Science Review* (February 1924): 110.

I would call a "soft" science of politics. It rejects a priori truths, metaphysics, and philosophical generalization. It rejects normative speculation on what is just or what is the best regime. It advocates empirical research into the facts of politics, case studies that explore the political reality behind the rhetoric and platitudes of politics. More often than not the factual reality revealed by empirical research is conflict—conflict among individuals, and especially conflict among groups over power. Empirical research reveals, as one of its devotees wrote, that politics is a struggle over "who gets what, when and how." But this is not yet a "hard" political science (to which I will turn shortly), one that stresses quantification, hypothesis testing, and experimental verification.

By midcentury this soft political science could be found in many academic departments—which, in fact, had begun to call themselves political science departments. But alternative and older approaches to the study of politics persisted, often within the same political science departments. Many professors in political science departments who were labeled political scientists still studied politics with humanistic, normative, legal, or historical methodologies. A few places, like Harvard and Cornell, signaled their primary attachment to these more traditional approaches by calling themselves government departments.

Which brings us to the second wave of scientific enthusiasm in the discipline, the harder scientific initiative of the 1950s and 1960s, which is called behavioralism—and which involved an effort to completely rid the study of politics of these remaining traditional approaches. At the heart of this second wave of science was the ambition, as one of its 1951 manifestos put it, to describe "all the phenomena of government in terms of the observed and observable behavior of men."[4] Discussions of traditional concepts like the state were unscientific; especially useless was political philosophy.

Scientific political studies, behavioralists of the 50s and 60s claimed, look at the world of what is, and a nonscientific approach is concerned with what ought to be or what was, and therefore should be called either theology, philosophy, ideology, history, or poetry. Fueled by technological advances, such as new sophisticated survey techniques and refined methods of statistical analysis, postwar hard political scientists saw themselves as value-free collectors and manipulators of fact, like their natural science colleagues. Political truth had to be built on operationalizable hypotheses that were testable, i.e., verifiable or falsifiable—all in the service of producing uniform, regular, and predictive laws of political behavior. Insights into politics were scientific only if they could be proved or disproved, as

4. "Items," Social Science Research Council (December 1951): 37.

opposed to moral insights expressed in the language of values that cannot conclusively be validated or contradicted. Like natural scientists, the 1950s-60s hard political scientist was also convinced that scientific truth about politics was grounded in quantitative data and numerical indices.

Central to the behavioral political science initiative was a reified fact/value dichotomy, and much ink was spilled in the 1950s and 1960s analyzing the writings of Max Weber. The second-wave hard-science children faulted their first-wave softer political science fathers (there were fathers, no mothers) for having self-consciously wedded political science to a value-driven passion with reform. A political scientist's scholarly work is value-neutral, they insisted; the professor can have and express her or his values or beliefs outside the university. This points to another very important feature of hard political science: it is inquiry and scholarship on politics pursued by professors in universities, for an audience of other professors and graduate students. The first wave of political scientists had seen the academic study of politics as having public purpose outside the academy. I will come back to this all-important development.

The discipline of political science in the 1960s and 1970s was a bitter battle zone. Some departments, like Michigan, Yale, and Rochester, virtually converted to behavioralism, and some, like Harvard and Cornell, resisted. Behavioralism was attacked from both the academic left and the academic right. On the Marxist left, Herbert Marcuse complained that research into human political behavior did not provide truth value, but only the empirical reality of a particular social moment (capitalism) and described a historical temporary human being, not the real species being.

Important liberal scholars ridiculed behavioral political science as well. Cornell's Andrew Hacker wrote in 1967:

> What must be abandoned is the hope that political analysis can be either objective or scientific. . . . There may be cooperation among political scientists in the sense that they share and criticize each other's research. However, this communication does not produce an agreed-upon body of knowledge. . . . At this time, it is hard to point to any 'findings' that have been accepted by the scholarly community. As matters now stand, there are cliques, coteries, and lone wolves talking past one another or to themselves.[5]

Cornell's Theodore Lowi wrote in 1972:

> Political disorder does not favor political scientists; it deranges their theories and cracks their time-honored assumptions. But the shortcomings of political

5. Andy Hacker, "The Utility of Quantitative Methods in Political Science," in *Contemporary Political Analysis*, ed. James C. Charlesworth (New York: Free Press, 1967), 147.

science during . . . [the 1960s] are not to be found in the poor advice political scientists gave to authorities. . . . The somber fact of the matter was that,
on most of the fundamental questions underlying disorder, the discipline of
political science simply did not have anything to say one way or the other.[6]

From the academic right, Leo Strauss at Chicago thundered at the new
political science, and his disciples took up the cause. Behavioralism subverted the age-old moral focus of political studies, they claimed. This is
how Allan Bloom, formely of the Cornell government department, put it:

> students and citizens in general have an instinctive awareness of what politics
> is, but political science does not have any view of what it is, or at least not one
> that in any way corresponds to or refines that untutored awareness. . . . Now
> the awareness of which I speak is that politics has to do with justice and the
> realization of the good life . . . The citizen has . . . certainly been frustrated
> by political science, from which he had a right to expect instruction and clar-
> ification about the ends of politics and the means available for fulfilling
> them.[7]

Mention of these Cornell figures brings to mind that a minor skirmish
in the political science wars occurred right on Cornell's Arts Quad, literally in a battle over buildings. The history and government departments,
after World War II, were located in Sibley Hall, (all of you who have read
Alison Lurie's wonderful *War between the Tates* know that in her depiction
of the Cornell troubles, whose 30th anniversary we note this year, Professor Tate's government department office is properly housed in a building
with a dome). In the very early 1970s, expansion of the Art and Architec-
ture College required government and history to leave. Where to go? History chose McGraw, which the geologists were vacating. Meanwhile, Uris
Hall was conceived as the new home of scientific social science at Cornell.
Where would government go? To Uris with economics, sociology, and
psychology or to McGraw with history? It went to McGraw.

What about me? Time to bring me back into this story. In the late 1960s
and early 1970s I was an assistant professor at Yale, which was then probably the leading political science department in America, and decidedly
behavioral in its orientation. I taught history of political thought courses
and had published my first book, my *Bolingbroke and His Circle: The Politics*

6. Theodore Lowi, "The Politics of Higher Education: Political Science as a Case Study," in
The Post-Behavioral Era: Perspectives on Political Science, ed. George J. Grahm and George W.
Carey, (New York: McKay, 1972), 11.

7. Allan Bloom, "Political Science and the Undergraduate," in *Teaching Political Science: The
Professor and the Polity*, ed. Vernon Van Dyke (Atlantic Highlands, N.J.: Humanities Press,
1977), 118.

of Nostalgia in the Age of Walpole. In all honesty, I was utterly oblivious to the great methodological wars raging about me; I wrote nothing about Max Weber, nothing on the evils of value-free inquiry. I was uninterested in, and indifferent to, the "direction of the discipline" question. But I became a victim of that direction nonetheless, which is why I came to Cornell. In 1970 I was up for tenure at Yale. The chair of the department confided in me that it would be a breeze; his senior colleagues, it seemed, were very pleased with me. My book, by some miraculous throw of the dice, had been given a full-page, unsigned favorable review on the front page of the *Times Literary Supplement,* in the last year or so that it had both front-page and unsigned reviews. It had also won a prize. It was clear from the chair's tone that this was the sort of recognition that brought credit to a political science department that saw itself as the best in America.

The problem was that my senior colleagues had not read the book itself and when they did they were deeply troubled. Even for political philosophy it was, as they told me, too far removed from Yale political science. I was given a term associate professorship during which time they hoped I would produce a second book that was in their words "less synchronic and more diachronic," which I took to mean that I had to write about either two people or two eras. How else could I produce comparisons, from which I could then derive patterns and regularities, which would enable me to make testable hypotheses and predictions about a third person, text, or time.

I had transgressed the discipline's dominant norms in another way as well. I had violated the value-free neutrality of political science in another piece of writing I had published in 1971, a satirical lefty attack on my lefty Yale colleague Charles Reich, whose *Greening of America* was then number one on the nonfiction best seller list. (Yale was a vibrant place in the early 70s, for a Yale professor also was on top of the bestselling fiction list—the classics professor Erich Segal, with his profoundly memorable *Love Story.*) My piece on Reich bothered my senior colleagues because of "its lack of objectivity." The promised tenure was to be delayed while I learned how to be a better, i.e., more "rigorous" political scientist (rigor was the best thing you could have as a social scientist in the 1970s).

In retrospect, I should be thankful for having been victimized by behavioral political science at Yale because it enables me to answer truthfully and perhaps even poignantly one of the key questions the charge from the writing program laid out for us in describing what we might talk about in our lectures for this series. I quote from the "prospectus" for this lecture series: "Have there been periods when you felt yourself an unwitting or unwilling captive to disciplinary practices? If so, how did you escape captivity, or didn't you?" Yes, I was a captive and yes, I did escape captivity to disciplinary practices, and how I did it was simple—I came to Cornell in 1972. My sad writing story, indeed, has a happy ending. And for that, I am most thankful to my former senior colleagues in political science at Yale.

OUR WRITER AND THE MODES OF WRITING AT THE NEW MILLENNIUM

The methodological wars have continued unabated. Hard social scientists in their latest iteration as "rational choice" theorists still dismiss the more traditional historico-ethical kind of work I do as literature or ideology or journalism. Founded several decades ago by William Riker at the University of Rochester and helped by generous grants from the National Science Foundation, "rational choice" theory is everywhere in American political science today. Its true believers chair Ivy League departments and author about 40% of the articles in the prestigious *American Political Science Review.*

"Rational choice" scholars assume they can find universal and logically compelling explanations for all political phenomena, by looking at politics the way a scientist looks at particles of matter. Very much influenced by economics and its recent mathematical turn as well as by the mathematical theory of games, they take as a given that people in politics act rationally, i.e., pursue certain ends, usually maximization of self-interest, not the community's good. Rational people's behavior in politics can be predicted, according to "rational choice" theory, by generating abstract, formal mathematical models and numerical equations.

"Rational choice" theorists see themselves as the true scientists of politics, producing truth through the scientific method of deductive reasoning. Since values, beliefs, and historical insights can't be quantified, only interests and preference are studied. And when they write on politics, they seldom analyze texts, consult history, compare case studies, or even do survey research; they marshal and manipulate numbers. And in more and more graduate programs, the political science curriculum is requiring increased training in mathematical modeling and statistics.

Meanwhile, new methodologies have also entered the disciplinary struggle. Postmodernism is the most important new contender for the soul of political studies. Its assumptions are a mirror opposite of those of behavioral political science. While hard political science emphasizes regularity, predictability, and objectivity, postmodernism stresses irregularity, unpredictability, and subjectivity. Nietzsche, postmodernism's philosophical mentor, wrote that "objectivity" was a "nonsensical absurdity." He insisted that one could not find "knowledge in itself," since all knowledge carries the stamp of the situated individuals who create it.

Unlike my own indifference to and tolerance of hard political science, postmodernists challenge it head on, ridiculing any effort to uncover regular universal patterns that operate through inexorable logic or scientific laws. Postmodernists also repudiate conventional assumptions about individual human agency. Human identity, they argue, is socially constructed by an infinite number of institutions and social forces. Instead of "a single, uniform human nature," postmodernists see human beings as products of historical development and social process. As Richard Rorty has succinctly put it, "the postmodern assumption is that socialization, and thus historical circumstance, goes all the way down—that there is nothing 'beneath' socialization or prior to history which is definatory of the human."[8]

I am not concerned here with the validity or profundity of the postmodern approach to the study of politics, nor of the hard social scientist committed to "rational choice." Both approaches have much to say about the world of politics that is insightful and valuable. My interest here is the kind of writing produced by these disciplinary camps, writing quite different from the writing found in the once dominant historico-ethical camp. Most scholarly writing on politics today is pervaded by professional jargon, and technical data, wielded by college professors for the edification of other college professors and their graduate students. I would remind us all that Max Weber, that venerable touchstone in the methodology debates, once suggested that the development of new private terminologies is less concerned with precision than with the imperatives of professional exclusiveness. Packaging knowledge with jargon, he wrote, is a way of excluding others from access to it. In his famous essay on bureaucracy, Weber noted that Persian treasury officials actually invented a secret script in order to keep control over financial affairs—much like, we might add, the professional monopoly of the law maintained today through the inaccessible secret language of lawyers.[9]

When I write on politics I see my audience as that mythical collectivity some of us still hold dear, the general lay educated public. I want academics to read my work, but like my eighteenth-century antecedents, Bolingbroke, Burke, Paine, Rousseau, and Madison, none of whom were professors, I link writing on politics to wider public purpose. Neither they nor I

8. Richard Rorty, "Habermas and Lyotard on Postmodernity," in *Habermas and Modernity*, ed. Richard Bernstein, (Cambridge: MIT Press, 1985), 118.

9. H. H. Geron and C. Wright Mills, eds. *From Max Weber: Essays in Sociology* (New York: Oxford University Press, 1958), 233.

use a specialist language that a general readership finds inaccessible. Like them I am something of a relic, writing about politics as it was done before such writing became a professional monopoly of university professors.

In the new scholasticism that is much of contemporary political writing and social theory, arcane and virtually private languages make many texts inaccessible to all but the professionalized and the initiated and the implications of this for a democratic society are profound. If professors write only for each other and for each other's graduate students, who then writes for the broader public down in the "bustling town" upon which, Cornell's alma mater tells us, we "look proudly down?" More than any other scholarly discipline, the study of politics needs to rediscover its old voice, its public voice, the voice of public intellectuals who address the bustling town. It is difficult to have democratic deliberation and argumentation even in the academy if the terms of discourse are set and preserved by a priesthood writing in a private jargon or impenetrable numerology. Lost today is the earlier nineteenth-century American conviction that political scholarship is not just an intellectual exercise but an important service to a self-governing people, scholarship which speaks to the public square as well as to university quadrangles.

WHY WRITE?

Why do we write? Why do all of us write? Political scientists, English professors, historians, creative writers? Why do we write? Beyond the obvious clichéd response that we are driven to discover and distribute truth, what are the personal and private reasons we write?

First and foremost we write for the utter joy of writing. One reads often about the pain of writing, much less about the sheer pleasure of writing. There is the joy in its trivial aesthetic rituals, which differ for each of us. For me, who has not yet switched to a typewriter, let alone the word processor, it is my faithful mechanical pencil, my yellow pads, and the ceremony of ripping the just-filled page off the pad and watching the growing pile of loose pages of handwritten manuscript. Writing is full of the pleasures of repetitive routine. For me writing means the pleasure of quiet retreat, of being alone. There are few euphoric highs, sheer ecstatic joys, that compare with how one feels after a good day of writing.

Beyond joy, we write, of course, because we want to be noticed (itself no mean pleasure). As I observed in the brief psycho-biographical gloss I gave my own initiation into writing, writing is for many a safer way to be noticed than verbal self-assertion. And writers certainly want to be noticed, especially by the chattering class. Writers live and die by being noticed.

You could say that we also write, in part, to cheat death, to achieve some small form of immortality. One of my very published colleagues admits to having resolved as an undergraduate to be a writer on politics, after searching through the library card catalogue for entries on an author who had died before World War II. Each card trumpeted eternal life. Then it was cards in a catalogue, now it is a line on a computer screen; in both cases it is immortality.

Who knows—perhaps in the year 2099 a graduate student studying politics will tell her friends how she found her Ph.D. subject. "My professor asked me if I had a topic," she'll say. "When I told her no, she suggested I write about a person, someone not well known, about whom not much has been written."

"I asked the professor for some suggestions," the graduate student might go on. "My professor answered, 'What about Isaac Kramnick; in the late twentieth century he wrote some books on English and American politics. Someone should write on him.' "

Writing (and Quantifying) Sociology

RONALD L. BREIGER (Sociology)

UNDERGRADUATES in my course on quantitative reasoning in sociology soon encounter the homework problem illustrated in Exhibit 1. Having just been introduced to a review of some elementary concepts of statistical "averaging," they are asked to find the average class size of three sections of an introductory course.

Exhibit 1. Textbook Problem: Computing the Mean

At the local university, there are three sections of the basic accounting course, with 8, 12, and 120 students.
  A. For the three instructors who teach this course, what average class size do they face?
  B. Do the 140 students who are taking the course have a different view? Calculate the average class size that they sit in. (Wonnacott and Wonnacott 1990, 67)

Because sociology in the United States today is famously a numerical enterprise, one that my freshmen, sophomores, and juniors presume emphasizes objectivity of result and accuracy of calculation, and (more directly to the point) since these students have just been exposed to a discussion of the formula for the arithmetic mean, most students decide that part (a) of this textbook problem entails straightforward application of that formula. Thus, the average class size demanded in part (a) is given as the total of students in ratio to the number of sections: $(8 + 12 + 120) / 3 = 140/3 = 47$ students per section, rounding to the nearest whole student.

Part (b) of the same textbook problem stumps all but a very few of my students. Now they are asked about a possible difference in "view" between students and professors. The calculation in part (a) may be seen to have implicitly adopted the perspective of the faculty members who teach the three sections. On the other side of the desk, what do their students experience? Only a tiny fraction (8 of the 140 students considered in this homework problem) are in the smallest class section, the one with but 8 students. At the other extreme, the vast majority (120 of 140) are in the large section of 120 students. On average, the students considered in the homework problem experience a class size of

$$8\left(\frac{8}{140}\right) + 12\left(\frac{12}{140}\right) + 120\left(\frac{120}{140}\right) = 104$$

which is more than twice as big a class as the three professors believe they teach.

The arithmetic of parts (a) and (b) of this textbook problem using made-up data is not at all remarkable; no ambiguity in mathematics or logic is uncovered. However, the sociology is profound, and the policy implications consequential, as has been independently discovered by Cornell's dean of university faculty and expounded in a report on class size and curriculum (Cooke 1994).[1] I will emphasize four issue of sociological interpretation that seem implicated in an adequate analysis of this problem in average class sizes. These are considerations that many of my undergraduate students—and not a few of my professional colleagues—find startling.

Multiplicity. The same reality requires two different answers in order to compute a statistic as straightforward as the arithmetic mean. The professors on average teach relatively small classes of 47 students who themselves sit (on average) in relatively large classes of 104.

Reflexivity. In solving the textbook example that we have considered, coming to a single correct answer about the mean class size involves the analyst's placing herself, so to speak, inside the problem. Is one to look from the professors' "view" or from that of the students?

Duality. I propose to use the term "duality" to emphasize the co-constitution of elements existing at different levels of abstraction, as in the principle of geometric duality (Hodge and Pedoe 1968) by which a plane is defined by

1. This report noted the discrepancy in class sizes that confronted students and faculty members within the same university, in a manner quite similar qualitatively to that illustrated by the textbook problem of Exhibit 1. Feld and Grofman (1977) provide formal models of the class size paradox.

two intersecting lines, even as a line is determined by the intersection of two planes. In the textbook example considered here, the class size experienced by the students (104 students per professor) is dual to the class size for the professors (3 professors for the 140 students).

Institutional context, or power relations. The answer obtained—whether the class size is small or large on average—depends on which side of the desk is privileged in defining the calculation. As given in the statement of the problem, the instructors "face" a seemingly objective average class size, whereas it is allowed that the students might have a differing "view."

The textbook example helps me to convince my undergraduates that quantitative reasoning in sociology is not a straightforward matter of objectivity or of "letting the numbers speak for themselves," or a process that necessarily entails an omniscient analyst above the fray, or an analyst who could easily be replaced by some computing machinery.[2] Furthermore, these considerations do not (for the most part) lead to any form of nihilistic relativism but, on the contrary, can help the statistical modeler gain a great deal of clarity in describing the world and in comparing alternative accounts. In all these respects, there are deep analogies between writing quantitative analysis and other forms of writing. Issues raised by literary theorists of rhetoric and interpretation such as Steven Mailloux (1989; 1998) can be further illuminated in conversation with quantitative modelers in the social sciences. I will explore some of these analogies in this chapter, focusing on the writing of formulas as an activity that is not at all limited to formulaic writing.

WRITING MODELS

In a thoughtful essay on the relation of sociology and cultural studies, Michael Schudson (1997, 394) urges sociologists to recognize that "one

2. It seems still to be the case that, as Max Weber had it in his 1917 address, "Science as a Vocation" (Weber 1991), "Nowadays in circles of youth there is a widespread notion that science has become a problem in calculation, fabricated in laboratories or statistical filing systems just as 'in a factory,' a calculation involving only the cool intellect and not one's 'heart and soul.' First of all one must say that such comments lack all clarity about what goes on in a factory or in a laboratory. In both some idea has to occur to someone's mind, and it has to be a correct idea if one is to accomplish anything worthwhile. And such intuition cannot be forced. It has nothing to do with any cold calculation. Certainly calculation is also an indispensable prerequisite. No sociologist, for instance, should think himself too good, even in his old age, to make tens of thousands of quite trivial computations in his head and perhaps for months at a time. One cannot with impunity try to transfer this task entirely to mechanical assistants. . . ." This quotation appears at the head of the reading list for my undergraduate course in quantitative reasoning.

of the things we do when we 'commit a social science,' as W. H. Auden caustically put it, is to write, and that writing is a socially and culturally constructed act within a cultural field" and not, "as people still like to believe, a transparent record of data or observations."[3] If as Schudson and others allege there is too little reflexive reflection on the point that "sociology is itself a construction, a writerly construction,"[4] then this absence of self-consciousness would seem to be all the more relevant to sociologists who carry on and report the quantitative modeling and analysis at the core of the field in the U.S. today.

While indeed there is an egregious lack of systematic elaboration of the rhetorical dimensions of quantitative models and analysis, there are also countertendencies worthy of expounding, and openings to a recognition of some points of similarity as well as difference between literary analysis and quantitative analysis of social data. The social scientist who has thought most deeply about issues of rhetoric and quantitative method is an economist, Deirdre McCloskey. In elaborating a rhetoric of statistical significance tests, for example, McCloskey (1998) urges the proposition that good science is good conversation. McCloskey understands that she needs to convince social scientists that elaborating the rhetoric of quantitative analysis is much more than a negative, debunking activity.

> The invitation to rhetoric is not, I emphasize, an invitation to "replace careful analysis with rhetoric," or to abandon mathematics in favor of name-calling or flowery language. The good rhetorician loves care, precision, explicitness, and economy in argument as much as the next person. Since she has thought more carefully and explicitly than most people have about the place of such virtues in a larger system of scholarly values, she may even love them more. A rhetorical approach to economic texts is machine-building, not machine-breaking . . . an invitation to leave the irrationality of an artificially narrowed range of argument and to move to the rationality of arguing like human beings. (McCloskey 1998, 168)

Within sociology proper there is no elaborated linkage of quantitative modeling and analysis with strategies of rhetoric. There are, however, moves in this direction. Otis Dudley Duncan, a quantitative methodolo-

---

3. In addition to drawing guidance for sociology from cultural studies, Schudson's essay offers a trenchant critique of cultural studies from the perspective of sociology's concern with empirical observation, precision, and replicability.

4. Among those who do understand the importance of writing for argumentation in sociology are authors of writing guides, including some excellent ones (Becker 1986, 1998; see also citations in Reed 1989), analysts of the rhetoric of sociological research studies (see in particular the essays collected in Hunter 1990), and at least one author of a quantitative methods textbook (Levine 1993) who takes on rhetorical issues fairly directly.

gist *par excellence* in the American tradition, nonetheless argues for a sociology of social measurement inscribed within reflexivity: "the social roots
of social measurement are in the social process itself" (Duncan 1984a,
221). And Duncan has been a tireless critic of

> the syndrome that I have come to call *statisticism*: the notion that computing
> is synonymous with doing research, the naïve faith that statistics is a
> complete or sufficient basis for scientific methodology, the superstition that
> statistical formulas exist for evaluating such things as the relative merits of
> different substantive theories or the "importance" of the causes of a "depen-
> dent variable;" and the delusion that decomposing the covariations of some
> arbitrary and haphazardly assembled collection of variables can somehow
> justify not only a "causal model" but also, praise the mark, a "measurement
> model." (226)

Harrison White, a leading mathematical sociologist and—like Duncan—an elected member of the National Academy of Sciences, has recently argued that, "in avoiding and sidestepping the interpretive—and
thus any direct access to construction of social reality—mathematical
models have come to an era of decreasing returns to effort." White suggests that "interpretive approaches are central to achieving a next level of
adequacy in social data" (White 1997, 58).

One of the problems in furthering conversation between humanists
and quantitative sociologists on the subject of rhetoric and method is the
tendency of each group of scholars to use second-rank work in castigating
the other. It is not uncommon for humanists to imagine quantitative social scientists as modern descendants of Thomas Gradgrind, Dickens'
character in *Hard Times* who carries "the multiplication table always in his
pocket, sir, ready to weigh and measure any parcel of human nature, and
tell you exactly what it comes to," without acknowledging that we have
had quite a few successes in elaborating meaning, values, and social construction in ways that might inform humanistic inquiry.[5] And, for its part,

---

5. Graduate students in the Cornell English department's radical caucus point out "literature's disdain for engaging with social science methodologies" (Graduate Student Radical
Caucus 1998, 67). A counterexample, an essay by a literary theorist who engages applied social
science data analysis with great power, is Gates (1992). And I would cite Mohr (1998) as one
recent review of social science research in support of my contention on the value in overcom-
ing, or at least bracketing, such disdain. Mohr and Duquenne (1997) present and apply quantitative methods for analysis of the sorts of local cultural practices that are at the center of study
of at least some theorists of rhetoric (see Mailloux 1989, 145). Griswold (1993) reviews research studies as well as theoretical work in the sociology of literature pertaining to "the relationship between literature and group identities; connecting institutional and reader-response
analyses; reintroducing the role of authorial intentionality; and developing a clearer understanding of how literature is and is not like other media."

mainstream sociology seems resolute in not being impressed by "semi-otics, or hermeneutics, or any of the other tics of humanistic inquiry in these latter days," often dismissed as "the Paris fashions modish . . . in New Haven and Berkeley and the intellectual suburbs," as one presidential address to a regional sociological society had it (Reed 1989, 2), perhaps in an effort to call attention to the lack of dialogue and the degree to which sociologists are responsible for the absence. Useful conversation will have to step beyond the name-calling.

WRITING LOGLINEAR MODELS: CHANGES OVER THE PAST THREE DECADES

In order to begin a discussion, I would like to offer a reading of some accounts of quantitative modeling in sociology over the past three decades, as a way to understand some of the issues—both practical and general—in writing these formulas. I will refer to models for tables of counted data. Such tables are a stock-in-trade of contemporary sociology; a typical example might be "religious denomination by political party preference." Here we count the number of people in a random sample, taken from a population whose activities we hope to understand better, who are at the intersection of each denomination (perhaps "Baptist," "Presbyterian," and so on) and each party preference (such as "Republican" or "Libertarian"). If people of each religious denomination had the *same* distribution of party preferences, then we would say that the two variables (religion and party) were "statistically independent," and we could model the expected count in any cell of the table (say, Presbyterian Democrats) by multiplying the number of people in the sample by the overall probability of being Presbyterian and the overall probability of being a Democrat. Notice that this is a multiplicative model,[6] though statisticians and applied data analysts often prefer to replace the term "multiplicative" with "loglinear."[7] Of course in real societies people of different religious denominations *do* differ in their political party preferences, so the model of simple "statistical independence" that we have been dis-

---

6. Informally; the model is "multiplicative" due to the independence that I have invoked (for illustrative purposes) between religion and party preference. In analogy, the probability that two fair coins *both* land heads up is 1/2 "times" 1/2.

7. The product of terms that are multiplied together is, if transformed in a certain way (by taking its logarithm), equal to the linear sum of the logarithms of the given terms. The "linear" terminology is connotative of a major achievement of statistical science: the formulation of a "general linear model" of which both the usual forms of least-squares regression analysis and "loglinear models" are special cases.

cussing is virtually never adequate to the task of accounting for the observed data.[8]

From roughly the 1940s to the 1960s, the inadequacy of the simple independence model was exploited by developing indices of the lack of fit, allowing a sociologist to say for example that religion and party preference were associated however-much more than would be expected in the absence of a relation. While the loglinear model of simple statistical independence did in this way give sociologists a place to stand in assessing statistical relationships, clearly it is not entirely satisfactory to have a single model that the analyst hopes does *not* fit the data, if one believes that relationships among aspects of social life are important and capable of taking a variety of distinctive forms deserving of distinctive representations in social analysis.

From the mid-1960s through the 1990s, many researchers developed several very large families of generalizations of loglinear models (the model of statistical independence was often a special case of each of these families), the single most prominent contributor to this line of work being a professor of statistics and sociology named Leo Goodman. Historical accounts or glosses on this period of the elaboration of formal models emphasized increasing sophistication, "cumulation" and the production of "verifiable knowledge" (Breiger 1990, 225), and "progress" toward the goal of formulating "relevant models and methods" (Goodman and Clogg 1992 609). This language of cumulation and progress was especially likely to be found in the area of stratification and mobility research. James Coleman (1991, 3–4) contrasted nationally representative studies of individual attainment with an earlier tradition of stratification research based on community probes such as Lynd and Lynd's (1929) study of Middletown. In the earlier studies, analysis of community structure was synthetic, qualitative, concerned with the subjective views of persons located at different points in the structure, and regarded persons within the system as acting purposefully to make use of their resources. In sharp contrast, the more recent national studies of attainment take individual persons as the fundamental units; these studies are analytical and quantitative, provide no subjective views, and regard persons not as purposive actors but—as in much of the research employing loglinear models—as intersections of variables linked together in causal relations. Movement from the first research frame to the second captures for Coleman some as-

---

8. The "accounting" is done by comparing the observed table of counts to the table that would result by applying the multiplicative or "loglinear" formula reviewed above, where the comparison takes the form of assessment by means of a statistical distribution appropriate to the task of comparing the "observed" and "modeled" counts, the chi-square distribution.

pects of the transformation of social research in general over the past half
century. Moreover, Coleman, in contrast to many of his colleagues, was
distressed by this line of "progress" (see Breiger 1995 for a review).

Focusing in particular on the development of loglinear modeling in sociology over the past three decades, I find it useful to think of the many
different families of models that have been developed as inscribing stylistic differences in writing the structuring of social relationships, with the
styles in turn based on different images of the structuring of the cells of a
table of data. In introducing each style, I will consider the way in which
each path to new models provided a distinctive departure from the simple
model of statistical independence. To provide a sense of the images that
have been developed by loglinear analysts, consider the following.

Association models (Goodman 1984; Duncan 1979). The model of statistical independence introduced above may be seen as the "null association" model in that, if the model fits, Presbyterians and Baptists (for example) do not differ on average in their party preferences: there is zero
association between the row categories and the column categories. Other
models—models with definite formulas whose degree of fit can be as-
sessed empirically, not just efforts to exploit the lack of fit of the simple independence model—have been developed in which there is postulated to
be a "uniform association" across religious groups in party preference (to
continue our illustration), or according to which the association is row-
specific and/or column-specific (such that, for example, members of a
given religious group could be said on average to be particularly strong
supporters of a given political party), or perhaps multidimensional. Loglinear models were augmented by log-multiplicative models to handle
some of the principal extensions (Goodman 1984). As I have so far presented these matters it all sounds rather straightforward and quite possibly boring; however, by the end of the chapter I will be discussing some
major rumblings-up of fiery rhetoric associated with these developments.

Topological models (Hauser 1979; Goodman 1984; Erikson and Goldthorpe 1992a). The model of statistical independence consists of a series
of interaction terms (one such term for each of the table's cells) each of
which is zero. A generalization is to postulate an exhaustive partitioning
of the table's cells into sets each of which consists of cells sharing a "constant" interaction parameter (where these estimated constants differ from
one set of cells to another). The cells in any "level" may, in principle, be
drawn from anywhere in the table.

Class models (Breiger 1981, 1990; Goodman, 1984; Marsden 1985;
Hout and Hauser 1992). The model of statistical independence is a "one-
class" model in that association between rows and columns is homogeneously zero with respect to all rows and all columns. Generalization to a

"class" model results from postulating a rearrangement and partitioning of the rows and the columns of the table into clumps of rows and clumps of columns which produce an exhaustive set of rectangular subtables of the original table, each *subtable* characterized by the model of statistical independence (exhibiting homogeneously zero association internally) or by a simpler model of homogeneity.

Latent class models (Clogg 1981; Goodman 1987). A given table of counts that has R rows and C columns might not satisfy the model of statistical independence. However, it might be possible to represent the single observed table by a series of tables of imputed counts, each such table also having R rows and C columns, such that each of the constructed tables satisfies the model of simple independence *and* the imputed counts sum across any cell of the table to the count actually observed in that cell.

RHETORICAL MODELS

I have tried to suggest something of the innovation of loglinear modeling by focusing in my brief account on some of the images made available within this modeling framework for distinguishing various possibilities for the structuring of relationships among categories of people such as Presbyterians and Democrats. I would like to move closer now to a rhetorical analysis of these issues, applying a sense of rhetoric influenced by Steven Mailloux's building on Richard Rorty's proposal for "a theoretical discourse that focuses not on the *confrontation* between knower and object— the controlling visual metaphor of traditional epistemology—but on the *conversation* among knowers" (Mailloux 1989, 144, original emphasis). Following Rorty, Mailloux sees "recent theories of reading" as alternating between two major orientations. A Lockean realism argues that the meaning of a text is independent of the reader, the text consisting of objective facts that are reflected in correct interpretations. On the other side is a Kantian idealism according to which, as Mailloux (144) has it, the minds of readers "constitute the meaningful text," a text constructed by readers who share interpretive conventions that determine correct interpretations. Mailloux (144–49) argues for "pragmatist readings" according to which

> theory soon turns into rhetorical history. More precisely, it becomes a collection of more or less related histories of conversations about texts. These conversations consist of rhetorical exchanges taking place within traditions of arguments and figures, and these traditions of specific rhetorical practices are themselves part of the micropractices that make up a culture at any historical moment. (145).

Quantitative sociologists often flaunt a view of themselves as Lockean realists, and many graduate curricula in methodology are organized around positivist principles. However—and this seems especially true of the leading quantitative researchers and modelers—if one observes these analysts at work, in the midst of carrying out their "micropractices," a much more subtle picture emerges, fraught with ambiguities and prospects for further rhetorical elaboration. To provide some grounding for a pragmatic reading of the literature on loglinear modeling, I will have recourse to the four rubrics that served well to introduce my undergraduates to the subtleties of the "average class size" example: multiplicity, reflexivity, duality, and institutional relations.

Multiplicity

As is suggested by my enumeration of different families of loglinear models (association models, topological models, class models, and so forth), there has been a proliferation of loglinear models relative to the ability of a given set of data to help the analyst gain a preference for one model over another. A highly influential early paper of Goodman's, published in 1969 (reprinted in Goodman 1984, 302–41) was entitled "How to Ransack Social Mobility Tables and Other Kinds of Cross-Classification Tables." Such ransacking is evident in that article, for example, in Goodman's discussion (319) of 20 interactions in a table composed of just 9 cells.[9]

Analyses such as these suggest that our ability to either discover or construct meaning for tables of counted data exceeds the ability of the data to adjudicate between competing interpretive schemes. Panel A of Exhibit 2 (next page) is an excerpt from Otis Dudley Duncan's review of a volume collecting some of Goodman's papers on loglinear models (Duncan, 1982). Panel B of the same exhibit excerpts a gloss on Jacques Derrida's postmodern notion that texts are complex networks of unfinished meanings; for Derrida, therefore, the notion of text is no longer an easy or comfortable one.

In panel A we see Duncan endeavoring to resist the principle of multiple meanings, and we observe as well his difficulties in doing so with re-

---

9. "Ransacking" is a general issue of social science methodology, and it evokes considerable ambivalence. On the other side from many loglinear analysts, one critic who is a professional statistician comments (in an article directed at skepticism toward regression models), "Testing one model on 24 different data sets could open up a serious enquiry: Have we identified an empirical regularity that has some degree of invariance? Testing 24 models on one data set is less serious" (Freedman 1991, 306).

spect to the specifics of loglinear modeling. The first sentence of this excerpt establishes as a clear implication of Goodman's modeling work that models with "radically different conceptual interpretations may be about equally attractive on statistical grounds." The more inventive the analyst becomes in proliferating new families of models within incommensurable families (such that one model ceases logically to "imply" another), the more elusive become the quest for precision and the goal of testing models against data.

We can resolve dilemmas such as this one, Duncan suggests, by focusing our scarce resources for research on "adequate test" of "the really critical hypotheses in a given state of knowledge," pushing for ever larger sample sizes, which would (as the sample size, N, gets larger and larger) in principle allow rejection of any model. But larger N's will not resolve all questions of interpretation—and in some respects they exacerbate them, for if N is big enough we are in danger of rejecting a model even when the data were generated from that model. Hence we confront an "embarrassment" in loglinear modeling, the definition of which is that "the more ingenious we become in devising sophisticated models to reflect the fine points of conceptualization," the more likely we are to be unable to decide which of our models is "true." Greater precision is what leads to greater indeterminacy.

Exhibit 2. On Unfinished Meanings and Interpretive Stress

A. [Duncan on Goodman:] One of the clear implications of Goodman's examples is that models with radically different conceptual interpretations may be about equally attractive on statistical grounds, so far as one may judge from a particular sample. Thus, on pages 211 and 294 Goodman gives path diagrams for two models fitted to Coleman's two-wave, two-variable panel data on membership in and attitude toward the "leading crowd" for 3,398 high-school boys. In one model there are five (out of the possible six) direct associations linking pairs of observed variables; but in the other model, the observed variables have no direct associations at all, being linked indirectly by way of two latent variables. Both models fit well. Since neither model implies the other, one cannot make an explicit comparison of chi-square values in the manner prescribed for models that are hierarchically related. Nonetheless, both models cannot be "true." It just happens that they give closely similar estimates of expected frequencies in the particular population under study. It would require a much larger sample than 3,398 from that population to achieve rejection of one or both models. Or, one might decide between the models (or in favor of still another model) on the basis of comparative analyses in a variety of populations. The more ingenious we become in devising sophisticated models to reflect fine points of conceptualization, the more often we must find ourselves with this kind of an embarrassment of riches. The classic "need for additional research" will become increasingly urgent. Perhaps we will be led to a rather different allocation of resources among lines of inquiry such that the really critical hypotheses in a given state of knowledge receive an adequate test. This seldom happens today. A model-rich environment is not necessarily a comfortable one. (Duncan 1982, 961–62)

B. [Birch on Derrida:] Thus the text, for Derrida, is a complex network of unfinished meanings, a "fabric of traces referring endlessly to something other than itself" [Derrida 1979, 84]. The notion of text is, therefore, no longer an easy, comfortable one, in which openings and endings of meaning are recognizable by readers . . . As a consequence reading becomes a much more dynamic, but uncertain, activity. (Birch 1989, 9)

Duncan would prefer to see this embarrassment as an "embarrassment of riches," one that urges the researcher on to ever more ingenuity. Duncan recognizes that the success of the loglinear modeling endeavor has led to a surfeit of imposed meanings in the form of models, and he advocates not a formal but a pragmatic approach to living with the resulting indeterminacies, an approach that consists in an (unspecified) interaction between models and data. Duncan concludes the paragraph presented in panel A of Exhibit 2 with the understatement that "a model-rich environment is not necessarily a comfortable one." There is a useful parallelism between these concerns of the quantitative modeler and those of the literary theorist (glossed in panel B of the same exhibit) who recognizes that the notion of the text is no longer an easy or comfortable one, thus requiring "a much more dynamic, but uncertain, activity."

The foregoing example demonstrates that some problems of multiplicity in the fit of loglinear models pertain to considerations of sample size. However, other considerations generate similar discomfort. With respect to the topological models introduced earlier, it is possible that quite different specifications of the imputed "levels" of the table lead to the "same" model in that the expected cell frequencies and associated fit statistics produced by each of several models may be identical, to any number of decimal places (Macdonald 1981). Macdonald (562) claims that Robert Hauser, the most prominent researcher associated with the formulation of topological models, sometimes writes as if an assignment of

cells in a table to levels is "self-evident" and that the structure of association in a table may be uniquely captured in the modeling of that table's
levels. But such precision of representation is not in general possible,
Macdonald claims: " 'levels' talk reifies features which are not a necessary
component of the model" (562).

Exhibit 3. On Modeling as Narrative and Heuristic

A. [Robert Hauser:] Up to this point, I have worried along with Macdonald about the possibility of specifying equivalent models, but the
fact is that I do not share his concern about the matter. I do not believe that a model consists only of a set of expected values, but it also
(and mainly) consists of the structure or story that we use to interpret and explain those expected values. It is all well and good when
a model has no equivalents, that is, when it carries unique implications for population data, but that is rare indeed in the social sciences. Most of the time, a model is no more than a vehicle for rendering a complete and internally consistent interpretation of a body
of data in light of the ideas we draw from observation, theory, convention, or whatever. Sometimes, the model will illuminate a facet
of a phenomenon in a way that we had not anticipated. Sometimes,
the fit or findings of one model will lead us to reject other models.
In the usual course of social scientific modeling, we are rarely in a
position to regard the fit of one model to the data as grounds for rejecting all the other models, but this is the standard against which
Macdonald seeks to measure structural models of mobility. We can
(and do) learn a great deal from models that fall far short of this
goal, and I see no need to propose a special standard for mobility
models. (Hauser 1981, 576)

B. [Thomas Wilson:] [T]he line between mathematical models in
some pure sense and the use of mathematics as an aid to data analysis becomes blurred once all mathematical models in the social sciences are recognized as having primarily a heuristic function. For example, one of the major points that has become clear in the rapid
development of structural-equation modeling techniques is the importance of correctly specifying the causal structure, and this, it has
been repeatedly emphasized in the textbooks, depends on an adequate theoretical understanding of the phenomenon. But exactly
the same consideration arises with any mathematical model of social
phenomena. To be sure, the models employed in statistical data
analysis tend to be closer to the data and more ad hoc than models

motivated by more general concerns, but this is neither an automatic liability nor a guarantee of superiority. (Wilson 1987, 402)

In his reply to Macdonald, Hauser answers (in part) with a highly self-conscious rhetorical position given in panel A of Exhibit 3. Here Hauser claims that modeling the structure of a table is analogous to constructing an interpretive narrative. He acknowledges the innovative point that Macdonald has just demonstrated to his article's readers, who are mostly technical modelers and quantitative analysts: that two quite different topological models might indeed fit a given table exactly as well as each other. But now Hauser asserts that the interpretive force is not confined within the formalities of the models. Models do not consist of their expected values alone or (by extension) the equations that define them precisely; nor is there an easy correspondence between the statistical test of a hypothesis and the judgement we pass on the model generating the hypothesis. In Hauser's formulation in Exhibit 3 a model "also (and mainly) consists of the structure or story that we use to interpret and explain those expected values." What are governing are "the ideas we draw from observation, theory, convention, or whatever." The use of "or whatever" seems to suggest a certain distance, however, between Hauser's foregrounded interest in the technicalities of modeling and his more subdued interest in how social meanings might turn into stories that the omniscient "we" have available in some sort of repertoire. Hauser seems to be saying that, although it might be problematic that two different models can't be distinguished from each other, the same isn't true of two different stories; moreover, since models are like stories, Macdonald's critique is not as distressing as it might at first appear.

In this rhetorical moment a leading quantitative methodologist in the mainstream, Robert Hauser, in effect comes close to agreeing with Thomas Wilson, who has endeavored to reconcile interpretive and ethnomethodological approaches (Wilson 1970) and who writes, in an excerpt reproduced in panel B of Exhibit 3 (from Wilson, 1987), that mathematical models—in general—in the social sciences have primarily a heuristic function. Although they come from different traditions, Hauser and Wilson would seem to agree that interpretation of models is an activity that must take place, at least in part, outside the formal trappings of the models. Both of these highly talented contributors to sociology, in the excerpts of Exhibit 3, depart substantially from the Lockean realism with which Macdonald charges Hauser, with which humanists often charge social scientists, and by which social scientists often define ourselves.

Reflexivity

The notion of reflexivity as developed for example by writers in the traditions of ethnomethodology and conversation analysis draws attention to the fact that "descriptions are not just *about* something but they are also *doing* something; that is, they are not merely representing some facet of the world, they are also involved in that world in some practical way" (Potter 1996, 47). The question of whether a given loglinear model is a descriptive account of a table or a theory imposed on it by an analyst is a subtle one implicated in the discussion of the previous section. Even the question of how many rows and columns a table "should" have is an issue that has been brought far beyond the realm of pure description and, so to speak, "inside" the concerns of the formal modelers as an explicitly problematic feature of the analysis that can be modeled in various specific ways. Thus, it is possible to model the combination of row and column categories of a table on the basis of how the resulting combination acts in inducing some sort of an overall structuring among the categories, as in work of mine (Breiger 1981, 1990) and Goodman's (1984; see also Hout and Hauser 1992). These are the "class models" introduced in my earlier fourfold elaboration of loglinear imagery.

Again using Otis Dudley Duncan as my foil, panel B of Exhibit 4 excerpts Duncan's praise of Goodman's work on models for combining categories of tables. I read Duncan's comment as a critique of essentialism and praise for contextualizing the study of statistical relationships *within* a reflexively defined set of categories that, so to speak, make a given relationship (such as "homogeneity" of mobility flows within and between the categories) work. Emirbayer (1997) and Somers (1998) are elaborating epistemologies of "relational realism" (Somers's term) that aim to supply some theoretical foundations that I see as supporting this kind of modeling. Indeed, once again a parallel with Birch's gloss on Derrida (given in panel A of Exhibit 4) seems warranted.

Exhibit 4. On Classification and Context

A. [Birch on Derrida:] Following on from Derrida, there is no such thing as *the* single meaning, *the* correct meaning, *the* right meaning. . . . The "rightness" of a decision, of an act of classifying something, . . . is relative not to some inherent correct order for the world ordained somehow in nature, but to a theory, a position, a set of ideas, institutionally created and constructed. (Birch (1989, 25).

B. [Duncan on Goodman:] Goodman's results make it clear that the classification itself is part of the model specification. Hence it may make little sense to ask, What is "the" relationship between father's and son's occupation? Rather, we must ask, What models are consistent with the data in a cross-classification expressed in terms of the following (explicitly defined) categories? (Duncan 1984b, xi)

Duality

As I said in my discussion of Exhibit 1, I propose to use the term "duality"[10] to emphasize the co-constitution of elements existing at different levels of abstraction. Duality provides both analytical and rhetorical force to some sociological analyses. The French sociologist Pierre Bourdieu, for example, introduces his graduate students to a "convenient instrument of construction of the object: the *square-table of the pertinent properties of a set of agents or institutions*" (Bourdieu 1992, 230; original italics). "If, for example, my task is to analyze various combat sports (wrestling, judo, aikido, boxing, etc.), or different institutions of higher learning, or different Parisian newspapers," Bourdieu (230) tells his graduate students, "I will enter each of these institutions on a line and I will create a new column each time I discover a property necessary to characterize one of them." This very simple table (in which the number of rows and the number of columns will likely differ, despite its designation as "square") "has the virtue of forcing you to think relationally both about the social units under consideration and their properties" (230). A well-known example in Bourdieu's work is a table cross-classifying subjects that would make a beautiful photograph by the occupations of people choosing each subject (Bourdieu 1984, 526). In my terms the "duality" in this example is that categories of people are here defined in terms of their tastes, while the tastes themselves are simultaneously classified on the basis of the occupations of the people who manifest them (see also Breiger 2000). Bourdieu uses tables such as this one to construct "social spaces which, though they reveal themselves only in the form of highly abstract, objective relations, . . . are what makes the whole reality of the social world" (1992, 231).

The quantitative method that underlies the pictorial representations of social fields in Bourdieu's work is known as correspondence analysis. "If I make extensive use of correspondence analysis," Bourdieu affirms, "it is because correspondence analysis is a relational technique of data analysis whose philosophy corresponds exactly to what, in my view, the reality of the social world is." Specifically, "it is a technique which 'thinks' in terms of relation, as I try to do precisely with the notion of field" (Bourdieu and Wacquant 1992, 96). Correspondence analysis takes as its material the

10. Portions of this section and the next draw directly on Breiger (2000).

"square-table of pertinent properties of a set of agents or institutions" introduced in the preceding paragraph. Produced by the technique is a set of dimensions that (in a certain mathematical sense) may be said to underlie the structure. There is one set of dimensions for the rows ("occupations," in the above example) and one set for the columns ("subjects for a beautiful photograph"). Nonetheless, the two different types of phenomena (those named by the rows and those indexed by the columns) are mapped into a single space, which Bourdieu calls "the space of correspondences."[11] It is because of this duality that correspondence analysis often goes under the name of dual scaling (Levine 1979). Bourdieu often interprets these dimensions with respect to types of capital (e.g., economic capital, cultural capital) and volume of capital (see, e.g., Bourdieu [1979] 1984).

The connection of all this to loglinear modeling is the following. One of the main developments in Goodman's work in the 1980s and 1990s has been the elaboration of deep formal similarities between models of correspondence analysis and loglinear models, particularly the "association models" that I introduced earlier. Goodman never refers to Bourdieu—after all, Goodman is interested in statistical models, and Bourdieu is interested in social fields—and Goodman's references to the French methodologists who worked on developing correspondence analysis are few. Goodman is interested in furthering a different conversation (see, e.g., the title of Goodman, 1996), one in which classically different styles of statistical reasoning are "reconciled" and "synthesized." So the French social theorist and the American statistical methodologist are largely unaware of the implications of each man's work for that of the other. These implications are relevant, nonetheless, for the formal models (Breiger 2000) and for rhetorical development, as I now suggest.

Institutional Relations and Power Relations

Loglinear modeling and correspondence analysis, viewed by many of those who are uninterested in the enterprise and also by most sociology graduate students endeavoring to learn these procedures, are antiseptic activities far removed from contending social institutions and national culture differences. Such is not true of the statisticians and sociological methodologists who produce these models of data analysis.

---

11. Correspondence analysis ensures that the scale value produced for each row may be written as a weighted sum of the scale values produced for the set of columns (where the weights are proportional to cell frequencies in the table under analysis), and dually for the columns. In this sense the rows, so to speak, "are" the columns, and vice versa.

To begin with correspondence analysis: criticisms of correspondence analysis and related procedures as practiced by French, Dutch, and occasionally Japanese researchers have been legion, especially in America and England. Disputes among statisticians on this subject are so heated as to often result in a rhetoric of national character differences. "These national distinctions are more real than one might think," the eminent British statistician J. C. Gower writes in the pages of *Applied Statistics* (1989, 273), where he treats correspondence analysis as an instance of "Franco-Dutch statistics" which in confrontation with "Anglo-Saxon statistics" leads to "opportunity for confusion" on core issues of statistical practice: what is and is not a model, the importance or otherwise of graphical methods in defining a model, data description versus statistical testing, and other issues. For his part, Goodman, whose "style or rhetoric" was characterized by Duncan (1984b, xii) as so close to the technical issues of modeling that he "never allows us to relax our responsibility for the fine structure of an analysis in favor of a specious preoccupation with the big picture," nonetheless manages to aver in a leading American sociology journal (Goodman 1987, 535) that

> although it is not very relevant, I cannot forbear to include here the following . . . statement from [a French] . . . report: "French sociology will not 'follow' Anglo-Saxon sociology . . . in its mathematisation but will develop its own indigenous methodological research."

From the side of France, J.-P. Benzécri, an early shaper of the development of correspondence analysis in that country, commenting on a paper of Goodman's in a leading American journal of statistical science, and glancing in passing at "the three small tables that served as a grounding point in his article," goes on to proclaim (1991, 1115) that

> On both sides of the Atlantic, the same numerical algorithms are applied to data analysis. Bibliographical references cross over the ocean, but the very spirit of correspondence analysis, as we understand it, did not cross over yet.

Here the question of multiplicity—the same numbers are computed robustly on both sides of the Atlantic, but the "spirit" is weak—is inscribed within the differing institutions of national culture. My point is that conversations about loglinear modeling are not *only* related to communities of practitioners, but that such communities exist within national cultures that themselves provide some of the features to conversations among statisticians that we sometimes associate with communication across ethnic boundaries.

Often the Americans are seen, or are assumed, or are accused, of having the politically privileged position in this international methodological field. The authors of an extremely influential cross-national mobility study centering on European nations (Erikson and Goldthorpe 1992a) endeavor to maintain a contrast between two images, the "mobility" and "achievement" points of view, connoting respectively the topological models they formulate and—on the other hand—the image of a hierarchy of status attainment that they (and Duncan 1979) see as incorporated within the association models used by some American researchers and which Erikson and Goldthorpe (1992b) label "the American dream." In reply to the criticism of Hout and Hauser (1992), Erikson and Goldthorpe (1992b, 298) write that "we think that debate in the field of stratification and mobility research would be . . . made more productive if those pursuing the 'American Dream' were to recognize that . . . it is not in itself a fault for other investigators to have . . . different conceptions of what macro-sociology can and should aim to achieve." And so quantitative social scientists assert linkages between the technicalities of formal models and global ideological hegemony.

MODEL-RICH ENVIRONMENTS

Mailloux (1989, 19) argues with respect to literary analysis that we are in need of rhetorical histories that are interpretive, institutional, and cultural. In this chapter I have argued that very similar sorts of rhetorical histories can help us—whether we are sociological researchers, students, or curious denizens of other disciplines—to understand how formal modeling joins with data analysis and theorizing about our world in an active process that includes and needs to draw in with full consciousness the modeler and analyst. Although rhetorical analysis can of course be used to debunk and dismiss that which we do not like, the more serious scientific task is to deepen our understanding of a world that includes us.[12]

Literary analysts often speak of subjecting a text to interpretive stress. There is a useful analogy to the way quantitative social scientists such as Otis Dudley Duncan speak (as in Exhibit 2 of this chapter) of "a model-rich environment" as "not necessarily a comfortable one." In this chapter I have argued for a recognition of parallelism in issues of concern to literary analysts and to quantitative social science modelers. I have focused on

12. See also White (1997) on reflexive uses of mathematics in sociology, and Zald (1995) on the role of community practices, epistemic commitments, and organization in analyzing progress and cumulation within major subareas of sociology.

problems of multiplicity, reflexivity, duality, and institutional context and power relations.

The implications of this recognition run in both directions. Sociologists could benefit from engaging with questions raised by literary theorists as a means toward reevaluating the discipline's foundational issues. Pescosolido and Rubin (2000) provide a tentative step in this direction. It is possible to combine interpretive readings of sociologists' quantitative procedures with more usual methods of textual interpretation in order to understand relations among their contributions, as I have done with reference to writings of James Coleman and Pierre Bourdieu (Breiger 2000). For their part, literary analysts and, in particular, those interested in reception histories, could benefit substantially from the contributions of sociologists to frameworks for the empirical study of the sorts of local cultural practices that are at the center of study of at least some theorists of rhetoric. Note 5 of this chapter suggests some promising leads.

Graduate students in sociology are used to assuming that issues of theory are matters of contention and worth fighting over. When it comes to methods, however, they assume, and we often decline to challenge the assumption, that the quantitative models are somehow neutral, natural, bland (if not boring), and difficult to master (if not entirely irrelevant to theoretical and ideological struggles). Is it any wonder that we sociologists are often accused of poor writing? I urge more self-conscious, more wide-ranging conversation as a means to better writing of quantitative sociology.

Bibliography

Becker, Howard S. 1986. *Writing for Social Scientists: How to Start and Finish Your Thesis, Book, or Article*. Chicago: University of Chicago Press.
——. 1998. *Tricks of the Trade: How to Think about Your Research while You're Doing It*. Chicago; University of Chicago Press.
Benzécri, Jean-Paul. 1991. "Comment [on a paper of Leo A. Goodman]." *Journal of the American Statistical Association* 86: 1112–15.
Birch, David. 1989. *Language, Literature, and Critical Practice: Ways of Analysing Text*. London: Routledge.
Bourdieu, Pierre. [1979] 1984. *Distinction: A Social Critique Of The Judgement Of Taste*. Translated by Richard Nice. Cambridge, Mass: Harvard University Press.
——. [1988] 1992. "The Practice of Reflexive Sociology (The Paris Workshop)." In *An Invitation to Reflexive Sociology*, edited by Pierre Bourdieu and Loïc J. D. Wacquant.
Bourdieu, Pierre, and Loïc J. D. Wacquant. 1992. *An Invitation To Reflexive Sociology*. Chicago University of Chicago Press.
Breiger, Ronald L. 1981. "The Social Class Structure of Occupational Mobility." *American Journal of Sociology* 87: 578–611.
——. 1990. "Intermediate Classes and the Structure of Mobility." In *Social Mobility and Social Structure*, edited by R. L. Breiger. Cambridge: Cambridge University Press.

——. 1995. "Social Structure and the Phenomenology of Attainment." *Annual Review of Sociology* 21: 115–36.

——. 2000. "A Tool Kit for Practice Theory." *Poetics: Journal of Empirical Research on Literature, the Media, and the Arts* 27: 91–115.

Clogg, Clifford C. 1981. "Latent Structure Models of Mobility." *American Journal of Sociology* 86: 836–68.

Coleman, James S. 1991. "Matching Processes in the Labor Market." *Acta Sociologica* 34: 3–12.

Cooke, J. Robert. 1994. *Cornell Courses: A Quantitative Overview.* October 17. Prepared for the Cornell Faculty Commission on Higher Education.

Dickens, Charles. 1854. *Hard Times.* London: Bradbury and Evans.

Duncan, Otis Dudley. 1979. "How Destination Depends on Origin in the Occupational Mobility Table." *American Journal of Sociology* 84: 793–803.

——. 1982. "Statistical Methods for Categorical Data [review of Goodman 1978]." *American Journal of Sociology* 87: 957–64.

——. 1984a. *Notes on Social Measurement, Historical and Critical.* New York: Russell Sage Foundation.

——. 1984b. Foreword to *The Analysis of Cross-Classified Data Having Ordered Categories,* by Leo A. Goodman. Cambridge, Mass.: Harvard University Press.

Emirbayer, Mustafa. 1997. "Manifesto for a Relational Sociology." *American Journal of Sociology* 103: 281–317.

Erikson, Robert, and John H. Goldthorpe. 1992a. *The Constant Flux: A Study of Class Mobility in Industrial Societies.* Oxford: Clarendon.

——. 1992b. "The CASMIN Project and the American Dream." *European Sociological Review* 8: 283–305.

Feld, Scott L., and Bernard Grofman. 1977. "Variations in Class Size, the Class Size Paradox, and some Consequences for Students." *Research in Higher Education* 6:215–22.

Freedman, David A. 1991. "Statistical Models and Shoe Leather." In *Sociological Methodology 1991,* edited by Peter V. Marsden. Washington, D.C.: American Sociological Association.

Gates, Henry Louis. 1992. "Statistical Stigmata." In *Deconstruction and the Possibility of Justice,* edited Drucilla Cornell, Michael Rosenfeld, and David Gary Carlson. New York: Routledge.

Goodman, Leo A. 1978. *Analyzing Qualitative/Categorical Data: Log-linear Models and Latent-Structure Analysis.* Edited by Jay Magidson. Cambridge, MA: Abt Associates.

——. 1984. *The Analysis of Cross-Classified Data Having Ordered Categories.* Cambridge Mass.: Harvard University Press.

——. 1987. "New Methods for Analyzing the Intrinsic Character of Qualitative Variables Using Cross-Classified Data." *American Journal of Sociology* 93: 529–83.

——. 1996. "A Single General Method for the Analysis of Cross-Classified Data: Reconciliation and Synthesis of Some Methods of Pearson, Yule, and Fisher, and Also Some Methods of Correspondence Analysis and Association Analysis." *Journal of the American Statistical Association* 91: 408–28.

Goodman, Leo A., and Clifford C. Clogg. 1992. "[Review Essay:] New Methods for the Analysis of Occupational Mobility Tables and other Kinds Of Cross-Classifications." *Contemporary Sociology* 21: 609–22.

Gower, J. C. 1989. "Discussion of the Paper by van der Heijden, de Falguerolles and de Leeuw." *Applied Statistics* 38: 273–76.

Graduate Student Radical Caucus, Cornell English Department. 1998. "A Report on the State of the Department." Spring.

Griswold, Wendy. 1993. "Recent Moves in the Sociology of Literature." *Annual Review of Sociology* 19: 455–67.

Hauser, Robert M. 1979. "Some Exploratory Methods for Modeling Mobility Tables and Other Cross-Classified Data." In *Sociological Methodology 1980*, edited by Karl F. Schuessler. San Francisco: Jossey-Bass.

———. 1981. "Hope for the Mobility Ratio." *Social Forces* 60: 572–84.

Hodge, W. V. D., and D. Pedoe. 1968. *Methods Of Algebraic Geometry*. Cambridge: Cambridge University Press.

Hout, Michael, and Robert M. Hauser. 1992. "Symmetry and Hierarchy in Social Mobility: A Methodological Analysis of the CASMIN Model of Class Mobility." *European Sociological Review* 8: 239–66.

Hunter, Albert, ed. 1990. *The Rhetoric of Social Research Understood and Believed*. New Brunswick, N.J.: Rutgers University Press.

Levine, Joel H. 1979. "Joint-Space Analysis of 'Pick-Any' Data: Analysis of Choices from an Unconstrained Set of Alternatives." *Psychometrika* 44: 85–92.

———. 1993. *Exceptions Are the Rule: An Inquiry into Methods in the Social Sciences*. Boulder, Colo.: Westview Press.

Lynd, Robert S., and Helen Merrell Lynd. 1929. *Middletown: A Study in American Culture*. New York: Harcourt.

Macdonald, K. I. 1981. "On the Formulation of a Structural Model of the Mobility Table." *Social Forces* 60: 557–71.

Mailloux, Steven. 1989. *Rhetorical Power*. Ithaca, N.Y.: Cornell University Press.

———. 1998. *Reception Histories: Rhetoric, Pragmatism, and American Cultural Politics*. Ithaca, N.Y.: Cornell University Press.

Marsden, Peter V. 1985. "Latent Structure Models for Relationally Defined Social Classes." *American Journal of Sociology* 90: 1002–21.

McCloskey, Deirdre N. 1998. *The Rhetoric of Economics*. 2d ed. Madison: University of Wisconsin Press.

Mohr, John W. 1998. "Measuring Meaning Structures." *Annual Review of Sociology* 24: 345–70.

Mohr, John W., and Vincent Duquenne. 1997. "The Duality Of Culture and Practice: Poverty Relief in New York City, 1888-1917." *Theory and Society* 26: 305–56.

Pescosolido, Bernice A., and Beth A. Rubin. 2000. "The Web of Group Affiliations Revisited: Social Life, Postmodernism, and Sociology." *American Sociological Review* 65: 52–76.

Potter, Jonathan. 1996. *Representing Reality: Discourse, Rhetoric, and Social Construction*. London: Sage Publications.

Reed, John Shelton. 1989. "On Narrative and Sociology." *Social Forces* 68: 1–14.

Schudson, Michael. 1997. "Cultural Studies and the Social Construction of 'Social Construction': Notes on 'Teddy Bear Patriarchy.' " In *From Sociology to Cultural Studies: New Perspectives*, edited by Elizabeth Long. Malden, Mass: Blackwell.

Somers, Margaret R. 1998. "Symposium on Historical Sociology and Rational Choice Theory. 'We're No Angels': Realism, Rational Choice, and Relationality in the Social Sciences." *American Journal of Sociology* 104: 722–84.

Weber, Max. 1991. *From Max Weber : Essays in Sociology*. Translated, edited, and with an introduction by H. H. Gerth and C. Wright Mills. London : Routledge, 1991.

White, Harrison C. 1997. "Can Mathematics Be Social? Flexible Representations for Interaction Process and Its Sociocultural Constructions." *Sociological Forum* 12: 53–71.

Wilson, Thomas P. 1970. "Conceptions of Interaction and Forms of Sociological Explanation." *American Sociological Review* 35: 697–710.

———. 1987. "Sociology and the Mathematical Method." In *Social Theory Today* edited by Anthony Giddens and Jonathan Turner. Cambridge: Polity Press.

Wonnacott, Thomas H., and Ronald J. Wonnacott. 1990. *Introductory Statistics*. 5th ed. New York: John Wiley.

Zald, Mayer N. 1995. "Progress and Cumulation in the Human Sciences after the Fall." *Sociological Forum* 10: 455–79.

ACKNOWLEDGMENT:

I am grateful for conversations with John Baldwin, Mitchell Duneier, Noah Friedkin, Roger Friedland, John Mohr, Bruce Straits, Thomas P. Wilson, and Raymond Wong during a sabbatical year at the University of California at Santa Barbara, and for continuing discussions with Peter Bearman, Elisabeth Clemens, Gerry Cox, Donald P. Hayes, Keith Hjortshoj, James P. Lantolf, Joel Levine, Calvin Morrill, Philippa Pattison, Alan Sica, David Stark, Henry A. Walker, Linda Waugh, Harrison White, Robin M. Williams, Jr., and Mayer Zald.

Writing Law

LARRY I. PALMER (Law)

WHEN I was a law student at Yale in the late 1960s, the phrase "legal fiction" was a term of disparagement. My professors used this term to describe those legal constructs or doctrines that judges manipulated in order to avoid explicit articulation of the social and economic consequences of their decisions. To label, for instance, some judicial prose about what a "reasonable man" would do a "legal fiction" certified that I had reached the pinnacle of analytical rigor I was being taught to apply to legal texts. In the discourse of the first-year law school classroom, "legal fiction" signified, at best, sloppy legal reasoning, and at worst, "bad law." I resisted this legal transformation of the meaning of fiction and its implicit method of interpreting legal texts. At a pragmatic level, I could not imagine ever using the term "legal fiction" in any legal text I might eventually write. Judges or other lawyers were unlikely to respond favorably to my text if I referred to terminology they treated as sacred as "legal fiction." I asked myself why I should bother adding "legal fiction" to the growing body of arcane lexicon the law was to me as a first-year law student.

The second form of my resistance to the legal fiction rhetoric came from my educational experience as an undergraduate. "Fiction" was not simply "pleasurable reading," but seminal for my own developing social and ethical discourse. I read numerous novels while at Harvard, and I was not a literature major. My fondness for fiction kept me clinging to the notion that novels, perhaps even poetry, plays, and short stories, provided critical social perspectives.

My professors must have known that their artful use of "legal fiction" was not a model for discourse in the practical world of lawyering, where people's money, hopes, and at times their liberty and very lives would depend upon the prose I created. Yet I don't recall anyone ever explicitly stating what I sensed early on in my career as a law student: the way lawyers who are scholars—law professors—speak and write about law is different from the way lawyers who represent clients—professionals—speak and write about law.

I would have to find some term other than "fiction" to serve as a euphemism for "bad" when applied to law or legal reasoning. "Science" would not do, because "legal science" was somehow "good," at least among some of my professors.[1] Further, science had the patina of progress, usefulness, objectivity, and universality that the more idealistic among us longed for at the time.

I remain to this day skeptical of the style of legal writing and discourse epitomized by the rhetoric of "legal fiction." The coiners of the legal fiction terminology were, of course, legal realists. The terms of their discourse were in direct opposition to a more formalistic way of writing about law as a set of principles discernible in cases which had dominated legal scholarship in this country prior to the 1930s.[2] The realists' agenda sought to embed law in social and economic reality—an early form of "deconstructing" law. These scholars employed perspectives from other academic disciplines to critique legal doctrines. Philosophy and economics remain to this day the source of what legal scholars often call "theory," although anthropology, sociology, psychology, history, political science, and even literature[3] are also employed as allies in legal scholarship's attempt to find both intellectual rigor and social relevance.[4]

Even the supposedly more radical legal scholars of my own generation—those engaged in critical legal studies and critical race theory—are, from my perspective, heirs to the legal realism tradition. In writing for other legal scholars, the dominant mode of discourse in legal writing today shares in common with legal realists of an earlier generation an assumption that law, as interpreted by judges, plays a central role in resolving the social, ethical, and policy dilemmas their texts examine or display.

My own writing, mostly dealing with issues related to law and medicine,

---

1. For example, during my tenure at Yale, the late Myres McDougal, a great influence on legal education internationally, was collaborating with a political scientist, Harold Lasswell, on a project to transform the nature of legal education by talking about a new legal methodology. Some of the materials used in seminars were eventually published. See Harold D. Lasswell and Myres S. McDougal, *Jurisprudence for a Free Society: Studies in Law, Science, and Policy* (New Haven, Conn.: New Haven Press, 1992).

2. Laura Kalman, *Legal Realism at Yale, 1920–1960* (Chapel Hill, N.C.: University of North Carolina Press, 1986).

3. See Jane B. Brown, "Law, Literature, and the Problems of Interdisciplinarity," *Yale Law Journal* 108 (1999): 1059–85.

4. See Donald A. Schön, *The Reflective Practioner: How Professionals Think in Action* (New York: Basic Books, 1983), 41–45.

often questions whether legal institutions are central to the social and ethical resolution of these issues for readers—some of whom are not judges, law professors, or lawyers. My readers bring their own experiences with birth, family, religion, and death to the texts I write. It might well be that they live in a world I can't imagine, but certainly they are trying to live in a world I can imagine for them.

As a writer, I attempt to find those receptors in my readers: I search for a way to construct a problem that persuades without preaching about the underlying ethical dilemmas I discuss. If my audience is other lawyers and judges, it must be critical without deconstructing law. Whether my audience is lawyers or non-lawyers, my texts often depart from the dominant mode of legal writing, legal realism, and its newer forms of critical legal studies, critical race theory, and what is sometimes called "outsider jurisprudence."[5]

My evolution as a writer begins with a description of how literary imagination—what we develop from reading good fiction—is important for the kinds of professional writing lawyers do. As an example, I describe the story of my professional representation of a criminal defendant before an appellate court. The kind of professional writing I had to employ on behalf of my client is very different from the way law professors write about law. To illustrate the difference, I will retell the story of my professional representation from the perspective of an imaginary critical race theorist.

Of course the issues of race are crucial in medicine, law, and all aspects of our culture, especially for an African American like myself, who came of age when racial segregation was legally enforced in the city where I grew up. So I must describe my method of confronting the issue of race in my own writing about law and medicine. This part of my evolution as a writer was nurtured, ironically, not by legal texts on race or great literature dealing with the issues of race, but by my encounter in the early 1980s with a seminal text on professionalism, Donald Schön's *The Reflective Practitioner: How Professionals Think in Action*. This book provided me with a theoretical framework for differentiating between writing about law as an academic discipline, writing law as a professional who serves clients, and writing about law for those educated in other disciplines.

To write about law for those without professional legal training, I discovered that I had to learn to teach non-professionals how to write about the intractable problems at the intersection of law and medicine. Finally, the process of teaching undergraduates to write about issues in law and medi-

5. One of the more gifted writers among those who are part of the "outsider jurisprudence" group is Patricia J. Williams. See her *The Alchemy of Race and Rights* (Cambridge, Mass.: Harvard University Press, 1991).

cine converted me: I have become an essay writer about law rather than a writer of more traditional law review articles for other law professors.

WHY SHOULD FUTURE LAWYERS READ NOVELS?

I am often asked by undergraduates what was the most important thing that I did to prepare to become a lawyer, a very different question from what one *needs* to do these days to gain admission to law school. My response: I read all of Dostoyevsky's novels during the spring semester of 1966, my senior year in college.

Reading all of Dostoyevsky's novels gave me some insight into how another writer views the world morally, spiritually, and emotionally. It was the systematic reading of a great writer that prepared me for the many-layered manipulations of text that law is. To this day, my sense of satisfaction with my work as a lawyer comes when I have been able to listen to strangers as if they were novelists, telling me stories I must hear and help them interpret to others.

The last time I represented someone in an actual case, I had the most important professional "success" as a lawyer in my life. Back in 1976, I was asked by the clerk of the local court to undertake the representation of a man on appeal who had been convicted at trial of homicide. I was told that the lawyer representing the convicted man at trial had done a very fine job, but that he and other lawyers whom the clerk had approached had declined the appellate representation. While I knew the compensation for such court-appointed work was meager, I expressed surprise that no one would do it, and tried to decline because I was not a member of the bar in New York State, having been admitted only in California. The clerk assured me that the court would grant special permission for me to appear, so I accepted the assignment as my public duty.

Many disasters—this homicide, for instance—are learning experiences for future lawyers, so I hired a law student to help on the appeal. Writing the brief would be a learning experience for both of us. He would learn something about an actual appeal, and I would learn something about New York law and practice.

As soon as my research assistant and I began to work together, it was apparent that the novel reader in me, the lover of Dostoyevsky, would take over. The student immediately suggested that we should get in the car and drive to the state prison to interview the client, who was incarcerated without bail pending the appeal. I declined to follow the suggestion and said that we were both to read the thousand pages of trial transcript to understand what had actually happened at trial. The pragmatist in me told my assistant that a trip to the state prison would take at least an entire afternoon, time which would be better spent understanding the trial, the story of what happened from the defendant's and the state's perspectives.

Reading this transcript with empathy for what my client said, and objectively as to what others said, I could immediately see how the stories conflicted. My professional role was to search the cases and statutes of New York to determine how I could "give voice" to my client's story through a series of legal arguments about how juries should be charged about self-defense in homicide cases. In addition, by reading the transcript with literary empathy, I was convinced that despite a long previous record of imprisonments, my client was a very intelligent and literate individual. Letter writing would be my mode of communication—and my client would first be introduced to me as a writer.

I wrote a letter informing him of my appointment and how I planned to proceed in his case. My law student assistant, ever hopeful of meeting a real live client, expressed doubts that the prisoner would respond to my epistle from Ithaca. The lover of Dostoyevsky, the novel reader, won the bet: I received a very cogent letter from my client thanking me and agreeing with my overall strategy. As we worked on writing the brief, I gave in at one point to my research assistant's need to at least get out of the law library.

In order to write the "statement of facts" for our brief, I realized that we needed to leave the literary world of trial transcripts and judicial opinions and enter the world that existed at the time of the homicide in November 1971. We visited the courthouse and looked at some photographs, including a picture of the deceased, who had been shot at close range with a 38-caliber pistol—a terrifyingly gruesome experience—that the appellate court judges would have before them in addition to my brief. We also walked to an area of the city near Cornell, called Collegetown, the scene of the homicide. I was searching for a way to organize what would only be a two-page written description of the facts in a manner most likely to lead the judges towards my argument, and yet not misrepresent anything that was in the transcript.

As I viewed the photographs and walked down the street, I went over my client's story in my mind *and* in my imagination: during the afternoon of that November day, he had been drinking and injecting heroin at a bar; around 5 P.M., he called his girlfriend, a Cornell student, to meet him at a certain location in Collegetown; on his way there, my client encountered a man who accosted him with a gun. My client, fearful for his life, pulled out his 38-caliber pistol and shot the man. Almost immediately after the shooting, my client's girlfriend arrived in a taxi, and they left Ithaca, not to be found again until over three years later. The victim of the shooting was dead. I also remembered reading that the only eyewitness to the shooting was some distance away, not close enough to hear the conversation or to clearly recognize the two men.

As we walked back toward the law school on that sunny June day in 1976, I suddenly remembered that at 5 P.M. in November the sun is starting to set. I thought about the fact that the eyewitness was viewing the scene from a distance at twilight, a time of day when vision is impaired by shadows and rapidly changing light. In a moment of inspiration, the metaphor of my client's story came to me: romance at twilight interrupted by an assailant whom he killed in self-defense. I turned to my research assistant and shouted "Romance at twilight!" He looked puzzled. I explained that this would be the theme for our factual statement and saw him become as excited as I was about how the "facts" could be put together in a way that would allow our brief to have *passion*—a point of view—and yet be objective about the facts so that the judges might at least listen to our arguments.

So the brief began: "At twilight on November 12, 1971, the defendant had arranged to meet his girlfriend at the Sunoco gas station in a portion of the city of Ithaca called Collegetown, when he was accosted by the deceased, who was armed with a gun. . . ." The brief went on to argue that the manner in which the judge charged the jury about the interrelationship of the various homicide statutes was illegal because it deprived the jury of a fair opportunity to consider my client's claim of self-defense. I filed the brief in the appellate court and sent my client a copy. I lost the case in the appellate court and failed to receive a hearing in the highest court of appeals in New York.

Since I lost the case, why do I call it my greatest professional success? Writing this brief was a professional success in terms of service to a client. After the court's decision, I wrote my client, expressed my regret about the outcome, sent him a copy of the decision, and explained his remaining options regarding the federal courts through a process he could start on his own called a Writ of Habeas Corpus. I did not hear from him for some time, but at Christmastime 1977, a few months after my first son was born, I received a card from him, from the prison where he was then serving six to ten years. In the card he thanked me for my services on his behalf and wished me a Merry Christmas. I thought of the irony of the situation—I was about to spend my first Christmas as a father, and a man who was still in prison despite my efforts was sending me holiday greetings. His written words, the only way I really knew my client, had touched me as my written words must have touched something good and very human within him.

As a client, he wanted a human being to hear his story, and treat it with integrity within the peculiar written constructs of law—those things we call appellate cases and statutes. Unlawful homicide is divided into three constructs in New York: "murder," "manslaughter," and "criminally negligent homicide." Our theory was that "self-defense" should have the same meaning under all three rubrics of New York law, rather than two or three distinct theories of how a homicide might become "justifiable" homicide and therefore not unlawful. My client knew that not all stories fit within the legal structure, but he acknowledged my human efforts that went into researching and writing the brief. More important, he gave me some insights into true professionalism.

Professionalism is about hearing the other person at his or her deepest level and translating those broken dreams, hopes, thoughts, and value systems into a position within the existing institutional structure. I had "won" despite the appellate court decision because I had been faithful to my client's interests, values, and imagined world without violating my own standards of honesty, service, and reverence for human life. Again, when we act from that deep sense of what I call literary empathy, I believe we gain deeper knowledge about the meaning of being human in ways of which we are often unaware.

It is worth noting here that in some sense, all fiction is the same: it gives us resemblances, new ways of looking at things, that help us in that process of constantly remaking ourselves into the larger constructs of another's imagination. The best fiction gives us this, whether it is poetry or prose. I refer to Dostoyevsky because he is the writer who truly gave me the world. The late Dorothy West, a Harlem Renaissance author who died in 1998, was quoted as saying about her first encounter with Dostoyevsky at fourteen years of age, "I think I had read up to page 50. And all of a sudden I jumped up, and I walked up and down the floor of my room with tears in my eyes, and I said, 'this is genius; this is genius!' "

It is out of this encounter with the genius of fiction that I have developed my own sense of professionalism. As a lawyer—a person who must serve the interests of others who are strangers while maintaining one's own sense of values—my professional challenge is to have what I would call both professional empathy and professional distance.

CRITICAL RACE THEORY AND THE CASE

Let me now retell the facts of my representation from what I imagine is a "critical race theory"[6] perspective. What I omitted from the first version of

---

6. Legal scholars who identify themselves as critical race theorists often advocate race-conscious solutions in law and are skeptical of liberalism's claims of objectivity and neutrality. Critical race theory is not without its critics; see Randall Kennedy, *Race, Crime, and the Law* (New York: Pantheon Books, 1997).

the story was that the defendant, his girlfriend, and the deceased were all black or African American; that the defendant had grown up in Harlem and had spent over ten of his then twenty-seven years in prison; that the defendant and the deceased were both drug dealers from Harlem. To the critical race theorist, these are crucial facts which perhaps I should have explored in my text, especially since I had a hunch my own race was probably a factor in the clerk's decision when I was asked to take on the appeal.

Even though I recall being conscious of all of the possible racial implications of this case, I resisted exploring those issues for two reasons centered in my own sense of professionalism. First, the client himself never raised any of these issues in his own trial testimony or in any subsequent communications with me. I felt my obligation was to be client-centered in creating the text—his legal story. In other words, when writing for this client, I had a professional obligation to write the most convincing "story" he and his trial lawyer had constructed in the trial court.

Second, I assumed the appellate court would know of the racial background of the defendant and the victim from the context of the transcript or from some of the photographs introduced into the record at trial. I thus knew that race was a "subtext," and chose to cast my arguments in terms of narrow provisions of the statutes or general language in the United States Constitution about "due process of law."

In the institutional context in which I was operating as a professional, I left race out of my arguments because I thought it gave my client the best chance at liberty, or the least amount of time in prison. I am somewhat more cynical about the nature of racism than my colleagues who call themselves "critical race theorists." I do not believe that appellate court judges in upstate New York, or anywhere for that matter, would be sympathetic to claims about race unless they had clear backing in precedent. To this day, it is very difficult to make racial claims in the course of criminal adjudication, even in death penalty cases in which the American Bar Association has acknowledged apparent racial disparity in the infliction of the death penalty on convicted prisoners.

Of course, I must admit that my imaginary critical race theorist might point out that I never gave my client an effective opportunity to choose to make race an issue in the case. In 1971, the year of the homicide, when my client was in Ithaca, there were no African Americans or blacks on Cornell Law School's faculty. My client couldn't know I was black unless I interjected that fact in my letters, since I never saw this man. Our communication was always through letters. None of my published writing at the time had dealt explicitly with the issues of race. So even if he had managed to find any of my published work, he would probably have assumed I was Caucasian, with little interest in legal analysis of racial justice.

My point in recasting the facts is that some critical race theorists[7] give the impression that issues about race are important to arguments made by an African American like myself. What is often obscured about critical race legal scholarship is the problem of audience. Critical race theorists, like most academicians, write for other critical race theorists. I doubt if any of them, if presented with the facts of the case I described, would have made race an issue in the brief filed on behalf of the client. Or they would not have done so at the time. As I ponder these things nearly two decades later, it certainly occurs to me that a different person from myself, at that time, might have said something other than "Romance at twilight!" And of course another kind of imaginative empathy—another kind of metaphor—might or might not have led to a different outcome.

LAW AS A DISCIPLINE AND A PROFESSION

Race is a very powerful institutional influence in American life, politics, and art, and it must be confronted by writers. Given my own commitment to fiction as a form of moral discourse, it may come as no surprise that the appropriate vehicle for me to write about race was not a legal brief, but a work of fiction, the play *Miss Evers' Boys*.

A chance encounter with David Feldshuh in the summer of 1989 led me to one of the most exciting collaborations of my professional life. At the time, David was finishing the final draft of his prizing-winning play, *Miss Evers' Boys*, which is based on his reading about an actual event, the Tuskegee Study of Untreated Syphilis in the Negro Male. I was writing an article dealing with the work of Jay Katz, a psychiatrist and a member of the original government panel to review the ethical and policy consequences of the study in 1973. When David asked me to read and comment on a draft of his play, he would eventually provide me with a vehicle for writing about the intersection of race, social and economic justice, law, and professional ethics. As it happened, the experience was also multiracial and multidisciplinary: in addition to being a playwright, David, who is Caucasian, is also an emergency room physician.

After the national acclaim of David's play, he, along with several others, worked with me to bring a production of his play to Cornell in August 1991 and to produce an educational video based on *Miss Evers' Boys* and a study guide to accompany the video, *Susceptible to Kindness: Miss Evers' Boys and the Tuskegee Syphilis Study*. Although I was the "executive producer" of

---

7. See Stephen L. Carter, *The Dissent of the Governed: A Meditation on Law, Religion, and Loyalty* (Cambridge, Mass.: Harvard University Press, 1998), 68–69.

this entire project, the most exciting part of the project was writing the study guide.

Daniel Booth, a filmmaker at Cornell's Media Services, created a visual text from the many hours of video of the play and various interviews with experts from many fields. I then had to create an accompanying written text that would help a group leader frame questions for discussion of the many complex issues addressed in the final forty-two-minute video. Clearly, a two-hundred-page academic tome would not do. I realized that the text was intended to help a person turn directly to Booth's film, and saw my own piece as ephemeral. In effect, I was writing a pedagogical piece,[8] not a definitive statement about race, professional ethics, or health care delivery.

My writing task allowed me to raise questions about race and professional ethics and provide Booth with a metaphor for his visual text. In the study guide, I ask: "Does David Feldshuh present a sympathetic and realistic vision of the moral dilemma of a black public health nurse in the rural South of the 1930s?" And, "Can you describe a situation in which you have been susceptible to someone else's 'kindness'?"

Of course, the educational video was different from the two-hour prizewinning HBO film, *Miss Evers' Boys.* Some of the critics of the play and the HBO movie confused the historical reality of what happened during the Tuskegee Study with the characters David created to develop a moral dialogue with the audience. But—and I say this modestly—these critics were not following the study guide. They were fusing metaphor to reality.

My ability to use my professional knowledge to create a written text that resonated with both the historical reality of the Tuskegee Study and Booth's visual text was aided by my reading the work of the late Donald A. Schön nearly a decade earlier. His *The Reflective Practitioner: How Professionals Think in Action* demonstrates how important the construction of problems is to the work professionals in various disciplines do, and the tenuous relationship of the academic researcher to the work of the professions. In working with a video that students and teachers from all levels of education might use, I had to become mired in what Schön calls the "mess" of practice. My previously articulated theories of how law and medicine (and in the case of the Tuskegee Study, public health) ought to work were only the background knowledge that I brought to the task of writing about a visual text, a kind of reality very different from the legal cases and statutes I most often encounter and interpret. In Schön's words,

8. See Larry I. Palmer, "Research with Human Subjects as a Paradigm for Teaching," *Law, Medicine, and Health Care* 16 (1988): 183–89.

I could not rely upon "technical rationality" to solve my writing problem, but had to reflect upon the reality that the filmmaker had created through his imaginative juxtaposition of excerpts from the play with expert commentary.

Although Schön did not write much explicitly about law in his book, his theory of the kind of professional knowledge individuals like Booth use to create coherence for the viewer has much to offer law professors. As a law professor, I must constantly distinguish between the textual skills that students will use as lawyers and the critical analytical skills they have to acquire in law school. Despite popular images, lawyers spend most of their professional lives reading and creating texts from reading and interpreting other texts, and from what other people say and do. Schön's work helps me resolve the conflict between my role as a teacher of professionals and my role as writer. His book converted me from writing law review articles to writing essays about law. My first book on law and medicine, *Law, Medicine, and Social Justice*,[9] is an essay for the non-lawyer concerned about the role of law in resolving the problems of modern medicine.

TEACHING WRITING AS PROFESSIONAL PRACTICE

My commitment to the essay as my preferred mode of legal writing solidified when I taught an upper-division writing course to undergraduates in the Biology and Society Program at Cornell from the mid-1980s to the mid-1990s. Discovering a way to teach non-professionals to write critically about law led to a form of self-discovery: the teaching of writing is part of my vocation, at least at this point in my evolution as a professor, a scholar, and a teacher. In the course of this teaching, I found myself using fiction as a way of teaching students how to carefully formulate problems in law and medicine. Yet I am not a part of the "law and literature" crowd who write law review articles about the relationship between law and literature.

The problem I faced in my undergraduate seminar on law and medicine in the spring of 1992 was how to design a set of questions around a legal case in which a trial judge had authorized physicians to perform a Caesarean section on a comatose woman suffering from terminal cancer during the twenty-sixth week of her pregnancy. The physicians were attempting to save the fetus, which was delivered alive, but died shortly thereafter. Although the undergraduates in the seminar had not yet been

9. Larry I. Palmer, *Law, Medicine and Social Justice* (Louisville, Ky.: Westminster/John Knox Press, 1989).

officially professionalized in the discourse of either law or medicine, I knew from previous seminar discussions that they were well versed in media-generated slogans about "fetal rights," "choice," "rights to life," "women's rights," "men's rights," etc. As I read their short papers in preparation for class discussion, I realized that in order to get beyond their simplistic ideas of "rights," I needed to reach beyond the facts of the case to something in their collective human experience that just might turn the class into a conversation about their divergent ethical perspectives on the issues presented by the case.

The students knew that *The Brothers Karamazov* was my favorite novel, but I decided to tell the students the story of *The Little Fur Family,* by the well-known children's author, Margaret Wise Brown. I began relaying this story of a little furry creature who says good-bye to his father in the morning, goes out into the world to find his own biological connections to his little fur grandfather and the earth in the form of fish, insects, a little tiny fur animal, and a brilliant sunset. As darkness comes the little fur child returns home to his little fur family and his fur father is there. After eating his supper, his father takes him off to bed and both parents sing him a song. In effect, *The Little Fur Family* is a story about a child's view of family wholeness. I asked them to consider their own image of family as compared to the image of family in the children's story before asking them a question about the consequences of legal institutions deciding that a fetus might have a "family."

We moved well beyond competing, simplistic "right" versus "right" as we went through the process of thinking about the complexities of ethical perspectives. My evidence that the students moved beyond slogans about "rights" is their writing. These students had to produce group projects that required them to work and write collaboratively with students with whom they disagreed. And my own response to one of the finer group papers said, in part:

> Your paper is a wonderful combination of your own ideas, the questions raised in our classes, and good writing. . . . Having listened and debated with each of you in class, I am very impressed that with your strong views, you have learned how to maintain your intellectual integrity and yet produce an excellent group-written project.

Through shared imaginative experiences, we were able to grant validity to one another's perspectives.

It might be that my students were amused by my invoking *The Little Fur Family* as well as *The Brothers Karamazov*; it might be that there was something pleasantly jarring for them in the apparent dichotomy of their professor's literary preferences. From a psychiatrist's point of view, this is either very simple or very complex. But in the end, this was one of the best classes I have ever taught—one in which my questions led to various responses, where students listened and disagreed, and where they built new questions from mine—a class in which I could feel my own deep love of teaching.

I cannot "prove" that my use of the literary image of family from *The Little Fur Family* was the sole reason for the seminar's success. I do have some evidence that the students were moved by my telling them the story. When the class met one night at my house for dinner and discussion several weeks later, before we began to get down to work, the students asked me to read aloud *The Little Fur Family.* A strange request from a group of 20–21-year-olds? Not if one considers that *perhaps* this children's book helped them to think more deeply about issues, to hear arguments they had never heard before, to respect individuals with whom they had violently disagreed, and to feel a gratefulness for what the human mind can do. I granted their request.

My challenge as a teacher in this seminar was to help the students understand each other's feelings—empathy—but yet have enough distance to criticize each other's ideas. In my view, the dilemma for modern people beyond the classroom is how all the psychologizing in which we engage can move us from "information" to "knowledge" about our fellow human beings and ourselves.

What Is Law?

Legal scholars today are engaged in acrimonious debate about how their knowledge should be conveyed. The new legal realists, almost all of whom employ some discipline other than law in their writing, are dominant, particularly among those law professors who write books for the general audience. Yet the realists' opponents have not faded from the scene. Within the legal academy and among some judges, the formalists of various types seek to find the boundary of the law within legal cases, statutes, and the Constitution. The formalists' most prominent ally is Harvard Law School educated United States Supreme Court Justice Antonin Scalia, and his "new textualist" colleagues on the federal bench. Justice Scalia, formerly Professor Scalia at the University of Chicago, expresses his ideas in books as well as in his opinions. His recent book, *A Matter of Interpretation,*[10] will

---

10. Antonin Scalia, *A Matter of Interpretation* (Princeton, N.J.: Princeton University Press, 1997).

surely play a crucial role in the debate, if nothing else as the foil for many of the new realists. Underneath this debate lies the question: what is law?

When I began to write for non-lawyers, as I did in my first book, that task forced me to articulate my own view of law, despite all the controversy raging about the nature of law in legal writing. My writing treats law as a basic social institution. It—along with other basic institutions such as medicine, the family, religion, and even the market—provides individuals in a given society with assumptions about how everyday life is organized socially and morally. These "rules of the game" constrain individual behaviors[11] and generate ideologies.[12] The impact of any particular institution varies for each individual. Viewing law as an institution raises the interesting question of whether law is a more powerful institutional force than, say, people's conceptions of "families" in determining whether reproductive technology should be used.

This institutionalist perspective on law is not generally shared by other legal scholars, particularly those who write about law and medicine or "bioethics." Most scholars writing today about topics such as assisted suicide, cloning, or reproductive technology start with the assumption that our conflicts about these topics should be resolved through a theory of "rights." These rights can be derived by applying moral theory to constitutional analysis and thus ultimately decided by judges of the United States Supreme Court. The most widely known scholar of this type of writing is Ronald Dworkin. Dworkin's brief in the United States Supreme Court case dealing with physician-assisted suicide was deemed interesting to the general reading public—enough to be published in the *New York Review of Books*.[13] Why? Is a "theory of rights" more or less a "legal fiction" than other briefs? Assuredly not. But Dworkin keeps focused on the subject of "rights" in such a way that his construction of the problem as one of "rights" becomes equal to the facts of life and death themselves for many readers.

It is easy to miss that Dworkin's seductive metaphor of "rights" had almost no effect upon the judges who decided the case. Rather, the brief written by the lawyers from the American Medical Association had a tremendous influence on the Justices because their manner of constructing the problem fit within the institutional context of both law and medi-

---

11. Douglas C. North, *Institutions, Institutional Change and Economic Performance* (Cambridge: Cambridge University Press, 1990), 3.

12. Janet L. Dolgin, *Defining the Family: Law, Technology, and Reproduction in an Uneasy Age* (New York: New York University Press, 1997), 225 n. 1.

13. "Assisted Suicide: What the Court Really Said," *The New York Review of Books* 44 (March 27, 1997): 41–47.

cine.[14] The AMA brief was built around the metaphor of "access to health care, autonomy, and the relief of pain." Dworkin's "theory of rights" and his metaphors of "constitutional principles of liberty for courts and legislatures" seem far removed from the practical issues of deciding the case before the Justices.

When we think about what metaphors mean for us, we must think about *misrepresenting* as well as *representing*. Do creators of prose, fiction, or nonfiction, lie? All the time. They lie when they tell us what passes for the truth about their own lives—witness the appalling number of memoirs on "bestseller" lists. Do lawyers lie? Do clients lie to their lawyers? All the time.

But there are some overriding truths to the metaphors created by good fiction that help us understand law as a very human and fragile enterprise. The connections that individuals feel for one another are best explained to me by the sense of connectedness portrayed in *The Little Fur Family*. Its vision of wholeness is not some ideal of what families ought to be, but rather for me an antidote to the fragility of connections best symbolized by the brothers of many marriages and sexual liaisons in *The Brothers Karamazov*. The lawyer's role as text writer for individuals is not to assume that the individual is either like the child of the Fur Family or one of the children of the father Karamazov. The lawyer must meet the client as a stranger with a story to tell, before offering an interpretation.

When we examine writing by legal scholars, I suggest that the subject of their texts—judicial opinions—could benefit from a heavy dose of "literary imagination." Imagine for a moment if legal scholars thought of Justices Rehnquist and Scalia as writers invoking metaphors to frame and resolve cases rather than as proponents or defenders of liberty. Although these two Justices often agree, when they disagree we might discover their different conceptions of law and the institutional role of the United States Supreme Court if we paid attention to those metaphors in their writing. For instance, Justice Scalia and Justice Rehnquist have different approaches to the problem of abortion although they often vote for the same result.[15] In a 1989 case, Rehnquist avoided overruling *Roe v. Wade* by framing the question as whether state legislatures can prefer childbirth over abortion. Scalia chastised his colleague in a separate opinion for failing to overrule *Roe* by framing the question as a kind of "deconstruction"

14. Larry I. Palmer, "Institutional Analysis and Physicians' Rights after *Vacco v. Quill*," *Cornell Journal of Law and Public Policy* 7 (1998): 415–30, 420–21.

15. See Larry I. Palmer, *Endings and Beginnings: Law, Medicine, and Society in Assisted Life and Death* (Westport, Conn.: Praeger Publishers, 2000).

of what he called "the mansion of constitutionalized abortion law, constructed overnight in *Roe v. Wade.*"[16]

The importance of literary imagination[17] to the work of the professional lawyer cannot be overstated. The task of the lawyer, at least in the ethically complex areas in which I write, is to have both professional empathy and professional distance. It is essential to be able to feel compassion for a person or organization and to give that compassion shape within a legal institutional context. At the same time, in creating a text, the lawyer must step back and restore himself or herself to the role of reader and see the world from another perspective. To me this is the essence of "thinking" and acting like a lawyer and thus exercising professionalism.

When Richard Nixon's lawyer during the Watergate matter, James St. Clair, was asked what he thought of the fact that then-President Nixon had lied to him about the so-called Watergate tapes, his reply intrigued me. St. Clair said something like: "Clients are free to tell me whatever they please. I was hired to be his lawyer and have no comment about the truthfulness of what he told me." St. Clair in effect took Nixon's story and followed it to its tragic political end without public rancor. I suspect that Nixon's lawyer had overcome the ambiguity of client lies by treating his clients as if they were novelists telling him stories to be legally reconstructed. Lawyers often find themselves working in the twilight.

So I read and reread Dostoevsky, among other novelists, as part of my own evolution as a writer. Until I understood the importance of the frames we bring to problems in law, I—like a first-year law student—did more imitating of a rhetorical style than negotiating the writing tasks necessary for different occasions. As I learned the value of metaphor, I understood the value of reading fiction—in my case, sometimes rereading and recreating myself through literary imagination. The whole business of creating and recreating, it seems to me, is what we keep coming back to as we live our lives as well as pursue our professions. In the end, they are one and the same.

16. *Webster v. Reproductive Services* 492 U.S. 490, 537 (1989).
17. Martha C. Nussbaum, *Poetic Justice: The Literary Imagination and Public Life* (Boston: Beacon Press, 1995).

Part Three

THE HUMANITIES

Writing Criticism

JONATHAN CULLER
(English and Comparative Literature)

WRITING about writing academic criticism is a daunting task. Literature professors write about every manner of thing: the text of *Piers Plowman,* breast feeding in the French Revolution, the image of cigarettes in modern literature and culture. How to talk about writing criticism without being hopelessly pluralistic or excessively polemical? But the problem is graver than that. When Jonathan Monroe gave me the document outlining what I was to do, I felt quite overwhelmed. Analyzing one's discipline as a discursive practice, where knowledge is produced by its ways of writing, is hard enough. But we were also asked to analyze the changes in the discipline, examining crucial moments in its history and especially influential texts that have shaped it. Moreover, Jonathan invited us to discuss the history of our own involvement with the discipline: what first drew us to it, what has retained our interest in writing within the discipline over time, and how we have revised our own disciplinary practices over the course of our careers. When I raised with him the problem of the multifarious things he wished us to do, he told me, by way of reassurance I suppose, that I should just take as my model Eric Auerbach's book *Mimesis: The Representation of Reality in Western Literature,* which takes up a series of key texts through the ages, from Homer to Virginia Woolf. Well meant, I'm sure, but not very reassuring.

I shall try to combine these functions by focusing on some essays that have been important for me, that embody significant shifts in the discipline, and that involve distinctive ways of writing criticism. Certainly one's sense of what it is to work in a particular field derives from possibilities enacted in key texts.

I first gained a sense of literary study as a discipline based on principles of criticism in my first year at Harvard when my graduate student tutor assigned a comparison of essays by Cleanth Brooks and Douglas Bush. In 1962 this exchange was already ten years old, but it helps define shift in the practice of criticism after World War II. Brooks, a leader among the so-called New Critics, had published an essay on Andrew Marvell's "Horatian Ode," to which Douglas Bush, a literary historian, replied.[1]

Marvell wrote "An Horatian Ode upon Cromwell's Return from Ireland" after Oliver Cromwell, who had previously led the Parliament to victory in the English Civil War and brought about the execution of Charles I, had, with an English army, ruthlessly put down an Irish rebellion. Here's a problematic passage in the poem, about which Bush and Brooks argue.

> And now the Irish are asham'd
> To see themselves in one Year tam'd:
>   So much one Man can do,
>   That does both act and know.
> They can affirm his Praises best,
> And have, though overcome confest
>   How good he is, how just,
>   And fit for highest trust.

Is this jokey, facetious, sardonic, ironic, or a serious claim about the Irish? Brooks argued that if the poem is any good, this passage must make sense *dramatically*. As a straightforward claim—that the defeated Irish confess how good Cromwell is, how just,—it would be foolish, a blemish on the poem as a whole, which Brooks sees as a complex, balanced, portrait full of judicious but often double-edged praise of Cromwell. Brooks hears a grim irony in these lines: the Irish who have been crushed can tell just how just he is (with a sword at their throat, they confess how good he is . . .)

Bush calls this a "desperate solution." "Nothing in the wording seems to me to carry the faintest trace of irony; it is as straightforward a statement as we could have, however little we like it" (349). He is not worried about how it fits into the poem or whether it is a blemish: "we really must accept the unpalatable fact that Marvell wrote as an Englishman of 1650; and, in regard to what seems to us a strange assertion, we must say he is indulging in some wishful thinking—Cromwell is so great a conqueror that even the

---

1. Cleanth Brooks, "Literary Criticism," *English Institute Essays* (New York: Columbia University Press, 1946), 127–58; Douglas Bush, "Marvell's Horatian Ode," *Sewanee Review* 60 (1952), 363–76; Cleanth Brooks, "A Note on the Limits of 'History' and the Limits of 'Criticism,'" *Sewanee Review* 61 (1953), 129–35. The exchange is collected in W. R. Keast, ed., *Seventeenth-Century English Poetry: Modern Essays in Criticism* (Oxford: Oxford University Press, 1962), to which my citations refer.

Irish must share English sentiment and accept the course of history"
(349). But note that even Bush can't stomach the literal claim of these
lines—that the Irish have confessed how good he is, how just—and paraphrases "accept the course of history." Here, as often, writing criticism is a
matter of seeking a paraphrase or reformulation that bears a plausible relation to the text while fitting an argument. And critical debate at the
micro-level bears on the supposed distortions accomplished by others'
paraphrases.

At stake in this disagreement are several principles. Brooks insists that,
considering the poem as a critic, one must focus on whether its elements
contribute to an artistic unity—a matter which does not bother the literary
historian: "If we unify the poem," Brooks writes, "by saying that it reflects
the uncertainties and contradictions of a man who was uncertain and self-
contradictory, and sometimes foolish . . . then we may have a useful historical document, but I am not at all sure that we have a poem" (356). The
fact that he worries how to read these lines as contributing to the whole
and Bush does not shows, Brooks says, how different their aims are.

Second, while Bush in his response focuses on what historical evidence
can tell us about what Marvell thought at the time when he wrote the
Ode, for Brooks this is a "coarse method" that won't tell us what the poem
says because (1) even if we knew what Marvell the man thought of
Cromwell at the moment he was writing the poem, the man is not the
same as the poet (who is, for instance, composing an Horatian Ode); and
(2) even if we knew what Marvell the poet intended to say in his poem,
this wouldn't prove that the poem actually said this. Brooks writes, "there
is surely a sense in which anyone must agree that a poem has a life of its
own . . . the poet sometimes writes better than he knows" (322). We are
trying to read the poem and thus appeal "to the full context of the poem
itself," not to Marvell's mind. For Brooks, what determines the meaning
of these lines is how they function in the context of the poem as a whole,
not what we imagine Marvell the man thought at the time. It is a problem
of poetic organization, not of biography or history.

Bush disputes what he calls "such an arbitrary doctrine of criticism"
(341). He quarrels with Brooks's identification of ironies and ambiguities, casting himself as a historian for whom the text means what it says
(given historical knowledge), and he accuses Brooks of forcing the poem
to fit the prejudices of a good modern liberal, for whom it goes without
saying that a smart sensitive fellow like Marvell couldn't have admired a
crude, ruthless man of action like Cromwell, who must have been something like a Puritan Stalin (342).

Brooks replies, "the title *liberal* alas, is one that I am scarcely entitled to
claim. I am more often called a reactionary, and I have been called a

proto-fascist" (354). This particular point shows the difficulty of relating what a text says to the opinions of its historical author: Bush's incorrect inference from Brooks's text to the supposedly liberal opinions of its historical author shows that one can't presume continuity between what the text says and what the historical individual believes.

What is at stake here for writing criticism? First, the principle, central to the New Criticism, of separating what the text says from what the empirical author may have thought, instead of assuming that the way to determine what a text means is to investigate the historical experience of the author. The reasons for driving a wedge between what is in the author's mind and what is on the page are two: writing a poem is different from, say, recording one's thoughts, and poets may not in any event accomplish what they intend. This separation of the meaning of the text from the historical experience of the author retains considerable critical importance today. In a post-New Critical age, it gives new interest to biographical criticism, which, in taking for granted this separation, can then work on the relation between the historical intentions of authors and what their works actually achieve. For instance, Jacques Derrida in his reading of Rousseau contrasts what Rousseau wants to say and what his text ends up doing.[2]

Second, the New Critical separation between thinking of the poem as a work of art and thinking of it as a historical document has in our day made possible a new historicist criticism which returns to that scene, not, like the old historicism, to equate the meaning of the work with what Marvell the historical author thought, but to contrast the work's aesthetic purpose and unity with its status as a historical act. As a historical event, its relations to other discourses of the day give it a particular ideological function. The separation permits a better historicism than one that must claim that what it investigates is the meaning of the work.

Brooks claimed in 1943 that the New Criticism had almost no influence in universities; by 1962 it was still contested—a minority position at Harvard, for instance, which added to its appeal for me.[3] An orthodox New Criticism never became hegemonic, but one respect in which it undoubtedly did triumph was in establishing the assumption, which still holds sway, that in general the test of any critical activity is whether it helps us produce new, richer, more compelling interpretations of particular literary works. One effect of this assumption is the creation of a new type of knowledge: previously, to put it crudely, what had counted as knowledge

2. Jacques Derrida, *Of Grammatology* (Baltimore: Johns Hopkins University Press, 1976), 141–64, for example.

3. Cleanth Brooks, "Mr. Kazin's America," *Sewanee Review* 51 (1943), 59.

was historical and philological information; now to produce interpretations of poems is to make a contribution to knowledge, and this knowledge is a form of writing, something that must be written, not just written up. Historical or philological investigations may achieve a positive result—a demonstration that Marvell did serve in the Civil War or that a poem falsely attributed to others is really his; but interpretative criticism yields not a result that can be summed up but a text that tries to render explicit the structure of meaning and implication woven through a poem.

Let me present a few more lines of this writing. Bush quotes Brooks on the two lines that immediately follow the passage about the Irish that we have been discussing.

> How good he is, how just,
> And fit for highest trust,
> Nor yet grown stiffer with Command,
> But still in the Republic's hand.

Says Mr. Brooks: "Does the emphasis on 'still' mean that the speaker is surprised that Cromwell has continued to pay homage to the republic? Does he imply that Cromwell may not always do so? Perhaps not: the emphasis is upon the fact that he need not obey and yet does. Yet the compliment derives its full force from the fact that the homage is not forced but voluntary and even somewhat unexpected. And a recognition of the point implies the recognition of the possibility that Cromwell will not always so defer to the commonwealth." But such "darker connotations" are quite gratuitous. "Still" here—as later in "Still keep thy sword erect"—has its normal seventeenth-century meaning, "always." (350)

Bush is rejecting what he calls illegitimate ambiguities that Brooks detects, such as the possibility that "still" does imply that Cromwell may not always defer.

Brooks writes this paragraph to argue that Marvell's praise of Cromwell at this point is ambiguous, but notice how obliquely Brooks puts it. "Does he imply . . . ? Perhaps not." He is bending over backward to fit into a critical consensus, to avoid appearing to deny anything about the meaning of a poem that other critics might think, while nevertheless opening the possibility of a slight ambiguity that he hopes others will find plausible. Recall the passage from Brooks I quoted earlier: "Surely everyone would agree that there is a sense in which a poem has a life of its own." There seems a presumption that there will be a critical consensus, that one must be careful not to say something blatant that might seem extreme, so that others will be brought along with you by virtue of your very reasonableness. Interpretation has to be new (otherwise why write it) but acceptable, convincing to those who had previously read things differently. It is as if that ability to enter the consensus one seeks mildly to expand were the test of critical writing. But note that this is a *convention* of critical writing rather than a reality of critical debate, as we see from the fact that Douglas Bush isn't seduced or deceived: he takes Brooks, for all his modest reasonableness, to be making a strong claim which Bush disputes. In this mode of writing, "Surely . . ." or "we would all agree that . . ." becomes a sign that something contestable is being said. Brooks's method of writing criticism works to suggest the ambiguity, plant the seed, so that the reader will find it plausible, as something he or she now sees in the poem. That is how this sort of knowledge is written.

Another thing to notice about this passage is that neither critic even thinks of alluding to what is likely to leap off the page to a modern reader in "Nor yet grown stiffer with Command,/ But still in the Republic's hand"—lines that seems to cast Cromwell as a phallus which might grow stiff by itself in the thrill of command but may also be a tool in the republic's hand, whereby it experiences its potency and pleasures itself. (The poem proceeds to declare that it is wonderful for England to have a Caesar who will conquer new empires for it.) Today, critics might feel it necessary at least to acknowledge the possibility of some such line of reflection, so as not to be thought obtuse about the suggestiveness of words or blinkered by conventional thinking. An age where videotapes of the sex life of the President are shown on TV knows different standards of what can be entertained.

Such texts as Brooks's encouraged me to adopt a resolutely New Critical attitude in my college years. The critical task was to show how the various parts of a poem fit together, to track as closely and sensitively as possible the stances, tones, and attitudes of a poem, treating it as the act of a speaker (not to be equated with the biographical author) whose shifting affects and tones were to be captured in a work of writing: a response which explains and espouses the poem. If critical writing shows that the work is more complicated, ironical and self-reflexive than others had thought, all the better.

The New Critical task is not one of which you can ever feel master: trying to translate the experience of the poem into knowledge, to analyze poetry in prose, you find that there always remain puzzling elements in the poem or aspects of its tone that are hard to identify or assess. There is a continuing challenge for writing, for the imagination. But the parameters of the task seemed well-known—work out what is being said with what affect; demonstrate the subtlety, complexity, and unity of the work as a whole— and debates like the Brooks/Bush exchange made it clear that the rules could be challenged. By the end of my undergraduate years, I felt ready to question both conventions of the interpretive project (such as treating the poem as, in effect, a dramatic monologue) and the project itself, the presuppositions of criticism. I began to study philosophy, linguistics, and literary theory, not to leave criticism but to reflect on its presuppositions.

There are lots of possible texts here. Let me offer a slim example by Roland Barthes. As the leading French structuralist in the field of literary studies, Barthes was of great importance to me (in 1979, Wayne Booth even called him "the man who may well be the strongest influence on American criticism today"—though I think that was above all a complaint about people like me). In a little paper from 1968 called "L'effet de réel" [the reality effect], Barthes begins with a sentence from Flaubert's "Un Coeur simple." Describing a room, the narrator tells us that "an old piano supported, beneath a barometer, a pyramidal heap of boxes and cartons."

For Brooks the task of critical writing is to show how every detail of a text contributes to the organic effect of the whole, but what of descriptive details like these? Barthes writes,

> if it is possible to see in the notation of the piano an indication of its owner's bourgeois standing and in that of the cartons a sign of disorder and a kind of lapse in status likely to connote the atmosphere of the Aubain household, no purpose seems to justify a reference to the barometer, an object neither incongruous nor significant, and therefore not participating, at first glance, in the order of the *notable*.[4]

Barthes concludes that in modern literature there is an opposition between meaning or function on the one hand and reality on the other. There is an assumption, deeply ingrained in Western culture, that the world—reality—is what is simply there, prior to our perception of it or interpretation of it. What does not bear meaning or is not being interpreted may thus stand for the real. When there occur items which have no role in the plot and don't tell us anything about the character, this very absence of meaning enables them to anchor the story in the real—but, Barthes emphasizes, not by denoting reality but by connoting it. "It is the category of the real which is then signified" (148). The more meaningless the details, Barthes concludes, the more vigorously they signify, "we are the real."

Now what is different in this kind of criticism is, most obviously, the goal, which is not to produce a new and improved interpretation of Flaubert's story. Barthes is working to advance a theoretical understand-

4. Roland Barthes, "L'effet de réel," *Communications XI* (1968). Quoted from Barthes, *The Rustle of Language* (Berkeley: University of California Press, 1989), 142.

ing of literary discourse. This is poetics rather than hermeneutics. That is a distinction made clear by an analogy with linguistics, which offered a model for literary studies in the structuralist ambiance of the late 60s and 70s. Linguistics does not produce new interpretations of English sentences but attempts to make explicit the underlying set of rules—the grammar of a language—that enables these sequences of sounds to have the meanings they do for speakers of the language. So a poetics modeled on linguistics seeks *not* to provide new interpretations of literary works but to understand the conventions and techniques that enable them to have the effects they do (what makes this passage ironic, why is the ending of a poem ambiguous, etc.)

I wrote a book called *Structuralist Poetics* arguing that literary studies should abandon hermeneutics for poetics.[5] We have plenty of interpretations of literary works, and people will certainly go on interpreting in any event, but we still don't understand very well how literature works. But this attempt to change the paradigm did not succeed, and critics and theorists in America were incredibly swift to embrace the idea of *post-structuralism*, so they could believe that the systematic projects of structuralism were passé, and so we could happily go on interpreting, though in a new, decentered way.

Why should this have happened? Well, there are good reasons for doubting the possibility of a comprehensive poetics, for as soon as any convention is recognized as such, literary works seek to outplay it. But the main reason is the lure of interpretation, which is extraordinarily powerful in literary studies. If people study works of literature, it is generally because they think these works have important things to tell them and they want to know what those things are. Moreover, it is easy enough to convince oneself that the payoff for investigating some aspect of narrative or of literary discourse generally should be the ability to understand better the works that interest you. What tends to happen, then, is that interesting work in poetics is mistaken for or converted into an interpretive claim. Thus, the payoff of Barthes's identification of the "reality effect" is the possibility of reinterpreting "Un Coeur simple," for instance as "really about" (as we say in the business) the problematic relation between reality and signification. I wrote a book on Flaubert at the same time as my *Structuralist Poetics* and essentially argued that what these novels are really about is the exposure of the contingent and conventional nature of human attempts to make sense of experience, and thus the ultimate van-

5. Jonathan Culler, *Structuralist Poetics: Structuralism, Linguistics, and the Study of Literature* (Ithaca: Cornell University Press, 1975).

ity (though inescapable necessity) of the attempt to impose meaning on things.[6]

This propensity in literary studies to convert poetics into hermeneutics applies not just to formal investigations like Barthes's but to all sorts of claims about conditions of possibility of literary effects. For instance, Toni Morrison, in *Playing in the Dark: Whiteness and the American Literary Imagination*, offers a brilliant account of how the distinctive characteristics of American literature have as their condition of possibility what she terms the Africanist presence—the 400–year-old presence in the United States of first Africans and then African-Americans. She writes, "The imaginative and historical terrain upon which early American writers journeyed is in large measure shaped by the presence of the racial other."[7] Such concerns as "autonomy, authority, newness and difference, absolute power," which "become the major themes and presumptions of American literature," are "made possible by, shaped by, activated by a complex awareness of a constituted Africanism. It was this Africanism, deployed as rawness and savagery, that provided the staging ground and arena for the elaboration of the quintessential American identity" (44). Thus, for instance, "The concept of freedom did not emerge in a vacuum. Nothing highlighted freedom—if it did not in fact create it—like slavery" (38).

This is poetics; this is theory—a speculative account of a framework for the explanation of literary productions—but it becomes available as resources for interpretation, so that after Morrison one can write about the hidden (occulted) Africanist presence in a given work. (Indeed, if the Africanist presence is a condition of possibility, then the fact that there aren't overt traces of it in a given work—that it is repressed—is all the more noteworthy.) This situation can give rise to interpretations that seem extreme, strained, partial—a familiar experience in reading contemporary critical writing, where what has been posited as an important aspect of literary discourse of a period or in general is transformed, by the conversion of poetics into hermeneutics, into what the work at some level is *really about*. Let me stress that if it is true that the thematic concerns of American literature are the product of the presence of an Africanist other, then this is true even for those works that conceal it best, but it does not follow that interpretation of those works should focus on a concealed Africanism. Hermeneutics is not poetics. The assumption that the payoff of critical work should be the interpretation of individual works is

6. Jonathan Culler, *Flaubert: The Uses of Uncertainty* (Ithaca: Cornell University Press, 1974).

7. Toni Morrison, *Playing in the Dark: Whiteness and the American Literary Imagination* (Cambridge: Harvard University Press, 1992), 46.

what can lead from powerful theoretical investigations to what are perceived as partial or strained interpretations.

Many of the so-called schools of modern criticism derive from theoretical accounts of what it held to be most important in language, culture,
and society, but when converted to hermeneutic enterprises, these
schools give rise to particular interpretations, easily satirized as what each
predictably takes the literary work to be ultimately about: the class struggle (Marxism), the Oedipal conflict (psychoanalysis), the containment of
subversive energies (new historicism), the self-deconstructive nature of
the text (deconstruction), the asymmetry of gender relations (feminism),
imperialism and the hybridities it generates (post-colonial theory).[8] It is
the persistence of the notion of interpretation as the task and goal of literary study that generates this result.

But I have leaped ahead of my autobiographical narrative. A way to gauge
the shifts in conventions of writing interpretive criticism is to juxtapose an
essay by Cleanth Brooks with Paul de Man's reflections on the same text,
W. B. Yeats's poem "Among School Children." In *The Well-Wrought Urn*,
Brooks devotes a chapter to this poem, exploring its dramatic structure
and its complex attitudes by following the movement of the poetic
speaker's mind. De Man, on the other hand, is not interested in the
speaker, his tone, or the complexity of his attitude toward love, mortality,
his past, and the "presences" that break hearts, but in the relation between
grammatical structure and rhetorical figure in the concluding stanza:

> O chestnut tree, great-rooted blossomer,
> Are you the leaf, the blossom, or the bole?
> O body swayed to music, O brightening glance,
> How can we know the dancer from the dance?

Critics read these sentences as rhetorical questions asserting the impossibility of telling the dancer from the dance or the inappropriateness of trying to divide a living unity into its constituents. Brooks writes, with a characteristic twist of turning the poem on itself, "Certainly, we ought to do no
less here than to apply Yeats's doctrine to his own poem. The poem, like
the 'great-rooted blossomer' that it celebrates, is not to be isolated in the
'statement' made by Stanza V or by Stanza VII, or by Stanza VIII." We
must not mistake a part of the poem or tree for the whole, investigating,
as Brooks puts it, "the root system (the study of literary sources) or sniff-
ing the blossoms (impressionism) or . . . questioning the quondam

---

8. For discussion, see Jonathan Culler, *Literary Theory: A Very Short Introduction* (Oxford: Oxford University Press, 1997).

dancer about her life history (the study of the poet's biography)."[9] We must experience the dramatic structure of the whole.

Brooks confidently takes the apostrophes to the chestnut tree and the body swayed to music as rhetorical questions: obviously the tree is not to be equated with one of its parts or the dancer distinguished from the dance. But "it is equally possible," de Man writes, "to read the last line literally rather than figuratively, as asking with some urgency the question . . . how can we possibly make the distinctions that would shelter us from the error of identifying what cannot be identified? . . . The figural reading, which assumes the question to be rhetorical, is perhaps naive, whereas the literal reading leads to greater complication of theme and statement."[10]

Now the normal standard of critical judgment would be to ask which interpretation—literal question or rhetorical question—better accords with the rest of the poem. But de Man goes out of his way to note that the figural reading can yield a coherent interpretation, and he sketches the alternative (literal) line of interpretation in a most offhand fashion without attempting to convince. He is not trying to produce a more complete or convincing interpretation. In fact, what is at issue is precisely the critical principle of using notions of unity and thematic coherence to exclude possibilities awakened by structures of the language. The literal reading of Yeats's question, as urgently asking how we can make the distinction so as not to be misled, cannot be dismissed as irrelevant. "The two readings," de Man writes, "have to engage each other in direct confrontation, for the one reading is precisely the error denounced by the other and has to be undone by it" (12). We cannot justifiably choose one and reject the other, but we are compelled to choose: "the authority of the meaning engendered by the grammatical structure is fully obscured by the duplicity of a figure that cries out for the differentiation that it conceals"(12).

How to explain this sentence that twists around itself? The rhetorical question here is a duplicitous figure that conceals a differentiation (between dancer and dance) while demanding or relying on or crying out for a version of the same differentiation (between entity and performance). To take Yeats's question as a rhetorical question is to assume that we *can't* tell the difference between the dancer and the dance—say an entity and its performance. On the other hand, the very idea of a rhetorical question depends on the general possibility of distinguishing a form or grammatical structure from its rhetorical performance. How can we simultaneously distinguish the grammatical question from its rhetorical performance

9. Cleanth Brooks, *The Well-Wrought Urn* (New York: Harcourt Brace, 1947), 185, 191.
10. Paul de Man, *Allegories of Reading: Figural Language in Rousseau, Nietzsche, Rilke, and Proust* (New Haven: Yale University Press, 1979), 11.

and take it for granted that we *cannot distinguish* the dancer from the dance? The claim that Brooks and others have interpreted the poem as making—the affirmation of fusion or continuity (the impossibility of making a distinction)—is subverted by the discontinuity (between the interrogative grammatical structure and the non-interrogative figure of the rhetorical question) that has to be assumed in order to infer the claim of continuity.

The contrast between de Man's and Brooks's essays gives us a number of differences. Most obviously, perhaps, de Man's key sentences, whose twistedness is an emblem of the complexities of a thought interrogating the relations between levels of discourse, are engaged in a different activity from Brooks's conciliatory appeals to a critical consensus that he attempts to enrich. De Man isn't alerting us to a new possibility we might want to consider but identifying what he claims is an ineluctable necessity, whether or not we see it. Though he is not here attempting to put forward a new interpretation of the poem, his emphasis on the necessity of choosing an interpretation without valid grounds for choice—what he elsewhere calls an "aporia"—could itself be a type of interpretation, and de Man usually undertakes powerful and detailed interpretations of texts or portions thereof in pursuing a theoretical issue.

The unity of the poem, Brooks's watchword, has not vanished, but it is no longer conceived as an *organic* unity—harmonious balance and continuous functionality, with every part contributing to the effect of the whole. It is the *presumption* of unity, though, that highlights dissonance or self-division, as here between what has to be assumed to infer the figural meaning and the implications of the meaning inferred. A most striking contrast here is the different understandings of the self-reflexivity of literature. For the New Criticism, poems are ultimately about poetry or sense-making, and a strategy of critical writing is to work out what the poem says about poetry and interpretation (Brooks, you recall, asks us to apply Yeats's doctrine to his own poem). In effect, self-referentiality closes off interpretation, which is how it came to be associated with a poem's organic unity. But for de Man, the self-referentiality of the text is what ruins any organic unity: the poem fails to practice what it preaches; self-reference opens a gap, as in the notorious logical paradoxes of the Cretan liar (if his claim that all Cretans lie is true, then he lies, but if he lies, then his claim might be true). In general, self-referentiality creates not a self-enclosed organic unity but paradoxical relations between what is said and how it is said and inaugurates an impossible and therefore open-ended process of self-framing.

Finally, note that de Man does not focus on the posture and stance of the speaker as Brooks does. No longer unified as the act of a posited speaker (separated from the poet him- or herself), the poem is a rhetorical construction, subject to comparison with other sorts of discourses, in an investigation of aspects of language. (In de Man's previous example in the essay, Archie Bunker dismissively replies "What's the difference?" to Edith's question of whether he wants his bowling shoes laced under or laced over. To understand his utterance as denying difference, one must, as in the Yeats example, differentiate the grammatical form from rhetorical performance.)

But de Man's powerful text is itself now more than twenty years old. Let me, like Auerbach, leap another couple of decades to my last text—an instance of the critical writing I particularly admire today. Since difference from Cleanth Brooks seems my principle of selection, I turn to an essay that starts from Keats's "Ode on a Grecian Urn," the poem which furnishes the title of Brooks's *The Well-Wrought Urn*. This is "Muteness Envy," by Barbara Johnson, from her book *The Feminist Difference: Literature, Psychoanalysis, Race, and Gender*.

This exemplary piece, which highlights the importance of cultural studies in the field of literary criticism, reads Keats's ode, with its "still unravished bride of quietness," against Jane Campion's film *The Piano* and the critical reception of the film, so as to explore the cultural construction and aestheticization of female muteness as a repository of feminine value. (Johnson notes, "It is no accident that every actress who has been nominated for playing the part of a mute woman—Jane Wyman, Patty Duke, Marlee Matlin, and Holly Hunter—has won an Oscar"—an astonishing fact).[11]

The feminine urn of Keats's ode—"Thou still unravished bride of quietness"—is celebrated for its mute tales and melodies, sweeter than poetry or audible music. Do male poets celebrating mute speech suffer from "muteness envy," as women are said to suffer from penis envy—envying that thing which they can't by definition have if they are to be poets? Jacques Lacan, notoriously, treats feminine *jouissance* as something about which women remain mute—"we been begging them on our knees to tell us about it—well, not a word!" and he looks to Bernini's silent statue of St. Teresa for information. With Keats's ode Johnson writes,

> the question of feminine *jouissance* (or lack of it) is very much at issue. By calling the urn a "still unravished bride," Keats implies that the urn's destiny is to become a *ravished* bride. The word "ravished" can mean either "raped" or "sent into ecstasy." Both possibilities are readable in the scenes depicted on the urn:

11. Barbara Johnson, *The Feminist Difference: Literature, Psychoanalysis, Race, and Gender* (Cambridge: Harvard University Press, 1998), 150.

What men or gods are these? What maidens loth?
What mad pursuit? What struggle to escape?
What pipes and timbrels? What wild ecstasy?

The privileged aesthetic moment is a freeze frame just prior to ravishment. But how does pressing the pause button here make us sublate the scene of male sexual violence into a scene of general ecstasy? How does the maidens' struggle to escape congeal into aesthetic triumph? (134–35).

The tradition provides similar scenarios: when Daphne turns into a laurel tree in order to escape rape at the hands of Apollo, he gets to pluck a laurel branch as sign of an aesthetic triumph that elides sexual violence. Glancing at some other examples, Johnson concludes that "the work performed by the idealization of woman's silence is that it helps culture not to be able to tell the difference between their pleasure and their violation" (137).

Johnson turns to Jane Campion's *The Piano*, with its mute heroine, Ada, where the question of violence or pleasure arises. "What is the movie *saying* about the muteness that articulates and confuses women's oppression and woman's desire?" (143).

Reactions to the film by viewers and critics have been remarkably varied. "Like the aesthetic tradition on which it implicitly comments, *The Piano* seems to be about telling or not telling the difference between women's violation and women's pleasure" (147). Those who view it as a love story concentrate on the characters: from this point of view, Ada's muteness is not passivity but a form of resistance and subjecthood; she is a vital character. But the *framework* within which the film places her makes her an object of male bargains and violence. The frame of the movie "says that women can find the way of their desire within a structure in which they are traded between men" (147).

Interestingly, the viewers intent on proving that Ada is not a victim, that her muteness is not silence, seem determined to produce a silenced woman elsewhere, castigating the *Boston Globe* for allowing its female reviewer to object to the film. And the question of muteness does not stop there. *The International Herald Tribune* reported that men who had felt silenced by the hoopla surrounding the film were finally daring to utter their dislike ("Slowly, timidly the naysayers are gathering courage to speak . . ." (150). The whole thing, Johnson writes, "becomes a political game of muteness, muteness, who's got the muteness" (150).

Why, she asks, are so many white men—from Petrarchan poets to today's self-proclaimed victims of political correctness—"so eager to claim a share in the victimhood sweepstakes? . . . To speak about female victimization is to imply that there is a model of male power and authority that is other than victimization," but perhaps this is not so(152). After all, the men in this movie are both depicted as in some sense powerless. "It is in this male two-step—the axe wielder plus the manipulative sufferer, *both* of whom see themselves as powerless—that patriarchal power lies. Far from being the opposite of authority, victimhood would seem be the most effective *model* for authority, particularly literary and cultural authority. . . . The most highly-valued speaker gets to claim victimhood" (153).

Several features of this essay are salient for me. First, in contrast with Brooks, it marks the remarkable insights and the concomitant changes that feminism has brought to criticism and theory. It's not for Johnson a matter of condemning the works of the literary tradition, much less of declining to read them, but of examining the gendered scenarios that they deploy and which can be exposed by critical readings drawing on the textual resources of these works. If we were reading Keats alone, her analysis might sound like simple condemnation, but that the "Ode on a Grecian Urn" shares many of these structures with a work of a contemporary feminist filmmaker suggests that the situation is not a simple one—certainly not one where we can easily or pertinently separate the virtuous productions from the compromised.

Second—in contrast with Bush's essay on Marvell with which I began— this reading doesn't use non-literary materials as documents to shed light on or to explain for us the literary work. Whether we are talking about movies, reviews and critical articles, or letters to the editor, these are all texts that have to be read, with the same kinds of techniques and attention—texts that share many of the same structures. This is in part because, as Johnson shows, reading or interpretation involves not so much judgment from a position of exteriority to the work being read as a repetition and displacement of the scenarios that structure the work and through which it draws in its readers. Thus the question of "muteness, muteness, whose got the muteness," as Johnson puts it, moves through the dramas of our culture.

Third, I want to note Johnson's development of what in de Man we encountered as the aporia of the rhetorical question, where it was structurally impossible to opt for one reading or the other because to generate one reading one had to assume a principle which the reading denied. Here we have a similar case of structural undecidability, between violation and pleasure, but it is even more evident that we have to choose one or another: readers can't just remain neutral. The undecidability here stems from the possibility of focusing on the subjectivity of the characters or on the objectivity of the framework: any attempt to sustain one interpretation will encounter compelling objections from the other perspective. What in de Man seems to appear as a property of language, here emerges more as a feature of the relations between levels of the work and of readers' necessary interpretive investments.

Finally, I want to single out what is for me the most powerfully seductive feature of this mode of writing criticism. I would love to write like Barbara Johnson but cannot manage it. She is the supreme master of the short critical essay, able to go straight to the heart of the matter with a telling example, and then jump to another example that not only confirms but neatly and elegantly advances the argument—like the brief turn to Lacan. Even when, with little space, I tell myself that I must try to write like Johnson, I find I can't do it. I always feel I have to give more background (explain who Cromwell is, what Marvell's "Horatian Ode" is about, for instance) or try to argue that the example I am offering is representative and not special pleading—an issue that bothers her not at all. She skips all the background, the filling, the justifications, judging (rightly, I think) that if you don't find her example telling, a paragraph claiming its representativeness won't help.

And she achieves great economy by using questions—"How does the maiden's struggle to escape congeal into an aesthetic triumph?"—letting the reader try to answer rather than herself laboriously filling all this in. There is a spareness and incisiveness to this writing that leaps daringly from the single example to the general proposition. That structure of argumentation—nothing could be farther from the idea of heaping up evidence until you have proved your point—marks this criticism as speculative and as theory, though it works by reading little bits of texts, always key texts that bring some interesting twist to the argument. Can this be a paradigm for the future of criticism? Since it's damnably hard to imitate it, probably not, but it alerts us to changes in what might be demanded in the discipline and provides a horizon toward which one might aspire in writing criticism.

Writing History, Writing Trauma

Dominick LaCapra
(History, Society for the Humanities)

I would initially distinguish between two approaches to historiography. The first is what I would term a documentary or self-sufficient research model, of which positivism is the extreme form. On this first approach, gathering evidence and making referential statements in the form of truth-claims based on that evidence constitute necessary and sufficient conditions of historiography. The second approach, which is the negative mirror image of the first, is radical constructivism. For it, referential statements making truth-claims apply at best only to events and are of restricted, indeed marginal, significance. By contrast, essential are performative, figurative, aesthetic, rhetorical, ideological, and political factors that "construct" structures—stories, plots, arguments, interpretations, explanations—in which referential statements are embedded and take on meaning and significance. As shall become evident, my own view falls at neither extreme represented by these two approaches. It is, however, not simply a *juste-milieu* between the extremes; rather it attempts to articulate problems and relations in a significantly different manner. In brief, I maintain that referential statements making truth-claims based on evidence apply in historiography to both the (problematic) levels of structures and events. Moreover, truth-claims are necessary but not sufficient conditions of historiography. A crucial question is how they do and ought to interact with other factors or forces in historiography, in other genres, and in hybridized forms or modes.[1]

A version of this chapter has appeared previously in Dominick LaCapra, *Writing History, Writing Trauma* (Baltimore, Md.: Johns Hopkins University Press), 1–42, © 2001 The Johns Hopkins University Press, and is reprinted here with the permission of the publisher.

1. I would note that a self-sufficient research model and radical constructivism form polar opposites, neither of which may adequately characterize the approach of certain historians. But both have played a significant role in the discipline as well as in analyses of it.

A documentary or self-sufficient research model was especially prominent toward the end of the nineteenth and the beginning of the twentieth
century, and it may even have been defensible in the attempt to profes-
sionalize history under the banner of objectivity and to distance, if not dis-
sociate, it from literature, especially in the form of *belles lettres*.[2] Since then
that model has to a significant extent persisted in professional historiography, but its value is more questionable, although it has been rendered
more sophisticated through its encounter with a radically constructivist
position.[3]

In a documentary or self-sufficient research model, priority is often
given to research based on primary (preferably archival) documents that
enable one to derive authenticated facts about the past which may be recounted in a narrative (the more "artistic" approach) or employed in a
mode of analysis which puts forth testable hypotheses (the more "social-
scientific" approach).[4] On this model, there is a sense in which writing is

2. On this issue, see Peter Novick, *That Noble Dream: The "Objectivity Question" and the American Historical Profession* (Cambridge: Cambridge University Press, 1988). For a discussion of
Novick's book by J. H. Hexter, Linda Gordon, David Hollinger, Allan Megill, Peter Novick, and
Dorothy Ross, based on a panel at the annual convention of the American Historical Associa-
tion, see *The American Historical Review* 96 (1991): 673–708. For a discussion that includes an
attempt to reconceptualize the problem of objectivity in normative terms, see Thomas Haskell,
"Objectivity Is Not Neutrality" in *History and Theory: Contemporary Readings*, ed. Brian Fay, Philip
Pomper, and Richard T. Vann (Malden, Mass.: Blackwell Publishers, 1998), 299–319. See also
Chris Lorenz's insightful essay in the same volume, "Historical Knowledge and Historical Reality: A Plea for 'Internal Realism,' " 342–76. This volume, to which I shall frequently refer, is in
general one of the best sources for contemporary views of historiography on the part of both
philosophers and historians. In addition to the essays in it, see as well those in *The Postmodern
History Reader*, ed. Keith Jenkins (New York: Routledge, 1997).

3. In the recent past, the affirmation of objectivity may even eventuate in what Hans Kellner has termed "a sort of postmodern literalism, a self-critical (or self-deconstructing, if you
will) literalism that points querulously to its own impossibility"—what might also be seen stylistically as a variant of minimalism evidenced, for example, in the work of Berel Lang. See Kellner's " 'Never Again' is Now," in Fay, Pomper, and Vann, *History and Theory*, 235. Kellner's discussion of Hayden White's notion of the middle voice in representing the Holocaust may be
compared and contrasted with what I write later.

4. The social-scientific approach is important for many historians but today not much discussed by philosophers treating historiography (for example, both Chris Lorenz in the analytic
tradition and Paul Ricoeur in the continental tradition) who tend to follow Hayden White,
even when they criticize him, by focusing on narrative. Although the conception of the relevant social-scientific theories and theorists changes over time, the concern with the relation of
history to the social sciences, at times correlated with a de-emphasis of the significance of narrative, has been a hallmark of both the Bielefeld school in Germany and the *Annales* in France.
A concern with the relation between history and the social sciences is crucial, but a primary if not exclusive orientation in the direction of the social sciences often implies a deval-
uation of literary studies, rhetoric, and (to a lesser degree) philosophy as relevant for the self-
understanding or conduct of historical inquiry (as well as of philosophers and literary theorists
as pertinent interlocutors for historians), and it constitutes philosophy and literature largely as
objects of historical and social-scientific analysis. The unfortunate result is often limited insight
into the work and play of philosophical and literary texts or the way they respond—at times

not a problem. Writing is subordinated to content in the form of facts, their narration, or their analysis. It is thus reduced to writing up the results of research, and style is limited to a restricted notion of mellifluous, immediately readable or accessible, well-crafted prose (or conventional *beau style*) in which form ideally has no significant effect on content. In other words, writing is a medium for expressing a content, and its ideal goal is to be transparent to content or an open window on the past—with figures of rhetoric serving only an instrumental role in illustrating what could be expressed without loss in literal terms. As Nancy Partner puts the point: "Correct modern historical style draws attention away from the verbal symbols chosen by the author and directs it to the words of others (or artifacts or natural objects), thus creating by literary convention the illusion [I would rather say, having the regulative ideal—DLC] of transparency, through the text into time."[5]

---

critically—to social categories and assumptions, however probing and complex may be the analysis of their social insertion in a collective representation, structure, field, or network. (The mutual reliance of history and the social sciences was in certain respects accentuated by the 1994 change in the title of the journal *Annales ESC [Economies Sociétés Civilisations]* to *Annales HSS [Histoires, Sciences Sociales]*.) Recently this orientation may be changing to allow a broader conception of inter-and cross-disciplinarity in which there is a critical, discriminating opening to the role of philosophy and literary theory as sites that, along with the social sciences, are relevant to a reconceptualization of (or "critical turn" in) history. For the editors' attempt to rethink the journal's approach, see "Histoire et sciences sociales: Un tournant critique?" in *Annales ESC* 43 (1988): 291–93 and *"Tentons l'expérience"* in *Annales ESC* 44 (1989): 1317–23. See also *Annales HSS* 49 (1994) on *"Littérature et histoire."* For a harsh critique of any turn in the *Annales* which would stress theoretical reflection or discourse analysis—much less a mutually thought-provoking interaction with philosophy and literary studies—see Gérard Noiriel, *Sur la "crise" de l'histoire* (Paris: Belin, 1996).

5. "Writing on the Writing of History," in *History and Theory* 77. I would note that the suspicion of a plain style and the advocacy of an opaque or at least a difficult style in the modern period are motivated by a number of considerations. One is the general idea that style should respond to the complexity and difficulty of the problems treated, thus that there is something dubious in the attempt to make certain problems easy or deceptively simple and accessible. (One finds this view, combined with a concern for religious intensity and demandingness, in Kierkegaard, for example.) Another is the idea that initiation, with its attendant trials, is necessary to understand and appreciate certain things—or, in Nietzsche's phrase, that all things rare are for the rare. A more democratic variant of this view is the notion that an intricate style may function as a strategy of resistance and ward off the grasp of dominant, oppressive (notably colonial or postcolonial) power. In the words of the Tunisian writer Abdelwahib Meddeb, "we will defend ourselves with arabesque, subversion, labyrinthine constructions, the incessant decentering of the sentence and of language so that the other will lose the way just as in the narrow streets of the *casbah.*" (Quoted in Jean Dejeux, *Situation de la littérature maghrébine de langue française,* [Algiers: Office des publications universitaires, 1982], 103–04.)

Still another reason, for writers such as Theodor Adorno and Paul Celan, is that language has been so distorted or corrupted by political and propagandistic uses that it must be made strange, difficult, even resistant to pleasure in order to be used again—a perspective intensified by the deceptions and euphemisms of Nazi discourse. Phrased differently, the last view criticizes a premature return to the pleasure principle in discourse before certain demanding if not intractable problems have been confronted and, to some viable extent, worked through

In its more extreme forms, a documentary or self-sufficient research model *may* bring with it a stress on quantitative methods (prominent in cliometrics), but it generally *does* involve the following features, which add further dimensions to a predominantly, if not exclusively, referential or constative use of language that conveys truth-claims based on evidence: (1) a strict separation or binary opposition between subject and object; (2) a tendency to conflate objectivity with objectivism or the objectification of the other which is addressed only in the form of third-person referential statements, direct quotations, and summaries or paraphrases; (3) an identification of historical understanding with causal explanation or with the fullest possible contextualization of the other (possibly in the form of thick description or narration); (4) a denial of transference or the problem of the implication of the observer in the object of observation; (5) an exclusion or downplaying of a dialogic relation to the other recognized as having a voice or perspective that may question the observer or even place him or her in question by generating problems about his or her assumptions, affective investments, and values. In general one might say that a self-sufficient research paradigm and, in even more pronounced form, its positivistic extreme confine historiography to constative or referential statements involving truth-claims made by an observer about a sharply differentiated object of research.

There are elements of a research paradigm which, extricated from a self-sufficient or autonomous framework, I (along with the overwhelming majority of historians) find indispensable, including the importance of contextualization, clarity, objectivity, footnoting, and the idea that historiography necessarily involves truth-claims based on evidence—or what might be called an irreducible "aboutness"—not only on the level of directly referential statements about events but on more structural and comprehensive levels such as narration, interpretation, and analysis. But I think that one has to situate these features in a manner not accommodated by their relatively unproblematic role in a self-sufficient research paradigm.[6]

---

in an empathetic, rigorous manner. In a more dubious form, an opaque or convoluted style may become mimetically prevalent when a difficult, demanding approach becomes an all-purpose methodology or stylistic tic.

6. The prevalence and importance of such a paradigm or model in the historical profession were perhaps stated in overly restrictive terms by Laurence Veysey when he asserted: "With all this greater sophistication about historical argument, it remains true that the very highest amount of prestige is still awarded to an historian who uncovers (no matter how he does it) some incontestable but previously unknown fact of major importance." "The United States," in *The International Handbook of Historical Studies: Contemporary Research and Theory*, ed. Georg G. Iggers and Harold T. Parker (Westport, Conn.: Greenwood, 1979) 168. Without denying the prevalence and importance of a documentary or self-sufficient research model in the profes-

The note (footnote or endnote) is the correlate of research, and its use as a referential component of research is one criterion that serves to differentiate history from fiction. The research paper or monograph is writing replete with referential notes, ideally, in a restricted research paradigm, a note per statement in the principal text. (More subjective moments are confined to a preface or coda or perhaps to notes not serving as references.) Fiction *may* have referential notes, notably when it blends fact and fiction, but historiography, to be professional historiography—even beyond a restricted research paradigm—*must* have notes that provide references for statements that function referentially and make truth-claims (except when these statements convey what is currently accepted as common knowledge at least among professionals).

For J. H. Hexter, the attitude toward footnotes distinguishes history not only from fiction but also from physics, and, in almost pastoral tones, he even seems to intimate that, at least in historiography, the note is a case wherein the last shall be first: "One difference becomes manifest in the divergent attitude of the historian and, say, the physicist to the lowly item in their common repertoire—the footnote. It is so lowly, indeed, that it may seem unworthy of notice; but we must remember that the lowly and humble things of the earth may be more instructive than the great and mighty—after all, geneticists learned a good deal more about genetics by considering the fruit fly than they could have learned in an equal span of time from a contemplation of the somewhat more impressive elephant."[7] Hexter unfortunately does not explicate what is implied by his shift from a putative contrast between historiography and physics to an analogy between the historian and the geneticist, and we are left mildly bewildered by the seeming aspersion cast on macrohistory by the allusion to the elephant as object of contemplation. But his affirmation of the importance of the note to historiography is unequivocal and unobjectionable.

Of course, notes may be used in both history and fiction in a manner that questions or even parodies a documentary or self-sufficient research paradigm, and there may be substantive footnotes that function not merely as references but as elaborations of points or even as significant qualifications of assertions or arguments in the principal text, at times to the point of establishing a critically dialogic relation between text and note or even something approximating a counter-text in the notes.[8] More-

sion, I qualified Veysey's assertion by observing that "the greatest prestige often goes to the historian who revises standard accounts on the basis of massive archival research." (*History and Criticism,* [Ithaca: Cornell University Press, 1985] 20).

7. "The Rhetoric of History," in *History and Theory,* 60. On the footnote, see also Anthony Grafton, *Footnote: A Curious History* (Cambridge, Mass.: Harvard University Press, 1997).

8. I think many historians and editors of historical texts get uncomfortable when the latter

over, with respect to a limit-event such as the Holocaust, even the eminent research scholar Raul Hilberg, whose formulation of problems usually tends toward understatement, was led to be hyperbolic and to paraphrase Adorno in posing this seemingly rhetorical question: "I am no poet, but the thought occurred to me that if [Adorno's] statement is true, then is it not equally barbaric to write footnotes after Auschwitz?" Hilberg added:

> I have had to reconstruct the process of destruction in my mind, combining the documents into paragraphs, the paragraphs into chapters, the chapters into a book. I always considered that I stood on solid ground: I had no anxieties about artistic failure. Now I have been told that I have indeed succeeded. And that is a cause of some worry, for we historians usurp history precisely when we are successful in our work, and that is to say that nowadays some people might read what I have written in the mistaken belief that here, on my printed pages, they will find the true ultimate Holocaust as it really happened.[9]

Still, the limit of history and the beginning of fiction is probably reached in the self-referential footnote (or entry) that goes beyond intertextual indications, related to the research findings or conclusions of other historians, and blocks reference by taking one back into the text with looplike or labyrinthine effects, as one has, for example, in Nabokov's *Pale Fire*. One might also invoke the ping-pong diplomacy of Flaubert's cross-references in *The Dictionary of Received Ideas*, where one has the following entries: "Blondes. Hotter than brunettes. See brunettes. Brunettes. Hotter than blondes. See blondes."

Let us now turn to the second position on historiography to which I referred earlier: radical constructivism. A radically constructivist position has received its most articulate defenders in such important figures as Hayden White and Frank Ankersmit, who accept the distinction between historical and fictional statements on the level of reference to events but question it on structural levels.[10] For them there is an identity or essential

---

process occurs, probably because it is a disconcerting departure from the more standard use of footnotes.

9. "I Was Not There," in *Writing and the Holocaust*, ed. Berel Lang (New York: Holmes & Meier, 1988), 25.

10. After completing this chapter, I read Chris Lorenz's "Can History Be True? Narrativism, Positivism, and the 'Metaphorical Turn,'" *History and Theory* 37 (1998): 309–29. It carefully elaborates certain of the points I touch on in terms of a somewhat more restricted frame of reference that focuses on narrative and involves a very limited if not dismissive treatment of fiction understood as the opposite of history. See also in the same volume, John H. Zammito, "Ankersmit's Postmodernist Historiography: The Hyperbole of 'Opacity,'" 330–46. Despite the force and cogency of certain of his arguments, in this essay (as in "Are We Being Theoretical Yet? The New Historicism, the New Philosophy of History, and 'Practicing Historians,'"

similarity between historiography and fiction, literature, or the aesthetic on structural levels, and their emphasis is on the fictionality of structures in all these areas. At the limit, they present historiography as a closed window so stained by one set of projective factors or another that, at least on a structural level, it reflects back only the historian's own distorted image. Yet at times their work takes them in directions that may go beyond a radically constructivist identification of history with fictionalization, rhetoric, poetics, performativity, or even self-referential discourse. After a brief elaboration of the better-known dimensions of their thought, I spend some time on what I find to be an insufficiently explored, difficult, and thought-provoking initiative in an essay by White, namely, the argument that a discursive analogue of the middle voice is most suitable at least for representing the most extreme, traumatic, limit-events in history, such as those of the Holocaust.

From what might be seen as a version of a self-sufficient research paradigm which has been rendered more sophisticated by its critical encounter with radical constructivism, Perez Zagorin provides this characterization of a position held by Frank Ankersmit, which Zagorin generalizes to apply to postmodernism and deconstruction in general:

> One of the characteristic moves of postmodern and deconstructionist theory has been to try to obliterate the boundaries between literature and other disciplines by reducing all modes of thought to the common condition of writing. So it maintains that philosophy, like historiography, is merely another kind of writing and subject to its laws, rather than a separate species of reflection concerned with distinctively philosophical questions. Putting aside, however, the identification of language and reality, a thesis construable in different ways (which in any case is well beyond the subject of my discussion), I venture to say that few historians would agree with Ankersmit's consignment of historiography to the category of the aesthetic. Nor would they be likely to approve a characterization that gives preeminence to its literariness. As the Russian formalists and Roman Jakobson have told us, the quality of literariness consists in the way it thrusts language and expression into the foreground and grants them an independent value and importance. Although

Journal of Modern History 65 [1993]: 784–814), Zammito shows little appreciation for the ways in which hyperbole and even opacity (or at least difficulty) may be understood and in a qualified manner defended, especially when they are framed in certain ways and are not simply indulged in all contexts. One might provide a limited, contextualized defense of hyperbole as a stylistic indication of one's involvement in the excess of an excessive or extreme (indeed at times traumatic) context or situation—a response (not a last word or a position) that must be undergone and even to some extent acted out if certain problems are to be understood empathetically and worked through. At the very least, one may argue that there is something questionable in a uniformly benign, mellifluous, blandly reasonable, or conventionally "realistic" response even to the most extreme situations or limit-cases.

Ankersmit holds that literary and historical works are similar in this respect, this is surely not the case. In historiography, the attempt by language to draw attention to itself would commonly be regarded as highly inappropriate and an obtrusive breach of the rule of historical writing. In history language is very largely subservient to the historian's effort to convey in the fullest, clearest, and most sensitive way an understanding or knowledge of something in the past.[11]

In his reply, Ankersmit makes a number of points worth taking seriously. He nonetheless seems to agree with important aspects of Zagorin's characterization of his position, although he here shifts or varies his emphasis from aesthetics to politics (as White often does). Ankersmit writes:

All that is essential and interesting in the writing of history (both in theory and practice) is not to be found at the level of the individual statements, but at that of the politics adopted by historians when they select the statements that individuate their "picture of the past." . . . Saying *true* things about the past is easy—anybody can do that—but saying *right* things about the past is difficult. That truly [*sic*] requires historical insight and originality . . . I have elsewhere called these "pictures of the past" narrative substances. The question everything turns on, then, is whether or not we are prepared to recognize these narrative substances as logical entities *next* to the logical entities like subject, predicate, theoretical concept, statement, and so on, we already know from philosophical logic. If we take seriously the text and its narrative substances we will become postmodernists; if we see only the statement we will remain modernist. Or, to put it in a slogan, the statement is modernist, the (historical) text is postmodernist.[12]

By narrative substance, Ankersmit means what White discussed in terms of prefigurative tropes and meaning-endowing, projective narrative structures. Like White, he sees the narrative substance or structure as fictive and politically or ideologically motivated, and he infers from the evident fact that "we can never test our conclusions by comparing the elected text with 'the past' itself," the questionable conclusion that "narrative substances do not refer to the past" (212). He also asserts that "we can only speak of causes and effects at the level of the statement" and that "narrative language is metaphorical (tropological)," indeed, that "the historical text is a substitute for the absent past" (220).

One may certainly agree with Ankersmit (or White) that it is of pressing importance to attend to current ideological and political dimensions or functions of historical accounts. Moreover, all narratives "construct" or

11. "Postmodernism: Reconsiderations," in *History and Theory*, 200.
12. "Reply to Professor Zagorin," in *History and Theory*, 209.

shape and some narratives more or less drastically distort their objects. But, without adopting Zagorin's limited frame of reference, one might still argue that the historical text becomes a substitute for the absent past only when it is construed as a totalized object that pretends to closure and is fetishized as such. (Put in somewhat ironic psychoanalytic terms, the historical text as fetish would become an avatar of the phallic mother giving birth to total history—at one time the dream of the *Annales* school.) One might also maintain that, although a past reality or object is for historians an inference from textual traces in the broad sense, the inference, while not exhausted by, nonetheless necessarily and crucially involves reference and truth-claims with respect to both events and structures or general interpretations and explanations. In other words, saying the right things may not be limited to, but it does constitutively require, saying true things on the levels of both statements referring to events and broader narrative, interpretive, or explanatory endeavors. How to adjudicate truth-claims may differ in significant ways with respect to events and to broader endeavors (such as interpretations or readings of the past), but truth-claims are at issue on both levels.

For example, in the debate about the Holocaust, in which White and Ankersmit have recently participated, reference and truth-claims pertain not only to statements such as "the Wannsee conference took place on January 20, 1942." They also apply to broader considerations such as those at issue in the debate between intentionalists (who stress the role of an intentional policy of genocide formulated by Hitler as well as the importance of that policy in a dictatorship) and functionalists (who stress the role of the "polycratic" or decentered nature of the Nazi regime, more impersonal bureaucratic processes, and the activities of middle-to-low-level functionaries in implementing and even at times initiating the "final solution"). Most historians of the Holocaust would now argue that an account both true and right is found neither in an intentionalist nor in a functionalist approach but in a more complex combination of their emphases as well as in a partial shift of attention to other factors not sufficiently accounted for by either. The more recent terms of the debate include facts (or statements of fact referring to events) that were important for both intentionalists and functionalists (notably the facts of the genocide itself as recounted by Raul Hilberg and others). But the debate is now about the relative weight to be given to (1) bureaucratic processes (including medicalized and hygienic concerns based on purportedly scientific race theory) linked to what Hilberg termed the "machinery of destruction," perhaps in relation to a broader concept such as modernization (with Zygmunt Bauman), a technological frame of reference (Heidegger's *Gestell*), and instrumental rationality (Horkheimer and

Adorno's "dialectic of Enlightenment") and (2) anti-Semitism as an ideology and practice, perhaps in relation to an expanded conception of victimization which would differentially refer to such groups as the handi-
capped, "Gypsies," homosexuals, and Slavs, including such issues as the
prevalence in Germany and elsewhere of rabid (or what Daniel Jonah
Goldhagen terms *eliminationist*) anti-Semitism and its relation to fears of
degeneration, quasi-ritual anxiety about contamination, and a quasi-
sacrificial desire for purification of the *Volksgemeinschaft* as well as its re-
generation or even redemption through violence. Of course there are still
more issues involved in contemporary debates—including in intricate
ways rhetorical, political, affective, and ideological matters—but these indications are enough to demonstrate that truth-claims are nonetheless at
issue on levels other than that of discrete statements referring to events.

When one moves from Ankersmit to White, it is important to note that
the former's opposition between modernism and postmodernism is repli-
cated in the latter's opposition between nineteenth-century realism and
modernism.[13] This very displacement might indicate that the oppositions
are less secure than they seem to either thinker and that both nineteenth-
century realism and modernism may be more internally complex than either allows in employing one or the other for purposes of contrast and
polemics. One might also observe that White tends to identify narrativization with fictionalization in a questionable manner.[14] As I have intimated,

---

13. In his most recent work, Ankersmit has moved from a constructivist aestheticism to the
concept of experience to which I turn in a somewhat different way later in this essay. Experience—conceived perhaps in too foundational and undifferentiated a form—is a key concept
in John Toews, "Intellectual History after the Linguistic Turn: The Autonomy of Meaning and
the Irreducibility of Experience," *American Historical Review* 92 (1987): 879–907. See also John
H. Zammito, "Are We Being Theoretical Enough Yet?" as well as my "History, Language, and
Reading: Waiting for Crillon," *American Historical Review* 100 (1995): 799–828 (a version of
which is republished as chap. 1 of my *History and Reading: Tocqueville, Foucault, French Studies*
[Toronto: University of Toronto Press, 2000] and in shorted form in *History and Theory*,
90–118). Curiously, neither Toews nor Zammito discusses the problem of empathy which
would seem to be crucial for any attempt to relate historiography and experience, particularly
one that insists on the distinction between the differentiated experience of those studied and
the differentiated experience of the historian. One may also note that utopian projects are always to some extent situated beyond historical experience even when they invoke a mythologi-
cal golden age.

14. I would note that one should not simply conflate the contrast between the literal and
the figurative with that between the factual and the fictive. Assertions of fact or truth-claims
may be conveyed in figurative language (for example, "war is hell" or "she has a heart as big as
all outdoors"). Conversely, fiction may be written in non-figurative, "literal" language, indeed
in language that tries to eliminate or render banal all metaphors (as, in different ways, in the
writing of Flaubert, Kafka, or Beckett). Of course, in ordinary language "literal" may be used as
the correlate of "factual" or in a seemingly pleonastic manner ("the literal truth"). The correlation if not identification of the figurative and the fictional (or, even more broadly, the literary) is an aspect of a special theory of language which is open to question.

narrative structures may involve truth-claims, either in terms of "correspondence" to lived narrative structures (such as those involved in more or less realized plans and projects) or in terms of references (for example, concerning patterns or more or less varied repetitions) that may retrospectively be seen to inform processes or activities in ways that may not have been entirely conscious to participants. (Here one may, for example, point to the role of secularization as a complex, often at least partly unconscious, displacement of the religious in the secular.)

The comparison of historiography and fiction may be taken in a different direction than that prominent in White. One might argue that narratives in fiction may also involve truth-claims on a structural or general level by providing insight into phenomena such as slavery or the Holocaust, by offering a reading of a process or period, or by giving at least a plausible "feel" for experience and emotion which may be difficult to arrive at through restricted documentary methods. One might, for example, make such a case for Toni Morrison's *Beloved* with respect to the aftermath of slavery and the role of transgenerational, phantomlike forces that haunt later generations, or for Albert Camus's *The Fall* with respect to the reception of the Holocaust.[15] (Indeed the more pertinent contrast between historiography and fiction might be on the level of events where historians, as distinguished from writers of fiction, may not imbricate or treat in the same way actual events and ones they invent.)

At the very least, the complex relation of narrative structures to truth-claims might provide a different understanding of modern and postmodern realism (including what has been termed *traumatic realism*) wherein correspondence itself is not to be understood in terms of positivism or essentialism but as a metaphor that signifies a referential relation (or truth-claim) that is more or less direct or indirect (probably generically more indirect in fiction than in historiography). Furthermore, one might maintain that truth-claims coming from historiography, on the levels of both events and structures, may be employed in the discussion and critique of art (including fiction) in a manner that is especially pressing with respect to extreme events that still particularly concern people at present. For example, one might justifiably criticize a work of art on historical as well as aesthetic and normative grounds if it treated the Third Reich in a manner that excluded or marginalized the Nazi genocide or even if it addressed the latter in terms of a harmonizing narrative that provided the reader or viewer with an unwarranted sense of spiritual uplift (as does the ending of

15. For a discussion of *The Fall* (as well as of Art Spiegelman's *Maus*) from the perspective suggested here, see my *History and Memory after Auschwitz* (Ithaca: Cornell University Press, 1998), chaps. 3 and 5.

Schindler's List, for example). On similar grounds, one might also criticize a work of art that addressed the relation between perpetrator and victim largely in terms of erotic titillation within the acting-out of a repetition compulsion (as the film *Night Porter* might be argued to do).[16]

Truth-claims are neither the only nor always the most important consideration in art and its analysis. Of obvious importance are poetic, rhetorical, and performative dimensions of art which not only mark but also make differences historically (dimensions that are differentially at play in historical writing as well). But my general point is that truth-claims are nonetheless relevant to works of art both on the level of their general structures or procedures of emplotment—which may offer significant insights (or, at times, oversights), suggesting lines of inquiry for the work of historians (for example, with respect to transgenerational processes of "possession" or haunting)—and on the level of justifiable questions addressed to art on the basis of historical knowledge and research. In brief, the interaction or mutually interrogative relation between historiography and art (including fiction) is more complicated than is suggested by either an identity or a binary opposition between the two, a point that is becoming increasingly forceful in recent attempts to reconceptualize the study of art and culture.[17]

One might also make explicit what is not thematized as such in White: narrativization is closest to fictionalization in the sense of a dubious de-

---

16. Here one may mention the more difficult case of Roberto Benigni's 1998 film *Life Is Beautiful*. I think this film tends to break into two parts—the pre-concentration camp and the camp experiences. The film does not recognize the break and is, if anything, too continuous in its techniques and approach to problems. The "magical realism" and humor that work effectively in the first, pre-concentration camp part (for example, in creating and sustaining the relationship between the couple or in protecting the child from harsh realities) become in many ways inappropriate in the context of the concentration camp. Life in the camp demanded more and is an unsuitable context for benign humor and the stylizations (or games) of protective denial. The second part of the film tends to be either too implausible or not implausible enough, and it discloses both the possibilities and limits of Benigni's type of humor and realism. (The camp itself remains a rather "utopian" space or nowhere land, underspecified in terms of location, duration of stay, and operation—itself magically stylized in questionable ways—and the uplifting end of the film might be seen as the Italian mother-and-child analogue of a Hollywood ending.) On the question of traumatic realism, see the thought-provoking book of Michael Rothberg, *Traumatic Realism: The Demands of Holocaust Representation* (Minneapolis: University of Minnesota Press, 2000).

17. This perspective has informed my own approach to problems. See especially my *"Madame Bovary" on Trial* (Ithaca: Cornell University Press, 1982) or, more recently, my discussion of Claude Lanzmann's film *Shoah* in *History and Memory after Auschwitz*, chap. 4. For an early attempt to rethink French studies in a manner relating history and art, see Maurice Crubellier, *Histoire Culturelle de la France XIXe-XXe siècle* (Paris: A. Colin, 1974). For a recent attempt, see Kristin Ross, *Fast Cars, Clean Bodies: Decolonization and the Reordering of French Culture* (Cambridge, Mass.: MIT Press, 1995). See also the final chapter of my *History and Reading: Tocqueville, Foucault, French Studies*.

parture from, or distortion of, historical reality when it conveys relatively unproblematic closure (or what Frank Kermode terms a sense of an ending).[18] Indeed, White sometimes tends to identify narrative with conventional or formulaic narrative involving closure and to move from this limited identification to a general critique of narrative. (This move is pronounced in Sande Cohen's *Historical Culture*.[19]) Yet White also defends what he sees as modernist narrative and argues that historiography would do better to emulate its resistance to closure and its experimentalism in general rather than to rely on nineteenth-century realism in its putative modes of representation and emplotment. Hans Kellner has attempted to show how Fernand Braudel's study of the Mediterranean at the time of Philip II does just that by enacting a satiric and carnivalesque interaction of various levels of meaning, interpretation, and explanation.[20] In any case, White's critiques of narrative are most convincing when applied to conventional narratives (or the conventional dimension of narrative) seeking resonant closure, and his claims about the possible role of experimental narrative with respect to historiography are often thought-provoking even when he does not show precisely how they might be applied or enacted.

Rather than track further White's movements that have already been extensively discussed in the literature and, if anything, have overly predetermined the terms of debate even for his critics, I would like to turn to a relatively recent essay of his in which he discusses the Holocaust.[21] In it he relates what he sees as an appropriately modernist representation with a discursive analogue of the middle voice as discussed by Roland Barthes in his famous essay "To Write: An Intransitive Verb?"[22] White seems to pull back somewhat from radical constructivism and an "endowment" or projective theory of meaning involving the idea that a historian could choose

18. *The Sense of an Ending: Studies in the Theory of Fiction* (New York: Oxford University Press, 1967).

19. *Historical Culture: On the Recoding of an Academic Discipline* (Berkeley: University of California Press, 1986).

20. "Disorderly Conduct: Braudel's Mediterranean Satire," *History and Theory* 18 (1979): 187–222, reprinted in *Language and Historical Representation: Getting the Story Crooked* (Madison: University of Wisconsin Press, 1989), 153–89. See also Philippe Carrard, *Poetics of the New History: French Historical Discourse from Braudel to Chartier* (Baltimore: The Johns Hopkins University Press, 1992).

21. "Historical Emplotment and the Story of Truth," in *Probing the Limits of Representation: Nazism and the "Final Solution,"* ed. Saul Friedlander (Cambridge, Mass.: Harvard University Press, 1992), 37–53. I shall mention points at which White himself turns to the concept of experience in this essay.

22. Included with a discussion in *The Structuralist Controversy: The Languages of Criticism and the Sciences of Man*, ed. Richard Macksey and Eugenio Donato (Baltimore: Johns Hopkins University Press, 1970), 134–56.

to plot any series of (inherently meaningless or chaotic) events with any given plot structure or mode. He continues to assert that "narrative accounts do not consist only of factual statements (singular existential propositions) and arguments; they consist also of poetic and rhetorical elements by which *what would otherwise be a list of facts is transformed into a story* [my emphasis]." Furthermore, "this raises the question of the relation of the various generic plot types that can be used to endow events with different kinds of meaning—tragic, epic, comic, romance, pastoral, farcical, and the like—to the events themselves" (39). White also asserts: "We can confidently presume that the facts of the matter set limits on the *kinds* of stories that can *properly* (in the sense of both veraciously and appropriately) be told about them only if we believe that the events themselves possess a 'story' kind of form and a 'plot' kind of meaning" (40).

In light of his earlier work, one might have expected White to argue that the latter presumption is untenable, whether entertained confidently or not, since plot structures are purportedly projective and fictive, perhaps politically or ideologically motivated, constructs that "endow" inherently meaningless events with meaning and structure. In the terms he borrowed from Sartre's *Nausea*, life (or reality) as lived is inherently chaotic or meaningless—one damned thing after another—and it is transformed retrospectively into a meaningful story only when told in a narrative. A lived story or a life with a determinate ("plotted") meaning, much less a true story, simply becomes a contradiction in terms. The reader might well do a double-take when White, contrary to expectations, writes: "In the case of an emplotment of the events of the Third Reich in a 'comic' or 'pastoral' mode, we would be eminently justified in appealing to 'the facts' in order to dismiss it from the lists of 'competing narratives' of the Third Reich" (40). White goes on to make an exception for an ironic, metacritical twist on a comic or pastoral story, but how he is able to put forward the earlier dismissal as "eminently justified" is puzzling in terms of his earlier postulates. I would add that the possibility is not purely hypothetical, for some attempts to normalize the Nazi period rely on nostalgic, pastoral forms, as is the case, for example, in Edgar Reitz's monumental docudrama *Heimat*. In it a pastoral evocation of life in the provinces both air-brushes the Third Reich and marginalizes its treatment of the Jews.[23]

In responding to White's essay, Martin Jay exclaimed: "In his anxiety to avoid inclusion in the ranks of those who argue for a kind of relativistic

---

23. See the excellent discussion of Reitz in Eric Santner, *Stranded Objects: Mourning, Melancholia, and Film in Postwar Germany* (Ithaca: Cornell University Press, 1990).

'anything goes,' which might provide ammunition for revisionist skeptics about the existence of the Holocaust, [White] undercuts what is most powerful in his celebrated critique of naive historical realism."[24] The problem encountered by White is not, however, unique to his treatment of the Holocaust. One might argue that the Holocaust raises in an accentuated form problems that arise with respect to other series of events, especially other extreme, traumatic series of events that are of particular concern at present because they are highly "cathected" or invested with affect and considerations of value. As I indicated earlier, one such problem is the manner in which truth-claims are at issue not only on the level of statements referring to events but on structural levels such as narrative plots, interpretations, and explanations.

I have alluded to the particularly difficult and knotty twist in White's argument represented by his appeal to the middle voice which he takes as the appropriate way to "write" trauma. Modern languages do not have a middle voice in grammar but may at best allow for a discursive analogue of it. Barthes sees as a primary task of modern writing the attempt to recuperate discursively what has been lost grammatically by working or playing out a middle-voiced alternative to the active and passive voices. White, however, tends to conflate the middle voice with intransitive writing and to ignore the question mark in Barthes's title. Still, one may distinguish two movements in Barthes's essay itself which White tends to follow. The first is to take writing as intransitive or to see it as self-referential, thereby bracketing the question of reference and focusing exclusively on the relation of speaker and discourse (or signifier and signified). Thus Barthes writes: "Modern literature is trying, through various experiments, to establish a new status in writing for the agent of writing. The meaning or the goal of this effort is to substitute the instance of discourse for the in-

---

24. "Of Plots, Witnesses, and Judgments," in *Probing the Limits of Representation*, 97. A further question is whether the writer of fiction, in contrast to the historian, may assume the victim's voice. I think that when this happens in an unmediated manner (for example, through identification) one tends to have confessional literature or perhaps the dubious *faux mémoire* whose literary qualities are quite limited. (Insofar as a text is taken as the expression of the actual victim's voice, notably as memoir, one may be inhibited from a rigorous critical examination of its literary qualities, an inhibition evident in the treatment of Elie Wiesel's *Night* or, at first, of Benjamin Wilkormirski's *Fragments: Memories of a Wartime Childhood* which I discuss later. In the case of a text written by a victim, this inhibition, which probably exists only for a time, may be partially defended in that it places the reader in a double bind between the desire to criticize and the fear of its inappropriateness—a bind analogous in some small way to that in which victims were placed by their experiences.) By contrast, in more significant literature, the relation of the author to the victim and the victim's voice is mediated and stylistically qualified, for example, by embodying the victim's voice in narrators or characters as well as in modulations of free indirect style.

stance of reality (or of the referent), which has been, and still is, a myth-ical 'alibi' dominating the idea of literature" (144). This formulation, which enjoins bracketing the referential function of language, is dubi-ous with respect to historiography, which involves referential statements and truth-claims, and I have indicated that I think it would even be ques-tionable, in certain respects, for fiction and, more generally, literature and art.[25]

The second tendency in Barthes is different, for it situates the middle voice not as homologous with intransitive or self-referential writing but as undecidable with respect to the opposition between the transitive and the intransitive. As Barthes succinctly puts it, "we place ourselves at the very heart of a problematic of *inter*locution" (144). In this sense the middle voice, as White suggests, would enact the play of Derridian *différance*—play resisting seemingly dichotomous binary opposites (such as transitive and intransitive, active and passive, past and present, or masculine and femi-nine) that effect something like a dubiously purifying, scapegoating process and repress an anxiety-ridden middle area of undecidability as well as the manner in which seeming opposites displace and internally mark each other. The middle voice would thus be the "in-between" voice of undecidability and the unavailability or radical ambivalence of clear-cut positions. It might, of course, also be seen as the voice Heidegger seeks in his "step back" from the history of metaphysics in a thinking that recalls more "originary" possibilities.[26]

Barthes himself relates the middle voice to the problem of the relation between the present and the past, notably in terms of one's relation as speaker to one's discourse in the present in contradistinction to one's ac-count of a past discourse or phenomenon. More precisely, he appeals to Benveniste's argument that many languages "have a double system of time. The first temporal system is that of the discourse itself, which is adapted to the temporality of the speaker [*énonciateur*] and for which the *énonciation* [speech-act—DLC] is always the point of origin [*moment généra-teur*]. The second is the system of history or narrative, which is adapted to the recounting of past events without any intervention by the speaker and

25. White does not comment on the fact that, while Barthes postulates a homology between the sentence and discourse, thus taking linguistics as an adequate model for discourse analysis, White himself asserts a dichotomy between the referential sentence in historiography and nar-rative structure. I would argue that both moves are deceptive and that the relation between the sentence and discourse is more complex and warrants differential analysis.

26. For an interesting discussion of the middle voice in Derrida and Heidegger which came to my attention after I wrote this chapter, see Thomas Pepper, *Singularities: Extremes of Theory in the Twentieth Century* (Cambridge: Cambridge University Press, 1997), chap. 2.

which is consequently deprived of present and future (except periphrastically)" (137).

As Derrida notes in his intervention, the distinction as posited by Barthes seems to function as a misleading binary opposition and, I would add, applies as such, in a manner open to criticism, only to a self-sufficient research paradigm in positivistic form.[27] I would further note that the deconstruction of binary oppositions does not automatically entail the blurring of all distinctions. In resisting the latter tendency, one may argue that deconstruction and undecidability, in casting doubt on binaries, raise the related issues of *both* the actual (often very important) role of binary oppositions in empirical reality (an issue demanding research) *and* the elaboration of nonbinary distinctions as well as the attribution to them of relative strength or weakness in fact and in right. In this sense distinctions are articulations (at times related to institutions) that counteract the "free" play of *différance* (or dissemination) and more or less problematically bind it by generating limits that resist that play in its unregulated form. They are to thought what judgments and decisions are to evaluation and practice.

I would make a correlation that will be significant in my later argument—a correlation that indicates the desirability of relating deconstructive and psychoanalytic concepts. I would argue, or at least suggest, that undecidability and unregulated *différance*, threatening to disarticulate relations, confuse self and other, and collapse all distinctions—including that between present and past—are related to transference and prevail in trauma and in post-traumatic acting-out in which one is haunted or possessed by the past and performatively caught up in the compulsive repetition of traumatic scenes—scenes in which the past returns and the future is blocked or fatalistically caught up in a melancholic feedback loop. In acting-out, tenses implode and it is as if one were back there in the past reliving the traumatic scene. Any duality (or double inscription) of time (past and present or future) is experientially collapsed or productive only of aporias and double-binds. In this sense, the aporia and the double-bind might be seen as marking a trauma that has not been worked through. Working-through is an articulatory practice: to the extent one works

27. Derrida questioned Barthes's opposition particularly with respect to a notion of the full presence of discursive time unmarked by the past, and he asserted that "the distinction between discursive time and historical time becomes fragile, perhaps" (155). I later argue that the problematic, perhaps fragile, distinction between discursive and historical time, or between present and past, is nonetheless especially significant with respect to acting-out and working-through. This distinction of course does not deny that the present is marked by the past and, in certain ways, haunted by revenants.

through trauma (as well as transferential relations in general), one is able to distinguish between past and present and to recall in memory that something happened to one (or one's people) back then while realizing that one is living here and now with openings to the future. This does not imply either that there is a pure opposition between past and present or that acting-out—whether for the traumatized or for those empathetically relating to them—can be fully transcended toward a state of closure or full ego-identity. But it does mean that processes of working-through may counteract the force of acting-out and the repetition compulsion. These processes of working-through, including mourning and modes of critical thought and practice, involve the possibility of making distinctions or developing articulations that are recognized as problematic but still function as limits and as possibly desirable resistances to undecidability, particularly when the latter is tantamount to confusion and the obliteration or blurring of all distinctions (states that may indeed occur in trauma or in acting-out post-traumatic conditions).[28]

Those traumatized by extreme events, as well as those empathizing with them, may resist working-through because of what might almost be termed a fidelity to trauma, a feeling that one must somehow keep faith with it. Part of this feeling may be the melancholic sentiment that, in working through the past in a manner that enables survival or a re-engagement in life, one is betraying those who were overwhelmed and consumed by that traumatic past. One's bond with the dead, especially with dead intimates, may invest trauma with value and make its reliving a painful but necessary commemoration or memorial to which one remains dedicated or at least bound. This situation may create a more or less unconscious desire to remain within trauma. It certainly invalidates any form of conceptual or narrative closure, and it may also generate resistances to the role of any counterforces, for example, those involved in mourning understood not simply as isolated grieving or endless bereavement but as a social process that may be at least partly effective in returning one to the demands and responsibilities of social life. Moreover, on a somewhat different level, there has been an important tendency in modern culture and thought to convert trauma into the occasion for sublimity, to transvalue it into a test of the self or the group and an entry into the extraordi-

---

28. One may also correlate acting-out and working-through with Walter Benjamin's notions of *Erlebnis* and *Erfahrung*—at least if these concepts are understood in a certain way. Trauma and its post-traumatic acting-act, reliving, or re-enactment are modes of *Erlebnis*—"experience" that is often radically disorienting and chaotic. Working-through is a mode of *Erfahrung* which need not be seen in stereotypically Hegelian terms as implying full dialectical transcendence or narrative closure.

nary. In the sublime, the excess of trauma becomes an uncanny source of elation or ecstasy. Even extremely destructive and disorienting events, such as the Holocaust or the dropping of atomic bombs on Hiroshima and Nagasaki, may become occasions of negative sublimity or displaced sacralization. They may also give rise to what may be termed founding traumas—traumas that paradoxically become the valorized or intensely cathected basis of identity for an individual or a group rather than events that pose the problematic question of identity.

Various modes of signification provide relatively safe havens for exploring the complex relations between acting out and working through trauma. Some of the most powerful forms of modern art and writing, as well as some of the most compelling forms of criticism (including forms of deconstruction), often seem to be traumatic writing or post-traumatic writing in closest proximity to trauma. They may also involve the feeling of keeping faith with trauma in a manner that leads to a compulsive preoccupation with aporia, an endlessly melancholic, impossible mourning, and a resistance to working-through. I think one is involved here in more or less secularized displacements of the sacred and its paradoxes. The hiddenness, death, or absence of a radically transcendent divinity or of absolute foundations makes of existence a fundamentally traumatic scene in which anxiety threatens to color, and perhaps confuse, all relations. One's relation to every other—instead of involving a tense, at times paradoxical, interaction of proximity and distance, solidarity and criticism, trust and wariness—may be figured on the model of one's anxiety-ridden "relation without relation" to a radically transcendent (now perhaps recognized as absent) divinity who is totally other. This is, of course, precisely the situation of everyone as described in Derrida's *Gift of Death*.[29]

Sacrifice—what Derrida discusses as the gift of death—is a mode of performatively re-enacting traumatic scenes in which victimization is combined with oblation or gift-giving (typically with the victim as the gift), a type of activity which, in its undisplaced or unsublimated form, involves actual killing.[30] Derrida stresses the excess of generosity or gift-giving and

29. Trans. David Wells (Chicago: University of Chicago Press, [1992] 1995).

30. Sacrifice itself can be seen as a relatively safe haven only on the problematic assumption that the institution of sacrifice, by localizing anxiety and projecting blame onto a particular victim—a scapegoat who is often an outsider to the community or one of its weak members not having the support of a potentially vengeful group—functions to limit a more generalized sacrificial crisis involving indiscriminate violence. Yet the scapegoating in sacrifice is bound up with binary oppositions (self and other, insider and outsider) that, in their putatively pure form, can become extremely unstable, as "suspect" insiders are projected to the outside and violence returns to characterize relations within the community that seemed to protect itself by selecting a discrete victim or set of victims. On these problems, compare the views of René Gi-

elides the problem of the victim in *The Gift of Death*. But disseminatory writing, as a supplement of the deconstruction of binaries which undercuts the basis of a scapegoating process, might be seen as a symbolic displacement of sacrifice which distributes the disarticulated, torn-apart, or fragmented self in a radically decentered discourse, perhaps in the hope of symbolically playing out a sacrificial process devoid of a differentiated, discriminated-against scapegoat or victim. The deconstruction of binary oppositions that subtend and are regenerated in sacrifice would thus be supplemented by their general displacement and the attempt to undo sacrifice, requiring a discrete victim—an attempt made in and through disseminatory writing that generalizes (rather than projectively localizing) anxiety, enacts (in the dual sense of both acting out and in part working through) transference, and scatters seeds of the self in signifying practices. Open to question is the manner in which this process may be related to the elaboration of problematic but nonarbitrary distinctions, judgments, and decisions required for responsible thought and practice as well as to the generation of alternative institutions necessary for an ongoing society and polity.

In any case, it is significant that as his primary "performative" example of the middle voice as distinguished from the active voice, Barthes himself invokes sacrifice, something White mentions without commentary in a footnote. Barthes writes (and here writing may, in a rather analytic, affectless manner, seem to be implicated in traumatization and to displace sacrifice):

> According to the classic example, given by Meillet and Benveniste, the verb *to sacrifice* (ritually) is active if the priest sacrifices the victim in my place for me, and it is middle voice if, taking the knife from the priest's hands, I make the sacrifice for myself. In the case of the active, the action is accomplished outside the subject, because, although the priest makes the sacrifice, he is not affected by it. In the case of the middle voice, on the contrary, the subject affects himself in acting; he always remains inside the action, even if an object is involved. The middle voice does not, therefore, exclude transitivity. Thus defined, the middle voice corresponds exactly to the state of the verb *to write*. (142)

Hayden White proposes the middle voice in undifferentiated terms as the proper way of representing the Holocaust. In a seeming performa-

---

rard, *Violence and the Sacred*, trans. Patrick Gregory (Baltimore: Johns Hopkins University Press, [1972] 1977) and *Things Hidden since the Foundation of the World*, trans. Stephen Bann and Michael Metteer (Stanford: Stanford University Press, [1978] 1987).

tive contradiction, he even writes that the middle voice is the way to represent realistically not only the Holocaust but modern experience in general:

> The best way to represent the Holocaust and the experience of it may well be by a kind of "intransitive writing" which lays no claim to the kind of realism aspired to by the nineteenth-century historians and writers. But we may want to consider that by intransitive writing we must intend something like the relationship to that event expressed in the middle voice. This is not to suggest that we will give up the effort to represent the Holocaust realistically, but rather that our notion of what constitutes realistic representation must be revised to take account of experiences that are unique to our century and for which older modes of representation have proven inadequate. (52)

Notions of uniqueness aside, perhaps the most generous way to interpret this passage is to see in it *both* an attempt to evoke the question of truth-claims in historiography (as well as in fiction) *and* a call for a traumatic realism that somehow attempts to come to terms, affectively and cognitively, with limit-experiences involving trauma and its aftereffects. What nonetheless remains questionable is White's indiscriminate affirmation of the middle voice as the only mode of representation suitable for the Holocaust and modernity in general, an affirmation that would seem to prescribe an insufficiently modulated rhetoric or mode of discourse and rule out or undermine the pertinence of third-person referential statements, direct quotations, and summaries or paraphrases. One may even ask in what sense it is possible to make truth-claims in the middle voice and to what extent that question is suspended by its use. In any case, without further qualification White's generalized middle voice would seem to imply a basically similar or at least insufficiently differentiated treatment of Hitler, Jewish Councils, victims of concentration and death camps, and others in significantly different subject-positions.

What is also elided in White's account, as in Barthes's (or in Derrida's *Gift of Death*), is the problem of the victim and the force of the distinction between victim and perpetrator. A rashly generalized middle voice would seem to undercut or undo systematically not only the binary opposition but any distinction, however problematic in certain cases, between victim and perpetrator, as it would seem to undercut the problems of agency and responsibility in general (except insofar as one is willing to identify responsibility with decisionism or an ungrounded if not blind leap of faith). Moreover, it would accord with White's dubious tendency to envision the Holocaust as an undifferentiated scene of horror and negative sublimity—a scene beneath or beyond ethical considerations and calling for representation in the middle voice. What would seem to be required (but lacking in White) is an account of relations of the middle voice to other uses of language as well as a subtle exploration of actual and desirable modulations of the middle voice itself in discourse addressing various, at times very different, topics or others.

One may further note that White's approach is facilitated, and its dubiousness concealed, by something implicit in Barthes's account and made explicit, but not recognized as dubious, in White's. The problem of the victim and the distinction between victim and perpetrator (or sacrificer) may be readily elided or obscured if one assumes the unproblematic identification of perpetrator and victim—or at least of observer or secondary witness and victim.[31] This identification is most plausible in the case of self-sacrifice. It is altogether dubious in the case of the sacrifice of another, whatever the bond between the sacrificer and sacrificed or between the sacrificed and the secondary witness. It is noteworthy that White cites as a case of middle voice Berel Lang's example, which (at least in White's rendering) involves unproblematic identification: "Lang explicitly commends intransitive writing (and speech) as appropriate to individual Jews who, as in the recounting of the story of the Exodus at Passover, 'should tell the story of the genocide as though he or she had passed through it' and in an exercise of self-identification specifically Jewish in nature" (48). I would observe that this form of identification is not specific to Jews. In fact it has been criticized by some Jews—one may recall the title of Hilberg's article from which I quoted earlier: "I Was Not There." And the analogy between the Holocaust and ritual recounting of the Exodus at Passover would seem pertinent only within a frame of reference that uncritically makes the Holocaust the sacralized center of a civil religion.[32]

31. By identification I mean the unmediated fusion of self and other in which the otherness or alterity of the other is not recognized and respected. It may involve what Melanie Klein treats as projective identification, in which aspects not acknowledged in the self are attributed to the other. It may also involve incorporation in which aspects of the other are taken into or encrypted in the self. Projective identification and incorporation may be necessary and inevitable processes in the relation of self and other—processes bound up with transference which are both particularly active with respect to highly "cathected" objects and especially pronounced in trauma and its aftermath. But counterforces to projective identification and incorporation may be generated in the self and society, and such counterforces are crucial for critical processes of inquiry, judgment, and practice. Moreover, empathy may be contrasted with identification (as fusion with the other) insofar as empathy marks the point at which the other is indeed recognized and respected as other, and one does not feel compelled or authorized to speak in the other's voice or take the other's place, for example, as surrogate victim or perpetrator. Not recognizing these points forms part of the problem in Giorgio Agamben's at times questionable argument in *Remnants of Auschwitz: The Witness and the Archive*, trans. Daniel Heller-Roazen (New York: Zone Books, 1999).

32. On these issues, see Charles Maier, "A Surfeit of Memory? Reflections on History, Melancholy, and Denial," *History & Memory* 5 (1992): 136–51; Anson Rabinbach, "From Ex-

Unchecked identification implies a confusion of self and other which may bring an incorporation of the experience and voice of the victim and its re-enactment or acting-out. As in acting-out in general, one possessed, however vicariously, by the past and reliving its traumatic scenes may be tragically incapable of acting responsibly or behaving in an ethical manner involving consideration for others as others. One need not blame the victim possessed by the past and unable to get beyond it to any viable extent in order to question the idea that it is desirable to identify with this victim, or to become a surrogate victim, and to write (or perform) in that incorporated voice. At least in its ability to question a rash generalization of the middle voice as a mode of writing or representation, Jean-Pierre Vernant's intervention after the delivery of Barthes's essay is worth quoting:

> [The middle voice designates] the type of action where the agent remains enveloped in the released action. Barthes considers that this furnishes a metaphorical model for the present state of writing. Then I would ask, is it by accident that the middle voice disappeared in the evolution of Indo-European? Already in ancient Greece the opposition was no longer situated between the active and the middle voice but between the active and the passive voice, so that the middle voice became a sort of vestige with which linguists wondered what to do. . . . In thought as expressed in Greek or ancient Indo-European there is no idea of the agent being the *source* of his action. Or, if I may translate that, as a historian of Greek civilization, there is no category of the *will* in Greece. But what we see in the Western world, through language, the evolution of law, the creation of a vocabulary of the will, is precisely the idea of the human subject as agent, the source of actions, creating them, assuming them, carrying responsibility for them. Therefore, what I ask you, Barthes, is this: Are we seeing, in the literary domain, a complete reversal of this evolution and do you believe that we are going to see, on the literary level, the reappearance of the middle voice in the linguistic domain? (152)

One may refer to the text for Barthes's answer, which I do not believe is up to the question (however contestable some of the latter's features may be).[33] Vernant's question suggests the manner in which the middle voice (and issues connected with it) may be further related to the Heideggerian "step back" (at times figured as a recourse to the pre-Socratic). The latter

---

plosion to Erosion: Holocaust Memorialization in America since Bitburg," *History & Memory* 9 (1997): 226–55; and Peter Novick, *The Holocaust in American Life* (Boston: Houghton Mifflin, 1999).

33. Vernant seems to have an unproblematic notion of the agent as creative source of his or her action as well as of the will as a category. I would further note that the free indirect style (or *Erlebte Rede*) is one more or less guarded mode of returning discursively to the middle voice. It is, in my judgment, an internally dialogized mode of discourse involving varying degrees of proximity and distance—not necessarily identification—between narrator and narrated ob-

converts the seemingly vestigial middle voice into a returning repressed and eventuates in a mode of discourse which, in insistently remaining undecidable, is suspicious of will as the most recent avatar of the metaphysical foundation. It simultaneously undercuts ethical discourse as superficial with respect to the call of Being (a call presumably to be answered in some discursive or poetic variant that recalls the middle voice). The larger question, as I suggested, is that of the possibilities and limits of the middle voice with respect to a wide range of issues, notably the legitimate role of distinctions and the problems of agency and ethical responsibility, including the ability to distinguish among accounts that are more or less true as well as among degrees of responsibility or liability in action.

In a sense one's response to the role of the middle voice may be intimately bound up with one's response to re-enacting or acting out trauma in relation to attempts to work it through. In my own tentative judgment, the use in historiography of some discursive analogue of the middle voice might be most justified with respect to one's most tangled and difficult relations of proximity and distance with respect to the other, notably when one is moved, even shaken or unsettled, in such a manner that one is unable or unwilling to judge or even to predicate with any degree of confidence. Hence something like a middle voice that suspended judgment or approached it only in the most tentative terms might be called for with respect to ambiguous figures in Primo Levi's gray zone, for example, certain well-intentioned but deceived and at times self-deceived members of Jewish Councils (such as Adam Czerniakow of the Warsaw Ghetto) who were indeed caught in double-binds not of their own making.[34] It might also be pertinent—and extremely difficult of attainment—in the case of certain victims who were also perpetrators, notably someone like Tadeusz Borowski, who reacted to his experience in an excruciating, unsettling manner both demanding and repelling the empathy of the reader.[35] The fate of certain victims in even more dire and less compromising circumstances is often such that it makes the use of any voice problematic for the historian, notably including a voice that enacts identification. In any

---

jects or characters, and it approaches undecidability at the limit. I also think there are problems in its indiscriminate use or rash generalization. For a discussion of free indirect style, see my *"Madame Bovary" on Trial*, chap. 6.

34. Levi recommends caution in judgment even with respect to the very compromised Chaim Rumkowski whose story "sums up in itself the entire theme of the gray zone and leaves one dangling." (*The Drowned and the Saved*, New York: Random House, [1986] 1989, 66–7) One of Agamben's most questionable moves in *Remnants of Auschwitz* is to generalize the gray zone into a zone of indeterminacy that collapses the distinction between perpetrator and victim.

35. See *This Way for the Gas, Ladies and Gentlemen*, selected and trans. Barbara Vedder, intro. Jan Kott (New York: Penguin Books, [1959] 1976).

event, the use of the middle voice would require modulations of proximity and distance, empathy and irony with respect to different "objects" of investigation, and it need not be understood as ruling out all forms of objectivity and objectification.

In yet another, more affirmative register, there is a sense in which the middle voice may be related to an unheard-of utopia of generosity or gift-giving beyond, or in excess of, calculation, positions, judgment, and victimization of the other. It may also exceed both delimited conceptions of justice and historiography in any form we would now recognize. The question is whether one can immediately leap to that utopia discursively (even deny that it is a utopia) or, assuming at least its partial value, it has to be approached or approximated in a different, more modulated and qualified fashion requiring the countervailing force of normative limits and the role of critical thought and practice. In realistic terms, the further question is whether or to what extent the unqualified enactment of what strives to be an affirmative middle-voiced (a)positionality attests to, or even furthers, a movement away from a binary, sacrificial logic and any totalizing belief that a regulative ideal (such as justice) may be fully realized (a movement that is in my judgment desirable) toward a problematic condition of social emergency or crisis marked by the generalization of trauma as trope, the conflation of the exception and the rule, the collapse of distinctions in an all-consuming zone of indeterminacy, arbitrary decision (or leaps of secular faith across antinomic or anomic abysses), extreme anxiety, and disorientation if not panic. It is unclear whether discourse in the middle voice, particularly when it is not supplemented and checked by other uses of language, is able to provide viable indications of desirable social and cultural articulations, including institutions and practices, other than in the generalized terms of a state of crisis or excess and open-ended hope (or messianicity without a messiah) that may induce indiscriminate hyperbole and undecidability (as well as a "contagiously" manneristic style at times verging on preciosity) in the face of proliferating aporias or double-binds.[36] In any case, to the extent that the notion of

---

36. Derrida himself rejects the applicability of the notion of "utopianism" to his thought with respect to "messianicity" (even to the point of seemingly denying in this crucial instance the displacement of the religious in the secular). However, he does so in questionable terms that might be read as affirming utopianism in another, "here-now" sense: "Messianicity (which I regard as a universal structure of experience, and which cannot be reduced to religious messianism of any stripe) is anything but Utopian: it refers, in every here-now, to the coming of an eminently real, concrete event, that is, to the most irreducibly heterogeneous otherness. Nothing is more 'realistic' or 'immediate' than this messianic apprehension, straining forward toward the event of him who/that which is coming. I say 'apprehension,' because this experience, strained forward toward the event, is at the same time a waiting without expectation [*une attente sans attente*] (an active preparation, anticipation against the backdrop of a horizon, but

a discursive analogue of the middle voice does indeed harbor an affirmative or even utopian dimension, it would be desirable to explicate that dimension as clearly and fully as possible in order to facilitate informed attempts to evaluate it and submit it critically to reality-testing without which affirmation becomes empty and utopianism is tantamount to wishful thinking and political romanticism.[37]

Without prejudging other possibilities, I would like to evoke a recent case in which the middle voice and undecidability are at issue in a particularly troubling and dubious manner. I am referring to Binjamin Wilkomirski's *Fragments: Memories of a Wartime Childhood*.[38] First thought to be the memoir of a child survivor of a concentration camp, the book has been called into question in that its author may never have been in a camp—indeed may have been born not in 1938 in Latvia but in 1941 in Switzerland. Problems of Holocaust denial and recovered memory make this case particularly controversial. And recent revelations concerning the retention and concealment of victims' wealth in Swiss banks have made Switzerland an object of special scrutiny.

I would enumerate at least four possibilities in the writing and reading of Wilkomirski's book. First, one may take it as a memoir, and this is the way it frames itself. It contains certain skeptical notes that may be read retrospectively to raise the question of whether the book at rare moments signals its fictionality, for example, the narrator's confused memories ("I was maybe ten or twelve, I just don't know" [139]) or the statement—

---

also exposure without horizon, and therefore an irreducible amalgam of desire and anguish, affirmation and fear, promise and threat). . . . This is an ineluctability whose imperative, always here-now, in singular fashion, can in no case yield to the allure of Utopia, at least not to what the word literally signifies or is ordinarily taken to mean." "Marx & Sons" in *Ghostly Demarcations: A Symposium on Jacques Derrida's Specters of Marx*, ed. Michael Sprinker (London: Verso, 1999), 248–49. The question, however, is the role of thought and practice in transitional or intermediate zones that fall neither at the extreme of universality nor at that of singularity (or "the most irreducibly heterogeneous otherness") as well as whether Derrida, especially in his more recent work ostensibly concerned with social and political issues, devotes to it the sustained attention it merits.

37. See the rather utopian, "deconstructive" approach to the "other" and trust in Derek Attridge, "Innovation, Literature, Ethics: Relating to the Other" in *PMLA* 114 (1999): 20–31 (special issue, *Ethics and Literary Study*, ed. Lawrence Buell). Attridge tries to combine the notion (derived from Derrida and Levinas) that every other is totally other with an affirmation of total trust in that other, who is an unknown stranger and may be a "monster." His argument includes the idea that responsibility for the other is not obligation, nor is it codified in any way: instead it is total openness and trust. This idea of trust seems devoid of all reality-testing and is other-worldly in the sense that it would require a total transformation of historical conditions to enable one to distinguish it from utter gullibility. The context of German-Jewish relations in the Shoah casts an especially uncanny light on Attridge's argument. (The issue of *PMLA* in which Attridge's essay appears includes an interesting set of instances of the state of reflection on ethics in literary studies today.)

38. Trans. Carol Brown Janeway (New York: Schocken Books, [1995] 1996).

ironic in different ways before and after the charges of imposture—that, in Switzerland, "everyone keeps saying I'm to forget, that it never happened, I only dreamed it" (129). But the doubts could readily be attributed to the confusion and disarray of a traumatized child from whose perspective the book is written. And certain events recounted in the book (such as tiny babies eating their own frozen fingers down to the bone [70–71]) may be seen with twenty-twenty hindsight as implausible. Still, what is plausible or implausible in events of the Holocaust is notoriously difficult to determine. And the book was initially accepted by many Holocaust experts and even by survivors and former hidden children (such as Saul Friedlander, who is an author of a memoir concerning his own childhood experiences). The book was obviously taken as authentic by those who granted it numerous awards, including the Jewish Book Award and the Prix de la Mémoire de la Shoah. The back cover of the paperback edition includes quotations from reviews that indicate how it was read. Jonathan Kozol wrote in the *Nation*: "This stunning and austerely written work is so profoundly moving, so morally important, and so free from literary artifice of any kind at all that I wonder if I even have the right to try to offer praise." And the blurb states unequivocally: "An extraordinary memoir of a small boy who spent his childhood in the Nazi death camps. Beautifully written, with an indelible impact that makes this a book that is not read but experienced." Indeed the passionate nature (but certainly not the existence or even the strength) of the negative reaction to the disclosure of Wilkomirski's possible if not probable imposture is related to the initial widespread acceptance of the book as a genuine memoir and the feeling of trust betrayed in the event it is not.

Second, one may take the book as fiction, but, as I have noted, this is not the way it is framed or presents itself. If it were explicitly framed as fiction, one might marvel at its ability to evoke certain feelings and states of mind in a remarkably empathetic fashion (although, once it is removed from actual experience of life in the camps, one might also see the book not as "austerely written" but at least at times as somewhat overwritten). Still, one might understand it as involving truth-claims not in terms of certain individual statements (such as those involving the identity of the author-narrator) but on more general levels, for example, with respect to how children in the camps might well have experienced certain events.

Third, one may take the book as a pathological case history of someone who may actually imagine or believe he was in a concentration camp as a child even if he was not. This reading might conceivably be justified, but it could easily function to eliminate disconcerting questions raised by the relation of the book to history and fiction. (Briefly put, my own view here is that one should have empathy for the author but provide criticism of the book as it bears on the public sphere—a distinction easily collapsed in a "clinical" approach to problems.)

Fourth, one can simply moot or bracket the question of the book's author or the status of his experience and see the text as undecidable with respect to its status as fiction or memoir. One might then analyze it either along with other works of fiction or with other memoirs. (Or perhaps one might see it as belonging to an emerging hybridized genre: the *faux mémoire.*) This as-you-like-it response seems to be recommended by Wilkomirski himself who stated in an interview: "It was always left freely up to readers to regard my book either as literature or as a personal document."[39]

But this affirmation of the undecidability of the text which leaves any decision or choice concerning its status up to the reader does not seem acceptable, and it may well be that some hybrids (such as the *faux mémoire*) are, in certain instances, undesirable. Indeed, Wilkomirski's is a case in which the appeal to undecidability seems inappropriate even if one were to claim that Wilkomirski was traumatized in a displaced or secondary manner by events of the Holocaust (or, as may be suggested at one point in the narrative, by a documentary film about it [148]) and wrote his book while reliving an imaginary or phantasmatic past he had never experienced in historical reality.[40]

My own views have partially emerged in my discussion and critique of others'. Since I have written extensively on them in other places, I shall be brief in stating them in condensed form here. I would begin by noting that the position I defend puts forth a conception of history as tensely involving both an objective (not objectivist) reconstruction of the past and a dialogic exchange with it and other inquirers into it wherein knowledge involves not only the processing of information but also affect, empathy, and questions of value.[41] This third position is not a straightforward dialectical synthesis of the other two, for it involves a critical and self-critical component that resists closure. Moreover, it does not simply eliminate hyperbole for a middling or *juste-milieu* reasonableness if not complacency. It involves the recognition of the possibly thought-provoking and fruitful role of hyperbole in emphasizing what one believes is given insufficient

39. Quoted in *Newsweek*, November 16, 1998, 84.

40. After I completed this chapter, there appeared Ellen Lappin's "The Man with Two Heads," *Granta* 66 (1999): 7–65, whose extensive analysis of Wilkomirski and his book may be compared with the brief one I offer.

41. For the importance of self-contextualization of the historian in a contemporary context of exchange and debate with other inquirers, see my *Representing the Holocaust: History, Theory, Trauma* (Ithaca: Cornell University Press, 1994), chap. 3.

weight at a given time in the ongoing attempt to articulate possibilities in a discipline or in the broader culture. (In this sense it may be justifiable, at a certain point in the history of historiography, to stress the role of rhetoric and performativity insofar as they are indeed largely ignored or downplayed and one does not see them as the exclusive generative or self-referential basis of a conception of the past.)[42] There may even be a legitimate role for polemic and parody as dialogic modes in a larger contest or agon of points of view or discourses. Hyperbole enacts stylistically the fact that one is affected by excess and trauma, but one can be excessive in many ways, prominently including a penchant for blandly generalized, unearned judiciousness that harmonizes problems and may even signal a numbing insensitivity to their import and implications. Still, the position I am defending does not entail a simple insertion within, or unrestrained enactment or acting-out of, hyperbole and excess. Instead it affirms the value of a difficultly achieved interaction between limits and excess, including the idea that hyperbole should in certain ways be framed as hyperbole (hence to some extent limited) and distinguished from other modes of address—including more understated and balanced ones—which may be called for in certain situations.

Truth-claims are at issue in differential ways at all levels of historical discourse. But the writings of Ankersmit, White, and others have, I think, made it evident that one cannot affirm a conventional stereotype of transparent representation or even a self-sufficient research paradigm. I think one begins investigation already inserted in an ongoing historical process, a positioning toward which one may attempt to acquire some transformative perspective or critical purchase. A crucial aspect of this positioning is the problem of the implication of the observer in the observed—what in psychoanalytic terms is treated as transference. Indeed, there is a sense in which transference indicates that one begins inquiry in a middle-voiced "position," which one engages in various ways. In historiography there are transferential relations between inquirers (especially pronounced in the relations between professor and graduate student) and between inquirers and the past, its figures, and processes. The basic sense of transference I would stress is the tendency to repeat or reenact performatively in one's own discourse or relations processes active in—or projected into—the object of study. I think transference in this sense occurs willy-nilly, and the problem is how one comes to terms with it in ways involving various com-

42. In this respect, see my "Rhetoric and History," in *History and Criticism*, 15–44. The argument there should be seen as complementing and supplementing the approach I develop in the present chapter. It should not be conflated with the radically constructivist positions taken by Hayden White or Frank Ankersmit.

binations, more or less subtle variations, and hybridized forms of acting-out and working-through.

As I have intimated, the question of experience (to which several historians have recently turned) is important in these respects—but experience not as an uncritically invoked, foundational concept or as an undifferentiated ground of historiography.[43] Rather, one has a series of interrelated problems involving the question of experience. For example, what is the relation between experience and non-experiential aspects of history such as demographic movements, price fluctuations, and objectified structural processes in general? How may one criticize a methodology focused only on objectified processes or employing only objectified modes of representation yet raise the question of objectivity in a post-positivist and post-deconstructive way?[44] What is the relation between the differentiated experience of agents or subjects in the past and the differentiated experience of observers or secondary witnesses, including historians in one of their roles, in a present marked in complicated ways by that past? How does one relate actual and imaginary or virtual experience? How is experience related to truth-claims and to critical value judgments? How does trauma—or traumatic "experience"—disrupt experience and raise specific problems for representation and writing? What is the gap or even the abyss between historical experience and utopian projects, including that intimated in certain discursive analogues of the middle voice?[45]

43. For some caveats about the concept of experience, see my "History, Language, and Reading," 822–24. In his diary entry for April 25, 1937, Victor Klemperer makes this chilling observation: "An always recurring word: 'Experience.' Whenever some Gauleiter or SS leader, one of the minor and most minor subordinate gods speaks, then one does not hear his speech, but 'experiences' it. Eva [Klemperer's non-Jewish wife] rightly says it was already there before National Socialism. Certainly, it is to be found in the currents that created it." *I Will Bear Witness: A Diary of the Nazi Years 1933–1941*, trans. Martin Chalmers (New York: Random House, [1995] 1998), 216. Klemperer was a German Jew (converted to Protestantism) who managed to live in Dresden through various forms of oppression throughout the Third Reich, and he strongly affirmed Enlightenment values. His observation should be seen as applying to one possible, important use (or abuse) of the concept of experience. It nonetheless serves to indicate that experience should not indiscriminately be seen as positive. See also Bernard Lepetit, ed., *Les formes de l'expérience: Une autre histoire sociale* (Paris: Albin Michel, 1995) and Jacques Revel, ed., *Jeux d'échelles: La micro-analyse à l'expérience* (Paris: Gallimard-Le Seuil, 1996). The turn to microhistory involves a concern for a history of experience, notably in figures such as Carlo Ginzburg and Giovanni Levi.

44. Satya Mohanty provides insight into this question in *Literary Theory and the Claims of History* (Ithaca: Cornell University Press, 1997). See also the excellent book of James Berger, *After the End: Representations of Post-apocalypse* (Minneapolis: University of Minnesota Press, 1999).

45. Compare Nietzsche: "Ultimately, nobody can get more out of things, including books, than he already knows. For what one lacks access to from experience one will have no ear. Now let us imagine an extreme case: that a book speaks of nothing but events that lie altogether beyond the possibility of any frequent or even rare experience—that it is the first language for a

I shall not pretend to answer these important questions. Rather, I would conclude by contending that the problem of experience should lead to the question of the role of empathy in historical understanding. This question was, at least in restricted ways, important for such figures as Wilhelm Dilthey and R. G. Collingwood but has by and large been stricken from the historical agenda in the more recent past.[46] One reason for the eclipse of concern with empathy was the relation of the ideal of objectivity to the professionalization of historiography along with the tendency to conflate objectivity with unrestrained objectification.[47] A closely related tendency, which facilitated the dismissal of empathy, was to conflate it with intuition or unproblematic identification implying the total fusion of self and other. Any attempt, however qualified, to rehabilitate a concern with empathy in historical understanding must distinguish it from these traditional conflations (as well as from patronizing sympathy). It must also critically engage professional identities or research strategies that marginalize or even eliminate the role of empathy along with dialogic exchange and affective (in contrast to narrowly cognitive) response in general. Especially open to question is a strategy of objectification and sustained ironic distance allowing only for unargued subjective asides—a

---

new series of experiences. In that case, simply nothing will be heard, but there will be the acoustic illusion that where nothing is heard, nothing is there." *Ecce Homo* ("Why I Write Such Good Books") in *The Genealogy of Morals and Ecce Homo*, ed. Walter Kaufmann (New York: Vintage Books, [1967] 1989), 261.

46. I employ the term *empathy* while trying to distance it from conventional or traditional associations with identification leading to a putative identity between self and other, whether through projection or incorporation. I am not employing *sympathy* both because that term has to some degree the connotation of condescension or pity (at least a superior position of the sympathizer) and because it has been commodified through its use in greeting cards and other relatively affectless or evacuated modes of expressing sorrow or fellow feeling. Moreover, *empathy* is the term that has a history both in historiography (or metahistory) and in psychoanalytic literature. One might, however, prefer the term *compassion*.

47. In *That Noble Dream* Peter Novick, in treating the role of objectivity in the historical profession, tends to replicate his sources in largely ignoring an explicit treatment of the problem of empathy, and the term does not appear in his index. Nor is Dilthey mentioned in the book. There are a few references to R. G. Collingwood. But it is significant that Collingwood's notion of historical explanation as rethinking or re-experiencing the past had little to do with affect and trauma. Collingwood praised Dilthey for conceiving of "the historian as living in his object, or rather making his object live in him." See *The Idea of History* (New York: Oxford University Press, [1946] 1956), 172. But he criticized Dilthey for positivistically understanding knowledge on the model of natural scientific universals and reducing history to psychology. Collingwood's idea of historical knowledge as the re-enactment of past experience in the historian's own mind was, however, largely focused on rethinking (or reawakening in the present) particular, reflective (or purposive), often rather elevated processes of deliberation such as an emperor's dealing with a certain situation or a philosopher's seeking a solution to a problem (283). Hence William Dray could plausibly be seen as taking up Collingwood's heritage in elaborating a "rational action" model of explanation explicitly linked to a libertarian metaphysical position. (See Novick, 397.)

strategy that both induces a denial of transferential implication in the object of study and obviates the problem of the actual and desirable interactions between self and other, including the possibilities and limits of a discursive middle voice.[48]

Such an objectifying strategy may well posit or assume a radical divide between objectivity and subjectivity (as well as between research and dialogic exchange) and lead to an either/or conception of the relation between empathy and critical analysis. When this occurs, objectification may be confined to treatment of the other, and subjectivity (or even radical constructivism) attributed to contemporaries or even the historian's own self, thereby obscuring the voices of the dead and the problem of one's own subject positions, projective tendencies, and investments. The historian may even eliminate or overly alleviate the diachronic weight of the past, including the after-effects of trauma, by seeing the past only in terms of contemporary uses and abuses, for example, as symbolic capital in memory politics.[49]

I think historiography involves an element of objectification, and objectification may perhaps be related to the phenomenon of numbing in trauma itself. As a counterforce to numbing, empathy may be understood in terms of attending to, even trying, in limited ways, to recapture the possibly split-off, affective dimension of the experience of others. Empathy may also be seen as counteracting victimization, including self-victimization. It involves affectivity as a crucial aspect of understanding in the historian or other observer or analyst. As in trauma, numbing (objectification and splitting of object from subject, including self-as-subject from self-as-object) may function for the historian as a protective shield or preservative against unproblematic identification with the experience of

48. Of the many works relying on such a strategy, I would mention only Richard J. Evans, *In Defense of History* (New York: W. W. Norton, 1997). The principal text, an objectifying, rapid survey of recent developments in historiography and metahistory, is supplemented by a section entitled "Further Reading," in which opinionated, subjective asides are adorned by a generous assortment of bouquets for some and barbs for others.

49. Such an orientation may be found even in Peter Novick's important *Holocaust in American Life* where—rather than being seen as possibly complementary to his concerns—the investigation of the problem of trauma, except in survivors, is "overall" seen as irrelevant in the case of Americans and opposed to a presentist, constructivist, at times debunking notion of historical understanding in terms of the uses and abuses of the Holocaust in "memory politics" (3–5). This orientation prevents Novick from elaborating a sufficiently complex and nuanced account of the transgenerational transmission of trauma (especially with respect to the children of survivors), the various (at times problematic) functions of trauma in the larger culture, and the role of empathy in historical understanding itself. Still, when detached from binarist, radically constructivist assumptions, inquiry into contemporary uses and "constructions" of the past is significant, including the constitution of the Holocaust as an identity-building icon and center of a civil religion—inquiry that Novick's book undertakes in a thought-provoking (indeed intentionally controversial and at times debatable) manner.

others and the possibility of being traumatized by it. But objectivity should not be identified with objectivism or exclusive objectification that denies or forecloses empathy, just as empathy should not be conflated with unchecked identification, vicarious experience, and surrogate victimage. Objectivity requires checks and resistances to full identification, and this is one important function of meticulous research, contextualization, and the attempt to be as attentive as possible to the voices of others whose alterity is recognized. Empathy in this sense is a form of virtual—not vicarious—experience related to what Kaja Silverman has termed *heteropathic identification* in which emotional response comes with respect for the other and the realization that the experience of the other is not one's own.[50]

Hence the experience, including the affective response, of the historian is at issue in a number of complicated ways with respect to understanding (or knowledge in a broad sense that includes cognition but is not limited to it). It helps to define the subject-positions of the historian and may serve as an initial warrant to speak in certain voices. In discussing the Holocaust, for example, it makes a difference—at least an initial difference—whether the historian is a survivor, the child of survivors, a Jew, a Palestinian, a German or an Austrian, a child of perpetrators, someone born later, and so forth—with subtle distinctions and variations that it would take a very long time even to touch upon. But part of the process of inquiry—involving both research and an attempt at dialogic exchange with the past and other inquirers into it—is to work over and through initial subject-positions in a manner that may enable one to write or say certain things that one would not have been able or inclined to write or say initially. Identity politics in a necessary sense may be defined in terms of subject-positions and one's work with and on them. Identity politics in a dubious sense may be defined as simply repeating and further legitimating or acting out the subject-positions with which one begins without subjecting them to critical testing that may either change or in certain ways validate them.

The import of my comments is that experience in relation to historical understanding should not be seen in a narrowly cognitive way that involves only a processing of information. Without diminishing the importance of research, contextualization, and objective reconstruction of the past, experience as it bears on understanding involves affect both in the observed and in the observer. Trauma is a disruptive experience that disarticulates the self and creates holes in existence; it has belated effects that are controlled only with difficulty and perhaps never fully mastered.

50. See Kaja Silverman, *The Threshold of the Visible World* (New York: Routledge, 1996).

The study of traumatic events poses especially difficult problems in representation and writing both for research and for any dialogic exchange with the past which acknowledges the claims it makes on people and relates it to the present and future. Being responsive to the traumatic experience of others, notably of victims, implies not the appropriation of their experience but what I would call empathic unsettlement, which should have stylistic effects or, more broadly, effects in writing which cannot be reduced to formulas or rules of method. (With respect to perpetrators, who may also be traumatized by their experience, I would argue that the historian should attempt to understand and explain such behavior and experience as far as possible—even recognize the unsettling possibility of such behavior and experience in him- or herself—but obviously attempt to counteract the realization of even its reduced analogues.) At the very least empathic unsettlement poses a barrier to closure in discourse and places in jeopardy harmonizing or spiritually uplifting accounts of extreme events from which we attempt to derive reassurance or a benefit (for example, unearned confidence about the ability of the human spirit to endure any adversity with dignity and nobility).[51] The question is whether historiography in its own way may help not speciously to heal but to come to terms with the wounds and scars of the past. Such a coming-to-terms would seek knowledge whose truth-claims are not one-dimensionally objectifying or narrowly cognitive, but involve affect, and may empathetically expose the self to an unsettlement—if not a secondary trauma—which should not be glorified or fixated upon, but addressed in a manner that strives to be cognitively and ethically responsible as well as open to the challenge of utopian aspiration.

51. Anne Frank is a recent figure who has been subjected to representation that attempts to bring to the reader or viewer unearned and incongruous spiritual uplift. For a recent biography that ends in this manner, see Melissa Mueller, *Anne Frank: The Biography* (New York: Henry Holt, 1998).

Writing the Humanities in the Twenty-first Century

Hunter R. Rawlings III
(Classics, University President)

In the early 1940s, Cornell's distinguished historian Carl Becker grasped that a certain amount of contentiousness is essential in a great university when he characterized professors as people "who think otherwise."[1] "(T)he essential quality of a great university," Becker maintained,

> derives from the corporate activities of such a community of otherwise-thinking men (and women). By virtue of a divergence as well as of a community of interests, by the sharp impress of their minds and temperaments and eccentricities upon each other and upon their pupils, there is created a continuing tradition of ideas and attitudes and habitual responses that has a life of its own. It is this continuing tradition that gives to a university its corporate character or personality—that intangible but living and dynamic influence which is the richest and most durable gift any university can confer upon those who come to it for instruction and guidance.[2]

Becker goes on to relate the story of the well-known professor of history: "passionate defender of majority rule, who, foreseeing that he would be outvoted in the faculty on the question of the location of Risley Hall, declared with emotion that he felt so strongly on the subject that he thought he ought to have two votes."[3]

This chapter is drawn from "The Role of the Humanities in the Twenty-first Century," the welcoming address for a symposium in honor of Dale Corson held at Cornell University on December 6, 1999.

1. Carl L. Becker, *Cornell University: Founders and the Founding* (Ithaca, N.Y.: Cornell University Press, 1967), 193.
2. Ibid., 194.
3. Ibid., 195.

Dale Corson, who assumed the presidency of Cornell in 1969, in an especially difficult moment when extremes of "otherwise" threatened the "corporate activities" that Becker celebrated, understood, far better than most, what it takes to make a great university: a strong and "otherwise-thinking" faculty with deep loyalty to the university, a willingness to take students seriously, and above all, a commitment to academic freedom, to informed debate, and a critical spirit, which recognizes differences of opinion not as disasters but as opportunities for dialogue that can lead to new understanding. Many of the qualities embodied by both Corson and Becker will remain central to the success of America's research universities in the twenty-first century, even as we move into an era of large and rapid change. Though science will make remarkable discoveries and many headlines in the new century, the humanities will be crucial to understanding, preserving, and extending the essential qualities of a great university. They, perhaps more than any other constellation of fields, can help guide us—but only if they can reclaim their central place within the university and return to purposes that are both broad and deep.

A HISTORICAL PERSPECTIVE

In the mid-1940s, as World War II was ending, President Franklin D. Roosevelt asked Vannevar Bush, who was then directing the federal Office of Scientific Research and Development, to suggest how science, which had contributed so dramatically to the Allied victory in World War II, could best serve the nation in the postwar era. Bush's report, *Science: The Endless Frontier*, completed after Roosevelt's death and delivered to his successor, President Harry S. Truman, made the case that the federal government could best strengthen American industry by supporting basic research and developing scientific talent at American universities.[4] *Science: The Endless Frontier* set the stage for the development of the National Science Foundation (NSF) and for a partnership between the federal government and American research universities that continues to this day. That partnership, which has endured since its establishment in 1950, has helped create great science at America's universities and made them the envy of the world. Through this potent collaboration—not only with NSF, but also with the National Institutes of Health, the Department of Energy, the Office of Naval Research, NASA, and others—American universities have pursued research and graduate teaching hand in hand, thus reaping the benefits of a remark-

---

4. Office of Scientific Research and Development, *Science, the Endless Frontier: A Report to the President by Vannevar Bush, Director of the Office of Scientific Research and Development* (Washington, D.C.: U.S. Government Printing Office, 1945).

able synergy that cannot be found in government research laboratories or in liberal arts colleges without graduate and research programs. These universities now attract the best young minds from the entire world, and they have spawned the lion's share of Nobel Prizes and other research awards that testify to scientific leadership. Cornell University has been a key player in the federal government–university research partnership and one of its major beneficiaries, as well as one of its major contributors.

Dale Corson, who remained president until 1977, played a major role in positioning Cornell for leadership in several important research areas, including materials science. In the early 1960s, during a trip to Washington, he learned that the nuclear power industry was finding that materials didn't hold up in the high-radiation, high-temperature atmosphere of their reactors. In an article in *Cornell Magazine*, Corson recalled, "I had a friend on the Atomic Energy Commission who told me what was going on. So I visited the AEC and talked to some of my old friends in the defense department. When I came back, I went straight to Day Hall and said, 'Here are the possibilities and here's what we ought to be doing.' "[5] Cornell's Center for Materials Research, as well as the Wilson Laboratory, the Cornell High Energy Synchrotron Source, the Cornell Nanofabrication Facility, and other facilities continue to be recognized as national and world leaders in their fields. So productive was the university-government-industry partnership, as evidenced by Cornell's success, that when Dale Corson finished his term as president, he and his wife, Nellie, moved to Washington, D.C., where he founded the Government University Industry Research Roundtable and led efforts to encourage more collaboration among those three sectors.

From 1950 to 1990, then, we saw an expanding university-government partnership and a healthy injection of industrial participation, from which American universities have benefited enormously. But since roughly 1990, we have experienced a dramatic acceleration of this trend, owing to several concurrent developments.

ACCELERATING REVOLUTIONS IN SCIENCE AND TECHNOLOGY AND IN GLOBAL CAPITALISM

We are witnessing two simultaneous revolutions in science and technology: the computing and information science revolution and the communications revolution. It is true that these revolutions began well before

---

5. Edward Hershey and Carol Stone, "The Man Who Would Be President (Really)," *Cornell Magazine On/Line* 101, no. 6 (May–June 1999): 7, http://cornell-magazine.cornell.edu/Archive/May1999/MayCorson.html.

1990, but they exploded in the last decade of the twentieth century. Each is significant in its own right. But because they are mutually reinforcing, they have become incredibly powerful tools, with a huge capacity to create change. There is no need to rehearse the elements of these revolutions; their potency and their tremendous impact on universities and on every other part of society is well acknowledged. In particular, they are fueling a third force: the conversion of multinational companies into powerful and truly "transnational" corporations, and the consequent emergence of American economic dominance. We live at a time when global capitalism, as carried out by transnational corporations, has become the principal driver of nearly everyone's agenda—from national governments making policy to individuals seeking jobs and their place in the world. The booming stock market of the mid and late 1990s created a huge amount of wealth in America. Transnational corporations such as Microsoft, Citigroup, General Electric, and Time-Warner have reshaped the economic geography of the United States and the world.

It is true that multinational corporations have been a feature of the global landscape for a century, but the old-style multinational corporations were headquartered in the United States and sold most of their goods here. That made them accountable to the federal government to a considerable degree. In contrast, as Walter LaFeber notes in his book *Michael Jordan and the New Global Capitalism,* the new transnationals have become so global—and so large—that any one government has power over only a limited part of their operations.[6] In fact, some have argued that the influence of global capitalism is so strong that it has supplanted the nation-state. Of the one hundred largest economic units in the world, fewer than half are nations. The rise of global capitalism is helping to drive the revolutions in communications and computing, and those revolutions, in turn, are fueling each other and also the market economy. These movements are powerful and difficult for governments to control. In fact, governments are starting to join them, as evidenced by the 1999 repeal of the Glass-Steagall Act, which prohibited companies from offering constellations of products and services under one roof.

It is not surprising that the rise of very large merged corporations, with their global economic power and weight, is beginning to occasion anxiety and alarm among a lot of people. Hence the real and symbolic power of the events in Seattle in the fall of 1999. The World Trade Organization, a group few people paid attention to five years before, met to develop ways to reduce barriers to global trade through negotiations largely shielded from

6. Walter LaFeber, *Michael Jordan and the New Global Capitalism* (New York: W. W. Norton, 1999), 57.

public scrutiny. And while it was billed by the Clinton administration as a way to showcase the benefits of free trade, it also showcased the fears that global capitalism is generating. More than forty thousand protesters, from more than five hundred different organizations and from several countries, descended on Seattle to make their voices heard on issues ranging from environmental protection to human and worker rights. We have not seen that level of protest since the Vietnam War. There were representatives of organized labor—the Teamsters, the United Steel Workers, and the AFL-CIO. There were environmental groups such as the Sierra Club and Friends of the Earth. There were farm organizations and fundamentalists and fringe groups ranging from the Ruckus Society to the Raging Grannies. Protestors spanned the political spectrum—from the far left to the far right. A great number of people seem uneasy about the implications of world trade, which is clearly symbolic of, or a surrogate for, triumphant global capitalism. *That* is what people were in Seattle to air their grievances about.

THE RISE OF THE UNIVERSITY-INDUSTRIAL COMPLEX

The protests in Seattle, in turn, should give universities pause, because universities have been willing participants in, and beneficiaries of, the scientific and economic revolutions that are generating so much economic momentum and power. By harnessing the two scientific revolutions and by hitching themselves to the global economic enterprise, research universities have met, and exceeded, the expectations of Vannevar Bush's *Science: The Endless Frontier.* Universities have linked directly and productively not only to government but to American industry and global capitalism. Research universities are among the most ardent and successful exponents of the computing-communications revolution. Because they are heavily engaged in science, and because science, in many of its most exciting domains, requires large infusions of capital, research universities seek funds not only from governments, which used to provide almost all of what they needed, but also from corporate "partners." This process began in the 1980s and by the turn of the century was accelerating and reaching maturity.

Large research universities are thus becoming a major driver of economic development. Colleges and universities in the United States collected more than $576 million in royalties from inventions licensed to industry in fiscal year 1998 and were awarded more than 2,681 patents.[7]

7. Goldie Blumenstyk, "Colleges Reaped $576 million in Licensing Royalties in 1998, Survey Finds," *Chronicle of Higher Education*, December 10, 1999, A-44.

And not only do universities' discoveries lead to patents and licenses as they have in the past, but now they are spawning start-up companies and partnering with corporations to produce and improve products and processes across a wide spectrum of commercial activity. Universities are expected by their states to be part of their economic development agenda and are, as a result, setting up research foundations, biotechnology centers, and incubator facilities on and off campus. They have thus become *complicit* in the creation of a university-industrial complex that produces tangible benefits for universities and for American society at large. Universities and industries have become willing collaborators, with government playing a supporting role. We can expect the university-industrial complex to expand its influence as the Internet and other communication technologies make national borders transparent and make possible global exchange and collaboration in both teaching and research. And they have only just begun. For-profit cyber-universities and other ventures, enabled by the Internet, are going to impact the university-industrial complex with a vengeance in the new millennium as universities and private industry team up to offer for-profit instruction on a global scale. University teaching using the Internet and other advanced communication technology is already raising troubling questions.

In the November 22, 1999, issue of the *Wall Street Journal*, there was a front page article about Harvard law professor Arthur Miller who was embroiled in a dispute with his dean over a series of eleven lectures he videotaped the prior summer for use in a course offered by Concord University School of Law, an on-line degree granting entity set up by the *Washington Post*'s Kaplan Educational Centers.[8] Harvard contends that Prof. Miller was violating its policy that bars its faculty members from teaching at another university, without permission, during the academic year. Professor Miller maintained that he wasn't teaching, since he did not deal directly with students, and asked how his Internet involvement differed from freelance work he had done for television. Harvard has since modified its "conflict of commitment" rule for faculty to include Internet teaching.

THE RESEARCH UNIVERSITY IN THE "AGE OF MONEY"

The rise of the university-industrial complex raises significant concerns about the role, about the very identity, of the university as an independent

---

8. Amy Dockser Marcus, "Seeing Crimson: Why Harvard Law Wants to Rein in One of Its Star Professors," *Wall Street Journal*, November 22, 1999, 1.

discoverer and conveyor of knowledge. Has it, in fact, become part of the global entrepreneurial enterprise, a transnational corporation with many of the same attributes as companies like General Electric, Citigroup, and Microsoft? In my view, the answer is yes. The ascendancy of science and the rise of the university-industrial complex contributing to and serving the needs of global capitalism have attractions and benefits on many levels. In fact, the advantages are nearly irresistible for universities. Who can complain about a booming economy and expanding markets and the resources universities receive from them? And who can object when universities, particularly land-grant universities such as Cornell, contribute to economic development and technological advances? But while universities reap many advantages from the revolutions they are helping to drive, they must also be aware of the risks and the downsides. The research university is increasingly abandoning its historical role as independent thinker and critic and is embracing a new role as collaborator with, beneficiary of, and enabler of government, business, and industry. As early as 1920, Max Weber saw universities becoming "state capitalist enterprises" in which free inquiry had given way to the production of knowledge useful to the state for economic or technological reasons, thereby helping to legitimize state authority.[9] But what he envisioned then is trivial compared to what we see now. Money has always been important to universities, but never so much as today in our information-based, highly competitive research and teaching environment. The revolutions in which we are ourselves complicit mean that the hallowed idea of the campus has just about disappeared. We are no longer, in Bill Chace's words, "removed from the every-day nature of American life—we are part of that life." We have been "desanctified."[10]

One of the risks of universities' new status is that they will be so driven by financial considerations that they make an unbalanced situation even more so by favoring the fields that attract resources and spawn economic activity, as opposed to fields that participate very little in economic development. James Engell, a Harvard professor, and Anthony Dangerfield, a Cornell Ph.D., wrote about "the market-model university" in an article titled "Humanities in the Age of Money," in *Harvard Magazine*[11] "In the Age

9. Max Weber, "Science as a Vocation," in *From Max Weber: Essays in Sociology*, trans., ed., and with introduction by H. H. Gerth and C. Wright Mills (New York: Oxford University Press, 1946), 131.

10. William Chace, "How Adult Learners Are Changing the University," paper presented at The Minary Conference on Alumni Education (Fallen Leaf Lake, Calif.: Stanford University Sierra Camp, October 11, 1999), 11.

11. James Engell and Anthony Dangerfield, "The Market-Model University: Humanities in the Age of Money," *Harvard Magazine* (May–June 1998): 52.

of Money," they assert, "the royal road to success" in the university is to offer at least one of the following:

- A Promise of Money. That is, the field is popularly linked to improved chances of securing an occupation or profession that promises above-average lifetime earnings.
- A Knowledge of Money—either practical or theoretical, as in the study of fiscal, business, financial, or economic matters.
- A Source of Money—such as support from research contracts, federal grants, corporate underwriting or other external sources.[12]

This formulation may be a little glib, but I cannot argue that it is altogether wrong. The humanities—with rare exceptions—meet none of Engell's and Dangerfield's criteria, and, therefore, have, in their words, lost "respect, students, and, yes, money."[13] Viewed from any perspective, the humanities have fallen behind their more worldly disciplinary cousins in the contemporary university. We could ignore this trend altogether, or simply lament it and move along, confident that the pragmatic disciplines in the university will prosper whatever happens to the humanities. That would be, in my view, a tragic error, for universities and for society at large. In his book, *American Culture, American Tastes*, the Cornell historian Michael Kammen quotes a revealing statement by the Council on Library Resources in 1985:

> Ways must be found to assure continuing attention for those aspects of culture and learning that are important but, in a commercial sense, not necessarily in fashion. . . . Uncritical adherence to the concept of information as a commodity will distort the agendas of institutions and disciplines alike. . . . Public interest in the principle of open access must appropriately influence the structure of the information system and its components. It is certain that the information needs of society cannot be defined by the marketplace alone.[14]

The Centrality of the Humanities in the New Millennium

The humanities remain central to research universities for several compelling and interrelated reasons. First, the humanities play a crucial role

---

12. Ibid.
13. Ibid.
14. Michael G. Kammen, *American Culture, American Tastes: Social Change and the 20th Century* (New York: Knopf, 1999), 61.

as the keepers and conveyors of culture in its many forms. The old aphorism is true: those who are ignorant of the past are indeed condemned to repeat it. It is essential in a democratic society that citizens be informed about the forces that have made them who they are. Second, the humanities, since the mid-1970s or so, have opened our eyes to formerly marginalized cultures and led in the development of gender studies and ethnic studies, which have enlarged the worldview of all of us. And while these fields have generated a certain amount of contentiousness within the academy and in political life, those individuals earning university degrees today are far more capable of broad thinking than those who graduated 25 years ago. Third, the humanities, and the arts, help mediate between high culture and mass culture, between elitism and populism. They thus extend our cultural reach, address problems of social structures, and raise enduring questions about what is worthy of our students' study. Fourth, the humanities have become especially important, given universities' shift toward science, technology, and global capitalism. Humanists, more than other scholars, have historically looked for insights in other areas of endeavor and used them to inform judgments of human value, relevance, and historical significance. As James Engell has pointed out, "The humanities absorb and interpret the results of science, knowledge, and technology for our inner lives, values, and ideals."[15]

Humanists give us not only a greater depth of knowledge and understanding for its own sake; they are also catalysts for change. "It has been the province of the humanities to preserve in order to reform," Engell writes, "to pay attention, even homage, to the past, but to criticize what we inherit, calibrating the fact that social and individual lives change in the present, and that the education of character, the shaping of society, balance what has been known with the pressure of what is discovered. The humanities openly cherish and brazenly criticize and see no contradiction in the two."[16] In the "Age of Money," a time of the commodification of nearly everything and *entirely* too much information, we desperately need *critique*—informed, disinterested, ethically-based, with the eye fixed steadily on long-term consequences. We require this critique for the global society and, in particular, for research universities themselves.

The humanities, ever since Socrates, have had not only a critical method, but also a critical *spirit*—a mind set upon argument, antithesis, and an urge, as Becker put it, to think "otherwise."[17] As universities speed

---

15. James Engell, "The Idea of Organic Growth in the University," *Forum for the Future of Higher Education* (September 1999): 18–19.

16. Ibid., 21.

17. Becker, *Cornell University*, 193.

into the new millennium on the backs of government and global corporations, they need to ask where they are going. A critique of global culture
should come not only from Luddites, fundamentalists, trade unions, and
Friends of the Earth; it should come from academic critics who think rationally and carefully about "why," not just about "how." Finally, the arts
and humanities perform a deep and essential role that goes to the heart of
universities and to the heart of individual women and men. As Max Weber
argued in "Science as a Vocation," "Scientific work is chained to the course
of progress; whereas in the realm of art there is no progress in the same
sense."[18] We generally see this as a problem, perhaps *the* problem for the
arts and humanities. But as Weber goes on to say, "A work of art which is
genuine 'fulfillment' is never surpassed; it will never be antiquated. Individuals may differ in appreciating the personal significance of works of art,
but no one will ever be able to say of such a work that it is outstripped by another work which is also 'fulfillment.' "[19] A work of art or literature, when
"read" by an informed observer, contains within itself a kind of knowledge
that is different from other kinds that depend upon the incremental
buildup of information: it has a human, moral dimension at its center.

THE DEVELOPMENT OF MORAL KNOWLEDGE

As W. Robert Connor, director of the National Humanities Center, has
written, moral knowledge differs in fundamental ways from knowledge of
the natural world. It is not of a body of facts or generalizations, but rather
an activity, "ongoing, constantly reacting to experience, monitoring responses, contemplating alternatives, seeking ways to understand how
things appear to affect others, confirming or revising patterns of actions
and habits of the heart, searching for ways to change. . . . It is, in other
words, a heuristic, a way of finding out, rather than a content or a set of
rigid moral laws."[20] It requires imagination as well as logic. "There are
methods that work," Connor notes, "but the knowledge can never be totally separated from the practice."[21]

Moral knowledge develops very slowly. While it is never actually stag-
nant, "glacial" might be a fair description of its pace. It grows, Connor
writes, "through a slow, sometimes agonizing examination of individual
cases, in the hope of eliminating obfuscatory and tendentious language,

18. Weber, "Science as a Vocation," 137.
19. Ibid., 138.
20. W. Robert Connor, "Moral Knowledge in the Modern University," *Ideas* 6, no. 1 (1999):
62, http://www.nhc.rtp.nc.us:8080/ideas61/connormoral.html.
21. Ibid.

cutting through self-deception, and trying to weigh alternative outcomes."[22] It is informed through studying history, reading a poem or novel, attending a play, looking at a painting, or listening to music, all of which help us imagine what it might be like to have a life different from our own. History and literature are particularly well-suited to developing a moral imagination because they challenge us to examine characters, both real and imagined, who confront difficult choices and to reflect on how those characters behave. As Cornell's eminent scholar of English Romanticism, M. H. Abrams has said, "The necessity, vitality, and vexatiousness of literary and other humanistic studies lies in the fact that they raise and reraise questions about the concerns we live by, to which they offer and reoffer answers that, however strongly supported, turn out never to be the last word."[23]

IMPLICATIONS FOR UNDERGRADUATE EDUCATION

In the final analysis, the development of moral knowledge demands that each of us answers the ultimate Socratic question: "Who am I, and what should I do with my life?" In universities, we must remember, a major part of our obligation is to help 18 year olds answer that question. In so doing, the example of the teacher is critical. As Alexander Nehamas of Princeton has written: "Teachers have to embody the principles that we are to teach our students. . . . Socrates was great because he did not just have theories—he lived and died for them. His power comes from being able to appear as a believable and admirable human type, not just because he claimed that reason is important."[24]

In recent years many of us have lamented the quality and level of our public discourse. This is not simply a complaint about scandals and gaffes; it is a deep concern about the increasingly superficial, sound bite, public-polling approach to complex issues we see in our public debates, in our political campaigns, and in our broadcast media generally. As the issues that confront us become more complex, our rhetoric becomes more simplistic. All of us are properly worried about the seemingly irresistible tide of materialism and the concomitant decline of intellectual life in America. We see these trends even on college campuses, where undergraduate life is often a series of formal academic challenges followed by a mad-dash

22. Ibid., 61.
23. M. H. Abrams, "The Transformation of English Studies, 1930–1995," *Daedalus* 126, no. 1 (winter 1997): 126.
24. Connor, "Moral Knowledge in the Modern University," 67.

seeking for relief in the form of games, drink, and social activity. That is why Cornell, along with a few of its peers, has embarked on a program to raise the level of the undergraduate experience by focusing attention on the quality of that experience in everyday life. As the 1998 "Report on the State of the Humanities at Cornell" well said, Cornell "should attempt a fundamental reorientation of undergraduate culture in a more intellectually challenging direction, and the humanities have a central role to play in the creation of an improved climate for undergraduate life at Cornell. Such a reorientation is a major undertaking, and it will require commitment and a sense of direction."[25]

Walt Whitman captured the spirit of what needs to be done in a memorable formulation:

> Books are to be called for and supplied on the assumption that the process of reading is not a half-sleep, but, in the highest sense, a gymnast's struggle; that the reader is to do something for himself, must be on the alert, must himself or herself construct indeed the poem, argument, history, metaphysical essay—the texts furnishing the hints, the clue, the start of the framework. Not the book so much needs to be the complete thing, but the reader of the book does. That was to make a nation of supple and athletic minds, well-trained, intuitive, used to depend on themselves and not on a few coteries of writers.[26]

In the age of transnational corporations and global capitalism, remarkable scientific and technological progress, the humanities have a more central place than ever in our struggle to become whole. It is time for the humanities themselves to shake off the ever-increasing specialization that has not served them nearly as well as it has served the sciences and to reclaim the broad and deep perspective, the personal example, and the integrating role on which the development of moral knowledge—and of morally grounded 18 year olds—depends. Only then can we ensure that we will maintain what Carl Becker called "the essential quality of a great university," its character and personality.[27]

25. Committee on the State of the Humanities, *Report on the State of the Humanities at Cornell* (Ithaca, N.Y.: Cornell University, May 15, 1998), 2.

26. Walt Whitman, *Democratic Vistas: With an Introduction by John Valente, Library of Liberal Arts,* no. 9, ed. Oskar Piest (New York: Liberal Arts Press, 1949), 67–68.

27. Becker, *Cornell University,* 194.

Contributors

RONALD L. BREIGER was Goldwin Smith Professor of Sociology at Cornell University when the first drafts of his chapter were written. He is currently a professor of sociology at the University of Arizona.

JONATHAN CULLER studied history and literature at Harvard College and French and comparative literature at Oxford University. He taught at Selwyn College, Cambridge, and Brasenose College, Oxford, before coming to Cornell University, where he is Class of 1916 Professor of English and Comparative Literature. His *Structuralist Poetics: Structuralism, Linguistics, and the Study of Literature* won the James Russell Lowell Prize of the Modern Language Association of America in 1975. His other publications include *Flaubert: The Uses of Uncertainty; On Deconstruction: Theory and Criticism after Structuralism*; brief introductions to the work of Ferdinand de Saussure and Roland Barthes; and two collections of essays, *The Pursuit of Signs: Semiotics, Literature, Deconstruction*; and *Framing the Sign: Criticism and Its Institutions*. His *Literary Theory: A Very Short Introduction* was published in 1997.

ROALD HOFFMANN was born in 1937 in Zloczow, Poland. He came to the U.S. in 1949, and studied chemistry at Columbia University and Harvard University (Ph.D. 1962). Since 1965 he has been at Cornell University, where he is now the Frank H. T. Rhodes Professor of Humane Letters. He has received many of the honors of his profession, including the 1981 Nobel Prize in Chemistry (shared with Kenichi Fukui).

Dr. Hoffmann also writes poems, essays, and plays. Two of his poetry collections, "The Metamict State," and "Gaps and Verges," have been published by the University Presses of Florida; his most recent collection, "Memory Effects," was published by the Calhoun Press of Columbia College, Chicago. His other publications inculde "Chemistry Imag-

ined," "The Same and Not the Same," and with Shira Leibowitz
Schmidt, "Old Wine, New Flasks; Reflections on Science and Jewish Tra-
dition." Dr. Hoffmann is also the presenter of a television course, "The
World of Chemistry," which has aired on many PBS stations and abroad.

ISAAC KRAMNICK is the Richard J. Schwartz Professor of Government
at Cornell, where he has taught since 1972. Prior to coming to Cornell,
he taught at Harvard, Brandeis, and Yale. He is from rural Massachusetts and was educated at Harvard and Cambridge Universities.

Professor Kramnick has taught and written principally in the area of
English and American political thought and history. He has written or
edited some 20 books, them his *Bolingbroke and His Circle: The Politics of
Nostalgia in the Age of Walpole*, which won the Conference of British Studies Prize for best book on British politics. His books also include studies
of Edmund Burke, a biography of the English socialist Harold Laski, an
edition of the Federalist Papers and the recent *Godless Constitution: The
Case against Religious Correctness*, which he co-authored with R. Laurence
Moore of Cornell's history department.

He has been the recipient of a number of awards, fellowships, and
honors. He is a fellow of Britain's Royal Historical Society and served in
1989 as President of the American Society for Eighteenth-Century Studies. In 1998 he was elected a fellow of the American Academy of Arts
and Sciences. At Cornell he has received the Clark Award for distinguished teaching and the Steven Weiss Prize for teaching, and in 1996
was chosen through student ballots to be the *Cornell Sun's* "favorite professor of the year."

Professor Kramnick has served his colleagues at Cornell as chair of
the government department from 1981 to 1985 and now from 1996 to
the present. He was associate dean of the College of Arts and Sciences
from 1986 to 1989 and faculty-elected trustee from 1990 to 1994.

DOMINICK LaCAPRA is professor of history, the Bryce and Edith M.
Bowmar Professor of Humanistic Studies, and director of the Society for
the Humanities at Cornell University, as well as director of the School of
Criticism and Theory. He is the author of eleven books, the most recent
of which are *History and Reading: Tocqueville, Foucault, French Studies* and
Writing History, Writing Trauma.

N. DAVID MERMIN received his Ph.D. in physics from Harvard in 1961.
In 1964, after two postdoctoral years in Birmingham, England, and a
third at the University of California, San Diego, he came to Cornell,
where he has been a member of the physics department ever since. In
1984–90 he served a term as director of Cornell's Laboratory of Atomic
and Solid State Physics. He is author of the semipopular "Space and
Time in Special Relativity" and "Boojums All the Way Through," and co-
author of the textbook "Solid State Physics." He enjoys teaching physics
to nonscientists, for which efforts he received the Russell Distinguished

Teaching Award of the College of Arts and Sciences. He is a member of the National Academy of Sciences and the American Academy of Arts and Sciences.

JONATHAN MONROE is professor of comparative literature, associate dean of the College of Arts and Sciences, and director of the John S. Knight Institute for Writing in the Disciplines at Cornell University. Author of *A Poverty of Objects: The Prose Poem and the Politics of Genre*, and coauthor and editor of *Local Knowledges, Local Practices: Cultures of Writing at Cornell* (forthcoming 2002), *Poetics of Avant-Garde Poetries* (*Poetics Today* special issue, winter 1999/spring 2000, with Brian McHale and Meir Sternberg) and *Poetry, Community, Movement* (*Diacritics* special issue, fall/winter 1996), he has published widely in his primary area of specialization, modern and contemporary poetry. His own poetry has appeared in a range of print and on-line journals, including *The American Poetry Review, The Barcelona Review, Combo, Epoch, Harvard Review, Slope, Verse*, and *Xcp: Cross-Cultural Poetics*. A former DAAD (German Academic Exchange Service) Fellow at the University of Konstanz and recipient of a travel award to Germany from the American Council of Learned Societies, he was a member of the project design team for the American Academy for Liberal Education, and since 1998 has served as a standing member of the Fulbright selection committee for creative writing.

LARRY I. PALMER is professor of law at Cornell Law School, where he has taught courses on law and medicine for many years. He is the author of *Endings and Beginning: Law, Medicine, and Society in Assisted Life and Death, Law, Medicine, and Social Justice*, and numerous journal articles dealing with law, medicine, and policy. He is executive producer and author of the study guide for the award-winning educational video, *Susceptible to Kindness: Miss Evers' Boys and the Tuskegee Syphilis Study*.

HUNTER R. RAWLINGS III, a classics scholar, became Cornell University's tenth president on July 1, 1995. He also holds the faculty rank of professor of classics.

Dr. Rawlings received his Ph.D. from Princeton University in 1970, and is a 1966 graduate of Haverford College, with honors in classics. At Princeton, he was a Woodrow Wilson Fellow and National Defense Education Act Fellow.

Rawlings came to Cornell from the University of Iowa, where he was president and professor of classics from 1988. Previously he served for four years as vice president for academic affairs at the University of Colorado.

Elected a member of the American Academy of Arts and Sciences in 1995, he has served as a member of the Board of Directors of the American Council on Education, and currently serves on the Executive Committee of the Association of American Universities, the Board of

Directors of the Baldrige Foundation, and the Business-Higher Education Forum.

MARGARET W. ROSSITER is the Marie Underhill Noll Professor of the History of Science in the department of science and technology studies at Cornell University, and the editor of *Isis* and *Osiris,* official journals of the History of Science Society. She has written three books: *Justus Liebig and the Americans: The Emergence of Agricultural Science; Women Scientists in America: Struggles and Strategies to 1940*; and *Women Scientists in America: Before Affirmative Action, 1940–1972.* She has also edited or coedited three other volumes.

She is a 1966 graduate of Radcliffe College of Harvard University and earned her Ph.D. at Yale University in 1971. She then held an NSF Postdoctoral Fellowship at Brown University and a fellowship at the Charles Warren Center for American History at Harvard University before moving to the University of California at Berkeley, where she taught for two years. In 1981 she was awarded a John Simon Guggenheim, Jr., Memorial Fellowship and in 1982–83 she was a program director at the National Science Foundation in Washington, D.C. She was then a lecturer in the history of science at Harvard University and continued as a research associate at the American Academy of Arts and Sciences. In 1986 she came to Cornell as an NSF Visiting Professor of the History of Science. She is the recipient of a Rockefeller Foundation Fellowship in Gender Roles and a MacArthur Prize Fellowship. Her books have been awarded the Berkshire Prize and the Pfizer Prize; in 1996–97 she was a fellow at the Institute for Advanced Study at Princeton.